Pictures of a Generation on Hold:
SELECTED PAPERS

Pictures of a Generation on Hold:
Selected Papers

edited by

Murray Pomerance
&
John Sakeris

Toronto • Media Studies Working Group • 1996

PICTURES OF A GENERATION ON HOLD: SELECTED PAPERS

Published in Canada and distributed worldwide by the
Media Studies Working Group
Ryerson Polytechnic University
350 Victoria Street, Toronto ON M5B 2K3

Canadian Cataloguing in Publication Data

Main entry under title:

Pictures of a generation on hold

Selected papers from a conference entitled Pictures of a generation on hold : youth in film and television in the 1990s, held at Ryerson Polytechnic University, May 18-19, 1996. Includes bibliographical references.

ISBN 0-9680859-0-3

1. Youth in motion pictures - Congresses. 2. Youth in television - Congresses. I. Pomerance, Murray, 1946- . II. Sakeris, John, 1945- . III. Ryerson Polytechnic University. Media Studies Working Group.

PN1995.9.Y6P53   791.43'652055   C96-931280-6

Designed at gecko graphics inc.
Printed in Canada

First Edition
September, 1996

Contents

Pictures of a Generation on Hold:
SELECTED PAPERS

When you're with another person, and you're
. . . *inside* them, you're so *vulnerable,* you're
revealing so much . . . there's no *protection.*
And . . . somebody could say or do something
to you while you're in this . . . state of . . .
nakedness. And they could hurt you without
even knowing it. In a way that you couldn't
even see. And you would withdraw. To make
sure it didn't happen again.

Steven Soderbergh, from the screenplay
of *sex, lies, and videotape.*

Michael DeAngelis

Gay Male Spectatorship and Keanu Reeves

Keanu Reeves has had a devoted following of gay male fans at various points in his career, and media speculations on the star's own sexual orientation were initiated by his portrayal of a homosexual character in the play *Wolfboy* in Toronto in 1984, two years before he became a film actor.[1] His role of a male hustler, Scott, who fields the sexual desire of River Phoenix' Mike in the 1991 film *My Own Private Idaho* only fueled public inquiries into the "truth" of the star's sexuality. Since 1994, with Keanu's rise to superstar status in *Speed,* speculations on his sexuality have become more strategic as a result of simultaneous cultural and industrial developments. The widespread success of the film *Philadelphia,* also released in 1994, has ushered in a new era of increased visibility of gay representations and themes in mainstream cinema. These changes in the production of images are linked to a proliferation of new reception strategies: with statistics indicating that homosexuals have higher levels of discretionary income, gays now constitute a targetable market sector from the perspectives of the film and advertising industries. In the past two years, new diversities of sexual orientation have been constructed, documented, and classified by the popular press, culminating in a series of articles in mainstream magazines in the summer of 1995, confirming the presence of a "New Bisexuality" in contemporary culture—a phenomenon which, not incidentally, opens up a new spectrum of possibilities in the realm of target marketing.[2]

If, as a result of these developments, there has been much greater interest in maintaining an image of the star persona that is accessible to multiple audience sectors across the lines of gender and sexuality, we can find a fascinating example of how such an image might be constructed by examining the case of Keanu Reeves. We can trace an interconnection of many of the media texts which Richard Dyer identifies as integral to the construction of the star image[3]—publicity materials, interviews, commentary and criticism, and character types and narrative—in order to see how the star image retains heterosexual appeal in the action adventure *Speed* while also becoming susceptible to queer readings. Facilitated in this process are gay male fantasy positions that depend upon the spectator's affective engagement. As I will demonstrate, this accessibility to both heterosexual and homosexual fans is facilitated by the strategic use of discursive ambiguities which promote the star's non-exclusivity and receptivity, and by the construction of a star image worthy of his audience's trust.

Fantasy operates as a structure which permits the spectator to introject him or herself as a participant in scenarios of desire. According to Elizabeth Cowie, pleasure in fantasy is derived not from the ultimate attainment of a desired object, but from the process of sustaining desire itself. Fantasy involves a "happening and continuing to happen," elicited through a series of stagings that enable the subject's continued participation.[4] Intersupportive yet ambiguous star texts can be seen as highly conducive to fantasy engagement: such texts afford pleasure not only by permitting spectators to fill in the gaps according to their desires, but also by promoting the ongoing work of staging and overcoming obstacles to fulfillment, which Cowie describes as "the making visible, present, of what isn't there, of what can never *directly* be seen (emphasis hers)."[5] Thus, in gay male fantasy relations between spectators and stars, the pleasure lies not in the prospect of a moment of closure when the star's sexual orientation will ultimately be known or verified, but in the negotiation of obstacles to the construction of a coherent and ideal fantasy figure.

Henry Jenkins stresses the importance of this notion of the obstacle in fantasy in his analysis of the Slash phenomenon.[6] Jenkins argues that the establishment of a "homosocial-homosexual continuum" poses the greatest challenge for Slash writers; at the same time, it offers the greatest pleasure because it dramatizes a crisis of a "traditional masculinity" in which intimacy between men is not socially tolerated.[7] In the star/spectator relations I examine here, the obstacle retains its potential for sustaining pleasure in fantasy only as long as the star earns and maintains the spectator's trust, and agrees not to disrupt the network of ambiguity that has been constructed within the star texts.

Although the publicity discourses surrounding the figure of Keanu Reeves often overtly emphasize his sexual appeal to women, the star's heterosexuality or heterosexual appeal is distinctly not constructed as exclusive, and the star is promoted as universally accessible. Reeves' *persona* is wrought with ambiguities: a writer for *The Independent* describes Keanu's "hyper-modern unisex quality. Reeves is, well, evolved. In interview he talks with an open-spirited, complex positivity that could easily come from either gender."[8] Other articles promote Reeves' passivity, and in attempting to explain his appeal, *Speed* director Jan De Bont remarks that "He's young, he has a vulnerable quality—open, romantic."[9]

Popular press constructions of Keanu's universal sex appeal are often enhanced through locative ambiguities, in an effort to construct the "pan-accessibility" of the star. Keanu has no determinate place: he does not comfortably or conveniently "fit in" with mainstream culture on the basis of national, ethnic, racial, or indeed domestic ties and allegiances. Keanu has no place to call home: he crashes occasionally at his sister's, but for the most part he lives in hotels. Several articles emphasize his multi-ethnic heritage (Hawaiian, Chinese, and British) as well as his nomadic wanderings (born in Lebanon, raised in Canada and Australia). *The Independent* remarks that Keanu is "fashionably ethnic-looking (but not too ethnic-looking, his name means 'cool breeze over the mountains')."[10] The *Chicago Tribune* remarks upon "the angular face with its ethnic and sexual ambiguities," and comments that "The actor's enigmatic face suggests a computer-generated composite of every known race and gender. His affect is pansexual and so is his appeal. At the trill of his name—say key-AH-noo—fans female and male heave libidinal sighs."[11] And Bernardo Bertolucci remarks that "[Reeves] has a beauty . . . that's not Eastern or Western."[12]

In these articles, star accessibility is often highlighted through discourses that construct the body as a site of receptivity and invitation. The body is firm and agile, muscular but not imposingly bulky; the hair is short; facial features resonate with an emotional, unthreatening quality. Receptivity at the site of the eye is mentioned in several of the articles about Keanu Reeves' performance in *Speed*; a *USA Today* piece includes Jan De Bont's observation that "[Keanu's] eyes are very open to the world";[13] with more focus, De Bont comments that "Most important are his eyes. You can read emotion in them. There's nothing going on behind the eyes of most action heroes."[14] Some popular press articles include testimonials for Keanu's receptivity, such as the following comment from a 19-year-old woman: "I feel I could step into his soul, just slide in."[15] And discussions of Keanu's sexual appeal on the active alt.fan.keanu-reeves newsgroup often focus on the expressiveness and impenetrable mystery of his face. In one heated debate over the range of Keanu's acting skills, a participant provides the following response, with indirect reference to his performance in *Johnny Mnemonic* (1995):

> I don't know how to distinguish acting from performing, Keanu aside. I DO know that his eyes, his looks—this man does NOT need morphing software, he's got the morph deep inside his DNA. I think a.lot [sic] about how he looks.. . . Our Keanu's appearance is not an average face or look."[16]

Out magazine relates Keanu's ocular receptivity to the probing eyes of his gay male fans: "Reeves can seem all things to all people. Why he has caught the eye of gay men isn't such a mystery, given his tough-but-tender looks, his dude-acious bod, those eyes."[17]

Receptivity is also figured as a "natural" sexuality which derives its power from its lack of self-consciousness, as well as from the star's refusal to take the constructed image too seriously. For example, Keanu offers objective, scientific and modest reactions to the course taught on his films by Prof. Stephen Prima at the Art Center College of Design in Pasadena:

> My understanding of it is that [Professor Prima]'s using an artist as a jumping-off point or a sort of strobe light on popular culture,. . . and I'm flattered he used me as that jumping-off point.[18]

One *People* article draws attention to the fact that, at De Bont's request, Keanu "pumped iron for two months at Gold's Gym in L.A. to add manly umpf to his formerly lanky frame";[19] however, the association of this active, goal-oriented labor with image construction serves to deflect any potential suspicions of the star's potentially distancing obsession with his sexual appeal. Keanu's own commentary on this subject confirms his disinterest in narcissism: "I like my body . . . and I know what it feels like when I'm in good shape—but I don't want to work at it all the time. Sometimes I do but if I'm not feeling as cool then I get into my whole other worlds and going to the gym is not at the top of my list."[20]

These constructed ambiguities are both reinforced and contextualized through elements of character and plot in the narrative of *Speed*. Certainly the character of Jack Traven demonstrates the strength, agility and resourcefulness which have come to be associated with the traditional action hero; however, these attributes are tempered by a physical and emotional vulnerability which adds resonance to the characterization, and which ultimately serves to expand the limits of acceptable masculine heroic behavior in the context of this genre. In conjunction with this vulnerability, the ravaged, strained body of the hero is frequently objectified sexually. Jack Traven's vulnerability is conveyed not only by frequent high angle and overhead shots which emphasize his helplessness, but also through plot devices which require that the hero's body undergo various gymnastic contortions. Toward the beginning of the film, Jack is suspended upside-down, then lowered and raised, by cable in an elevator shaft as he attempts to latch a hook to the top of a fallen car to rescue its terrified passengers. In several scenes, the hero is placed in a prone position to emphasize his passivity and vulnerability. Near the beginning of the film, an explosion propels him through the air and against a wall; groaning as rubble falls around his helpless body, he sinks to the floor in slow motion with his legs spread open. The scene in which he is transported by mechanic's dolly underneath the bus in an attempt to disassemble the bomb is marked by crosscutting between low-angle shots of Annie (Sandra Bullock) looking down at him from the driver's seat, and overhead shots of the helpless hero from Annie's point-of-view. Once he is underneath the bus, the shot composition changes to a series of close-ups of the hero's body in severely cramped quarters. The dolly is propelled out of control and ground-level shots show Jack frantically groping for any part of the underside of the bus that might provide a supportive, steadying anchor. The of one extreme close-up features Jack's left biceps flexing and straining in the foreground right, while in the background left his legs and feet dangle off the now wildly swerving dolly. After the dolly permanently veers away from his body a few shots later, another ground level shot offers a more dramatic fragmentation of body parts, revealing only a clenched torso and pair of legs that strain anxiously to avoid scraping against the pavement.

The most emphatic revelations of vulnerability are conveyed by the intensity of Jack's reactions to his own helplessness as he confronts the forces of the villain, Howard Payne (Dennis Hopper). After Payne telephones Jack to inform him that his partner Harry (Jeff Daniels) has been killed, the hero emits a slow, agonized, low-pitched groan; his head and back slumped over in despair, he suddenly erupts into a wild, convulsive state, gripping and shaking the handrail of the bus as the camera lingers on his straining arm muscles. After Annie manages to calm him down, he resignedly informs her, "We're gonna die." Interestingly, however, it is this very vulnerability that ultimately places Jack in a position of power both to defeat the villain and save his own life: in the closing moments of the final struggle between the two men on the roof of a speeding subway car, Howard manages to pin Jack underneath him, beating him senseless with a steel bomb trigger, and boasting that he has outsmarted and outmaneuvered him. But Jack's prone, submissive, and seemingly helpless position ironically becomes a position of safety; in a desperate effort, he succeeds in raising the head of his aggressor ever so slightly, just enough for it to be lopped off by a safety light mounted to the subway tunnel ceiling.

Vulnerability is also a function of locative ambiguities constructed through the publicity discourses and reinforced within the film narrative: both establish the hero as alone and socially unconnected, suggesting an alienation resulting from an unidentified loss. In *Speed*, Jack Traven's alienation depends upon his lack of personal history. A man without a past, Jack harbors a despair defined by various absences. While the viewer may assume that he belongs to a family and has a home, the narrative reveals no such domestic space. Despite the social connections afforded him as a police officer, he remains unconnected, unfixed. The day after receiving a medal for his rescue of the elevator passengers, when a local merchant comments that he must have celebrated his success the night before, Jack responds, "It can't have been too great—I woke up alone."

The narrative counterbalances this alienation by providing the hero with a temporary and functional alliance with a community, an alliance which is also integral to the construction of the star as a universal fantasy figure. In *Speed*, human survival depends upon the organized efforts of the community to withstand threats imposed by the outside world. Community is confined within tight, containable public spaces—an elevator car, a bus, a subway car—vulnerable to the forces which attempt to disband it. And it is the action hero who comes to assume responsibility for establishing and maintaining the community as a cohesive entity; he does so by encouraging cooperation, dispelling dissent, and establishing trust. Before Jack Traven arrives on the scene, community membership on the bus is distinguished only by common disadvantage: in a city plagued with traffic problems brought about to some extent by those who travel alone in cars, the group of bus passengers comprises those who can't afford private vehicles, those like Annie whose driving privileges have been revoked, and those like the tourist, Stephens (Alan Ruck), who cannot find their way. The common disadvantage uniting them in this public space of mass transit establishes a spirit of mutual tolerance more than unity of purpose, and while some passengers know each other by name, their interaction is fleeting and tentative, lasting only as long as it takes to reach their respective stops.

In an effort to establish its political correctness, *Speed* is insistent in emphasizing the diversity of the community by representing differences in age, race, ethnicity, gender, and domestic situation. Such differences appear to be tolerated until Jack makes the passengers aware of the bomb that threatens them. From this point forward, when the goal of the passengers is no longer to reach a specific destination, but to remain alive, differences between the community members become a source of conflict, and their cooperative effort is consistently in danger of being vitiated. Jack himself is initially greeted with suspicion and distrust, since he appears to them as a "madman" who disrupts their daily routine, and also because his identity as a police officer places him in a position of power and privilege. The disruption becomes life-threatening when one passenger, Ray (Daniel Villarreal), suspects that Jack will arrest him; the passenger panics, inadvertently shoots the bus driver, consequently risking the other passengers' lives.

Jack's mission is to organize cooperative activity according to rules that Howard, the "real" madman, has established: the bus must not decrease its speed below fifty miles per hour; no passenger may be permitted to alight. His mission is complicated because he must (a) impose order without posing himself as a threat; but also (b) neutralize the stratification of the community by establishing his trustworthiness and inspiring people to trust one another. His first goal requires him to prove that under the present circumstances, his role of police officer is secondary to his role as fellow human being who is willing to risk his life for them. He accomplishes this as soon as he boards the bus: after Ray pulls out his gun when Jack displays his police badge, Jack responds reflexively by pulling out his own gun, but then he makes a plea to the frightened passenger:

> I don't know you, man. I'm not here for you. Let's not do this.... Listen! I'm putting my gun away, okay? Okay? Now, listen. I don't care about your crime. Whatever you did, I'm sure that you're sorry. So it's cool now. It's over. I'm not a cop right now. See? We're just two cool guys hanging out.

To achieve the second goal he must serve as mediator of the conflicts which erupt as tension mounts within the enclosed space. When one passenger exclaims that he cannot die because he has a family to support, an unmarried passenger reacts vehemently that his own life is no more expendable because he is single; conflicts also arise between Ortiz (Carlos Carrasco) and Stephens, the tourist who is in one sense an "outsider" since he uses mass transportation by choice rather than out of necessity. Jack gradually guides the community to celebrate mutual accomplishments, and to identify and resolve differences. They attribute this resolution not only to Jack's organizing presence, but to their own resourcefulness. Through the trust that the action hero figure establishes in relation to this diverse community, spectators are invited to perceive the star *persona*'s absences and ambiguities not as contradictions, but as evidence of character depth, complexity, and coherence.

While these qualities support spectators' efforts to construct the star according to their own desires, his universal accessibility is not without deterrents. Perhaps the strongest of these are the markings or hints of the hero's heterosexuality, as evidenced by his relationship with Annie. While these deterrents cannot be disavowed, heterosexuality remains a negotiable element within the narrative. Although *Speed* concludes with the promise of Jack and Annie's romantic involvement, it is a promise that blooms only after his partner Harry is killed. Up to this point, the film stresses an evolving homosocial intimacy between the male partners. This "couple" is constructed as two aspects of a unifiable whole: Harry possesses technical knowledge and psychological insight, while Jack demonstrates a complementary physical agility and fearlessness. Together they are able to confound Howard's scheme and save the passengers in the falling elevator. Savoring their accomplishment immediately afterwards at the elevator shaft, Jack inquires, "Was it good for you?" "It was great for me," responds Harry. When he shoots Harry in the leg in order to confuse Howard, he loses not only his partner's active engagement, but also his own ability to perform his duties effectively; rendered impotent, he can now communicate with Harry only by phone, yet this separation of the partners does not result in a weakening of the homosocial bond between them.

If the ambiguous narrative of *Speed* poses surmountable obstacles in the realm of gay male fantasy relations, the ultimate challenge to this tenuous contractual arrangement between spectator and star occurs when the actor is asked to disclose his views on the issue of his own sexual orientation, or that of his fans. Since disclosure can settle the mystery of a star's sexuality, the trust which spectators have invested in the star figure is here most directly at risk of betrayal. A London *Gay Times* writer describes his emotional response to the news that male star figures whom he once desired have made homophobic remarks: "Yes , it does hurt: and you do what you did when you ended your first teenage love affair, when you tried madly to convince yourself the ex is ugly now, all attraction is gone."[21] But Keanu takes his appeal to gay audiences in stride. He remains entirely unmoved by the rumors of his secret marriage to David Geffen, and refuses to lend any definitive closure to the matter of his own sexual orientation; indeed, Keanu prefers not only to maintain the ambiguous, universal appeal of his image, but also to cultivate this ambiguity in the interests of a cool, progressive political correctness that echoes his community role in *Speed*. When asked whether or not he was gay in an article for *Interview* magazine in 1990, Keanu responded, "No, but ya never know."[22] And in a recent interview for *Vanity Fair*, when he is asked whether it might be better for him outwardly to deny rumors of his homosexuality, he replies: "Well, I mean, there's nothing wrong with being gay, so to deny it is to make a judgment. And why make a big deal of it? If someone doesn't want to hire me because they think I'm gay, well, then I have to deal with it, I guess. Or if people were picketing a theater. But otherwise, it's just gossip, isn't it?"[23]

In a 1995 cover article in the "straight" issue of *Out* magazine, the interviewer, aiming for a limiting and defining statement, boldly poses the hypothetical question, "What would be the best thing about being straight?" Keanu's response is appropriately opaque: "But wouldn't whatever that *thing* is be the best thing about being gay as well? There are no lines. I mean it's humans, man. I mean . . . what would I say?. . . We can go to different bathrooms in a restaurant!"[24] And it is the maintenance of such ambiguities which helps to perpetuate Keanu's accessibility to both gay and straight fans. Among the pages of the world wide web's KeanuNet is one entitled, "Is Keanu Gay?" And the writer's response?: "If Keanu is a fantasy figure for you, imagine that he prefers YOU. The truth is really not so important, is it?"[25]

Gay Male Spectatorship and Keanu Reeves

Notes

1 *Wolfboy*, by Brad Fraser and directed by John Palmer, was produced with Reeves as "Bernie" at the Main Space of Theatre Passe Muraille, Toronto, beginning February 10, 1984.

2 For accounts of this "new" sexual phenomenon, see John Leland, "Bisexuality Emerges as a New Sexual Identity," *Newsweek* (17 July 1995), 44ff; Lynn Darling, "Bisexuality," *Harper's Bazaar* (June 1995), 136ff; Rachel Cohen, "A Bisexual Journey," *Harper's Bazaar* (June 1995), 138ff; Robert S. Boynton, "Going Both Ways," *Vogue* (June 1995), 132, 143; Anastasia Higginbotham, "Chicks goin' at it," *Ms.* (May/June 1995), 29-33; and Greta Christina, "Are we having sex yet?" *Ms.* (November/December 1995), 60-2.

3 Richard Dyer, *Stars* (London: BFI Publishing, 1979), 68-72.

4 Elizabeth Cowie, "Fantasia," *m/f* 9 (1984), 159.

5 Cowie, "Fantasia," 154.

6 In *slash* fiction, fans rewrite old (and construct new) narratives around the presumably heterosexual relationships between television characters as homosexual relationships. Slash fiction is often circulated among the members of fan communities. The slash refers to the mark between the names of the two characters whose relationship is being established. For example, Jenkins documents "Kirk/Spock" slash written by *Star Trek* fans, and "Blake/Avon" slash written by fans of the British cult science fiction series *Blake's 7*.

7 Henry Jenkins, *Textual Poachers: Television Fans and Participatory Culture* (New York: Routledge, 1992), 204ff.

8 Angela Holden, "Blissed out, switched on perfect boy: what makes Keanu Reeves not just a movie star but a total babe?" *The Independent* (September 19, 1994), Living Page section, 22.

9 Mary Harron, "Picture that Majors on Motion," *The Independent* (October 9, 1994), Sunday Review section, 21.

10 Holden, "Blissed," 21.

11 Carrie Rickey, "The Importance of Being Keanu: the heartthrob hero of *Speed* talks about his transformation from airhead to man of action," *Chicago Tribune* (June 26, 1994), Arts section, 16.

12 Carrie Rickey, "Call it the cult of Keanu Reeves—Toronto actor is speeding away from adolescence at a record clip," *The Toronto Star* (June 13, 1994), F4.

13 Tom Green, "Built for *Speed*/Keanu Reeves, catching a bus to the big time/Former dude is a dynamo in demand," *USA Today* (June 9, 1994), Life section, 1-D.

14 Rickey, "Importance of Being Keanu," 16.

15 Holden, "Blissed," 22.

16 Entry in alt.fan.keanu-reeves Internet newsgroup, signed, "a.fan" (February 20, 1996).

17 Tim Allis, "Keanu Sets the Record Straight," *Out* (July/August 1995), 65.

18 Kristine McKenna, "Keanu's Eccentric Adventure: from stoner dude to computer brain, 29-year-old Keanu Reeves has racked up 16 films during his eight hard-working years of acting, and emerged almost untarnished by the corrosive glitter of Hollywood," *Los Angeles Times* (June 5, 1994), Calender Section, 3.

19 Natasha Stoynoff, et. al., "A Most Excellent Enigma," *People* (July 11, 1994), 49.

20 *Keanu Reeves: A Tear-Out Photo Book* (London: Oliver Books, 1994), 8.

21 Joseph Mills, "Can You Forgive Them?" *Gay Times* (March 1994), 40.

22 Dennis Cooper and Matthew Rolston, "Keanu Reeves," *Interview* 20 (September 1990), 132-137.

23 Michael Shnayerson, "Young and Restless," *Vanity Fair* (August 1995), 146.

24 Tim Allis, "Record," 117.

25 "Is Keanu Gay?" world wide web page, http://www.users.interport.net/~eperkins.gay.html.

DAVID DESSER

Anime: Its Origins in Japan and Its Appeal to Worldwide Youth

Anime is the Japanese term for animated film (it was *manga eiga* before recent times) and it refers in Japan and in the West to Japanese animated films and television series. There has been extremely little of a scholarly nature written on anime,[1] in contrast to the tremendous fan culture that has arisen and produced much writing in magazines and on the Internet. This absolutely astounding fandom, reflected most prominently in the tremendous availability of anime films in the U.S. and Canada as well as the fanzine work, testifies to a powerful phenomenon in contemporary popular culture, one apparently, though not entirely, generated by a subcultural formation aided by market forces, of course, though not at all by any official cultural institution in Japan or in the West. The lack of scholarship on anime works in conjunction with the lack of official cultural status accorded to it, to keep it more specifically in the realm of its fans. Indeed, one can imagine that as soon as anime becomes popular grist for the academic mill, its ability to speak to the subcultural formation which has grown up around it will be lessened, much as one might say that the canonization of much of narrative cinema in official culture, including the academy, served to lessen its impact on its most appropriate audience: youth.

Anime is, for the most part, but especially in the West, almost the strict province of youth, by which I mean adolescents rather than children, and more particularly not just college-aged youth, but college youths or those college grads who retain features of adolescence well into their 20s and even 30s. As Annalee Newitz describes it, "clubs, conventions, and fanzines dedicated to anime have sprung up on college campuses and in large cities all over the United States."[2] This fact might partially account for the lack of scholarly work on anime, a certain irony considering that anime is so prevalent on college campuses—scholars and critics tend to be outside the demographic to which the films and videos appeal. That the primary audience is adolescent as I have just defined it seems unarguable. That the major audience should be adolescent, and what that means more exactly, is the primary subject of this essay, written by someone who is himself a kind of outsider.

I'd also like to make the claim, based mostly on observation rather than a formal sociological analysis, that fans of anime are drawn from the same demographic group as fans of science fiction and horror films, and also comic books, especially those within SF and/or horror parameters. They also seem, though less exclusively, to be fans of the contemporary Hong Kong cinema, especially action or action-comedy. In addition, such fans are universally computer literate and facile with the Internet and the world wide web. Many such fans of anime, for instance, have their own home page dedicated to their favorite films, series, personalities, artists, etc. My sense is that the world of video games with an SF and fantasy bent, of CD-ROM interactive games, not to mention role-playing games on computers, alone or in groups, is another facet of the picture of anime's fans that I am attempting to draw. (So, too, are certain facets within pop and rock—heavy metal, for instance, with its tradition of cartoon-like violence onstage and the fantasy art derived from SF and fantasy known itself as heavy metal. Nevertheless, the world of rock music is so fragmented and so many fans of rock in any of its guises are not fans of anime and its related genres, that I'm afraid I must otherwise elide it, except for this: there is "*Bastard*, a sword and sorcery manga [from 1988] . . . in which all the characters are named after heavy metal bands."[3]) It is worthwhile to note, of course, that the primary demographic of anime, SF, horror, and interactive CDs and the like is the general demographic group from which all of cinema draws the major portion of its audience. Thus, to say that anime, SF, and horror appeal to this group should not come at the expense of recognizing that this is the group for gross-out comedies and the blockbuster action-adventure genre. Yet I would say that, in terms of more mainstream films, while boys aged 15-25 are the primary target audience, many, many films have either great crossover appeal or, alternately, a limited appeal to audiences outside of that grouping. Whereas mainstream films appeal to boys and often to others, anime, much SF, horror and the like, appeal almost solely to boys.[4] Similarly, while I'm not saying that all fans of anime are also fans of live-action SF, horror, gross-out comedies, comic books and computer games, I am saying that most, in fact, appear to be. Thus what I have to say about anime should be descriptive also of other popular film and quasi-literary genres.

Moreover, it is clear, given the basic components of virtually all anime, that its structure fits loosely into related genres like SF, horror and fantasy. All of the most popular and best-known anime in the West surely fit into that broad category: *Ultra-Man, Akira, Bubblegum Crisis, The Legend of the Overfiend, Ranma 1/2*, etc. However, unlike some of the best-loved, cult live-action horror films (from *Psycho*, to *The Texas Chainsaw Massacre*, to *Halloween*), anime are not usually low-budget, made-on-the-run films or television shows. Part of the appeal of anime is surely its high-tech gloss, its near-lavish production values, its generally "busy" frames. Obviously, this is also a quality associated with the Disney animated features in both their classic and modern incarnations. And the Disney films do have some fandom from anime's group (some) and certainly garner respect and admiration. But Disney films are not the objects of such fan cults. Therefore, it must be the case that while anime's high production values give it a certain appeal, that is not a sufficient explanation.

Background

Anime defines the corpus of Japanese animated works produced first for television in the 1960s and only later, in the 1980s, for theatrical feature films, and eventually also for OAV (original animation video—what we would call direct to video, but without the negative implications that has here). While television anime was popular in Japan, in the west it had only a minor cult following in the 60s and it was not until the 80s that it began to become the province of a burgeoning fan culture. Anime's roots in Japan are many. The primary ones seem to me to be: the older generations of animated films (*manga eiga*); the monster movies (*kaiju-eiga*) of the 1950s and 60s (*Godzilla, Mothra, Rodan,* etc.), television programs of the 60s, and, perhaps most particularly, manga (comic books, but perhaps graphic novels would be equally accurate).[5] Animated cinema was originally, and until quite recently, called *manga eiga*. Animation was never the regular feature of Japanese cinema-going that it was in the west during the golden age of the 1930s. Much of it, in fact, was produced independently throughout the decades immediately preceding the war. And, although I haven't come across a reference to this idea, it is possible that animation was looked on with some distrust in the later 1930s because of the clear influence of American animation.

Both before and after the war, Japanese critics of Japanese animation decried the influence of American animation on Japan, particularly Walt Disney. A typical critic is Imamura Taihei who issued a call for *manga eiga* based on Japan's own artistic heritage of scroll paintings (*emaki mono*), drawing, music, and theater.[6] Some animation, independently produced or officially sanctioned, was put to service in a propaganda role during the war, perhaps revitalizing the push toward a more "native" style and certainly a more native content.

After the war, and specifically after the Occupation and the rise of the Economic Miracle,[7] animation became more popular, with animation providing the background and some of the style, for instance, for Ichikawa Kon, one of Japan's premier directors of the 1950s and 60s (just as Oshima Nagisa would feel comfortable making an animated film in the 1960s, a background and influence he does not tend otherwise to manifest). Much of the energy in postwar animation went to special effects for the *kaiju-eiga*, but late in the 1950s it became a force in its own right in movies. Toei studios emerged as a major player in postwar animation, with their first feature film in 1958, *The Legend of the White Snake* (*Hakujya den*). The film is in color. I'd suggest that the more routine use of color in Japanese film, particularly due to its decreasing cost and the increasing success of Japanese films in Japan (and overseas, too, in the 50s) has a lot to do with the rise in the numbers of animated features and their popularity with audiences.

The prevalence of Hollywood's product in Japan and the continued impact of American popular culture on that country show up in a number of ways in most of the films produced in Japan in the post-Occupation period. Similarly, the mini-baby-boom in Japan after the war and especially after the economic miracle led to increased attention to children's programming in movies, even before the onset of television. This shows up in the films produced by Toei: "Toei's work in the 1960s continued with many feature-length animated films designed for audiences of children. Many source tales were not indigenous, and elements of science fiction often augmented the Disney-like worlds of these narratives."[8] Nor was Toei alone in producing animated films. Toho also had an important animated division in the 1960s, with their first feature, *Kamui gaiden* (*Kamui Story*) coming in 1965. Its focus was on ninja. It seems in retrospect to be a natural that Toho got into the anime business as they were the studio who dominated the monster mania.

But anime as we know it today grows not only out of the earlier *manga eiga*, but also out of changes in both style and content that emerged in the 1960s. Ed Small sees a major shift in animation technique after 1960, especially in the areas he calls intellectual montage (after Eisenstein) and metamorphosis—what is now often called, through the use of video effects, "morphing." Interestingly enough, one factor in the shift to new styles in animation was the Sogetsu Kaikan, which arranged for screenings of independent animation in Tokyo—international and Japanese. A major influence on the Sogetsu Kaikan's programming was Teshigahara Hiroshi, a central figure in the Japanese New Wave. The work of Norman McLaren and Stan Vanderbeek, for instance was screened at their facility.[9] The dominance of the major studios was beginning to crumble in the 1960s generally, as the era saw independent live-action feature production with major studio distribution along with alternate distribution and even non-theatrical films. So it was, too, in animation, with the formation of Mushi-Herald Productions by Tezuka Osamu.[10] Tezuka is one of the heroes, the cult figures, of anime; his *Astro Boy* is thought of as a watershed of the genre. And *Astro Boy* turns us, of course, to television, a major factor in the rise of anime and in the decline in live-action feature film production.

Television was later coming to Japan than in the U.S. Postwar economic conditions did not favor the rise of such a consumer item in a period of massively ruined infrastructures, after all. The housing shortage also did not help. But by the early 1960s television, especially in Japan's massive and massively growing urban areas, was a force to be reckoned with. The mini-baby-boom also contributed to the increasing centrality of television to Japanese life. The popularity of television was also helped by the fact that middle-class Japanese women rarely worked outside the home once they were married; and hardly ever when they had children. A cursory glance at Japanese TV reveals the dominance of women's programming and children's programming in the 1960s. Color was later coming to Japanese TV than in the West, which essentially turned to color around the time the Japanese turned to television. But by the late 1960s, color was prevalent and this, too, helped the popularity of animation.

The case of *kaiju-eiga* is fairly obvious as a precursor to anime. The generally sci-fi elements of anime are mirrored in monster movies; special effects in the movies are themselves often animated; the prevalence of monsters within anime is mirrored in 50s and early 60s monster movies, and the presence of robots and other techno-beings finds a precursor in such figures in *kaiju-eiga* as Mecha-Godzilla. And the general propensity to destroy Japan's major cities—to show such on-screen destruction or to situate the stories within a post-apocalyptic setting—is a notable feature of both monster movies and much anime. Similarly, the generally anti-nuclear stance of monster movies, the fear of nuclear Armageddon (understandable, needless to say, in Japan), finds expression, along with a strain of pacifism, in the nuclear nightmares of many anime, such as *Nausicaa of the Valley of the Wind*.

For all the importance of *manga eiga*, animated TV series and *kaiju-eiga*, unquestionably the impact of manga themselves are the predominate influence. The fact is that many of the most popular anime films and OVA began life as manga, and manga is concomitantly a cult-item in the West among anime fans. The world of manga is a complex one, but of tremendous significance in Japan, where it accounts for 20% of the publishing industry in the world's most literate nation. Manga of various sorts, published weekly or monthly or less regularly, appeal to a variety of demographic groups—businessmen, housewives, working men, and especially young children, adolescent boys and adolescent girls—each often having many manga addressed to it. Perhaps unsurprisingly the number addressed to adolescents and children exceeds the number for adults.

There are a number of theories advanced as to why manga should be so carefully devoted in Japan to so many age groups. "Experts such as Frederik Schodt point to cultural and historical predispositions, others to the fact that Japan is a nation of commuters using public transport . . ."[11] Personally, I favor cultural predisposition to public transport. Millions ride the subways in New York and their favorite reading is not manga but the *New York Daily News*.

My own sense is that Japan is a "graphic" nation. Perhaps it stems from the adoption of Chinese characters and the integration of these (called *kanji*) with the *hiragana* and *katakana* syllabaries which are phonetic; combined with the astonishing prevalence of English words and Arabic numerals. Surely no nation on earth is quite as comfortable with four separate alphabets as is Japan. For Gunther Nitschke, the written language of educated Japan is a clear source for manga. Manga are generally printed in black-and-white and Nitschke links this tonal printing to *kanji*: "the manga is an extension of Sino-Japanese calligraphy, the supreme art of the black and white line."[12] If that is so, surely China would be as manga-crazed as Japan. It is not. Still, this is certainly one factor.

Another is that graphics surround the Japanese in their daily life—whether that gives rise to manga or is a phenomenon of Japan as a "graphic" nation I don't know. Nevertheless, a trip to Japan is a veritable kaleidoscope. Billboards, including electronic as well as more traditional ones, dominate the urban landscape and are often a dazzling combination of pictures and multi-alphabetical written text. Magazines are glossy and omnipresent. Television is everywhere to be seen. Newspapers are numerous. To find manga amidst this pictorial-literary collage is no surprise. The cultural predisposition may extend as far back as certain traditional Japanese arts, such as *emaki-mono* mentioned above. For Gunther Nitschke, it's not just *emaki-mono* (narrative picture scrolls) but also *ukiyo-e* (woodblock prints) which are the clear predecessors of manga.[13] I think that's right about woodblock prints, recalling that they were a popular mass-produced art (as opposed originally to a high art, lacking the aura of authenticity brought about by uniqueness, of which Benjamin has so brilliantly written in "The Work of Art in an Age of Mechanical Reproduction"), whose subjects were drawn from popular cultural pursuits like tourism, the theatre, the pleasure districts and city sights.

Another factor, one that I find interesting and convincing, is also put forward by Nitschke: "Manga exhibit a creative energy similar to that of Japan's big urban centers, which are often chaotic with the potential to explode in yet new, uncharted dimensions.. . . [L]eafing through the pages of a manga is very much like going downtown."[14] Walking through Tokyo or Osaka is not only a dizzying experience of graphic patterns from billboards, magazines, television sets and, particularly in

Tokyo, some of the world's most exciting fashion trends; it is also a sometimes labyrinthine experience of winding streets and alleys, most with no names. The fact is that manga and anime cityscapes need only approximate Tokyo and Osaka to feel fantastic, dreadful, exciting, confusing, or all those things at once. (Consider that Ridley Scott's *Blade Runner* cityscape [1982] is modeled after Tokyo as much as Los Angeles, and his *Black Rain* [1989] adds very little to actual Osaka.) For Nitschke, "In manga and cityscape alike, the 'new visual generation' is exposed to a treat of the left and right sides of the brain simultaneously: to a stimulation of its verbal, discursive, and deductive as well as its spatial, holistic, and intuitive faculties."[15] This may be why many of the most popular manga and anime give older, pre-visual types (like me) a headache.

Anime Western-style

My sense of anime's appeal to youth in the West should not be taken as a statement on contemporary youth culture in Japan. The corpus of films I've looked at and studied are drawn, precisely, from what is available here through the network of fan-oriented video stores and through collectors and traders. Thus the facts I present are strictly indicative of anime across especially the U.S., Canada and Great Britain, though also Australia and New Zealand and, as far as I can tell, France, Germany and Spain. There are no less than thirty animated features and the same number of television series available in the US, to go along with at least fifty OAV movies and twenty OAV series. That is, there are more anime available from Japan than the entire corpus of live-action Japanese movies available on video in NTSC format for rent or for sale (even including 16mm and 35mm films available for non-theatrical rental). Of course, the films, TV shows and OAV videos were originally made in Japan for the Japanese market and thus their style and content may well be indicative of the culture in which they were meant to appeal.

This culture, as here, is the youth culture. There are, at least to my knowledge, no anime made from businessmen comics or from the startling variety of S&M or rape fantasy comics that appeal to working men and, apparently, to executives. And while there do exist strictly children's anime based on manga, the numbers pale before the broad spectrum of movies from adolescent-oriented manga. Though youth culture in Japan can be broadly defined, it can be broken into subcultures (mostly called *zoku*, or families, sometimes tribes), one being high school and college students, especially those boys now generally called "otaku." The easiest way to define *otaku* is to link it with the western "computer geek" or "nerd." Initially a term of derision in Japan, *otaku* came to be adapted by the computer-anime-CD subculture itself and became a potent force in the Japanese marketplace. For Ben Crawford, *otaku* had enormous impact on the shape and scope of anime:

> From the mid-1980s, a new genre of cartoon property emerged, which was responsive to an aesthetic championed by the otaku among audiences and filmmakers. These properties feature "pretty girls," whose surreal adventures shift minute-to-minute from domestic situation comedy to science-fiction action to eroticism to zany farce—taking in references to other cartoons and live-action properties.

Surely a certain adolescent discomfort with grown-up sexuality and sexual difference, a lack of social skills, and the ability to be aggressive in one's own defence are definitional properties of anime male characters and, consequently, of many of its fans.

Related to this manga-derivation and the youth audience to whom the films are geared is the fact that the most popular anime have been given over to serialization. Some began as television series, complete and whole by the time they got overseas—like the originary *Astro Boy* or the very popular *Urusei Yatsura* (*Those Obnoxious Aliens*) which ran on television from 1981-1986 to the tune of more than 250 episodes. Its popularity then resulted in six films, and at least three OAV movies. Others were serialized precisely at the time of their production due to their immediate popularity—such as *Dirty Pair*, which was a 1986 TV series that ran for one year of 26 episodes, then found life afterward in OAV to the tune of 10 more in 1988. *Ranma 1/2* and *Bubblegum Crisis*, and a sequel series, *AD Police*, each have a dozen or more videos with one or two episodes on each of them. This serialization may be likened to the sequelization of everything from *Halloween* to *Nightmare on Elm Street* to *Friday the 13th*, the latter two of which not only had film sequels but found life (so to speak) on television as well. Similarly, the *Star Trek* phenomenon, with four television series and seven feature films, is another important example. I suspect that there is something in the idea that things never change and never come to an end that is appealing to fan audiences on psychoanalytic grounds.

Most striking to me has not been the fact that anime are SF, horror or fantasy (even those which are comedy). For why shouldn't animation, the most "magical" of the cinematic modes, be given over precisely to the unreal, the impossible, the fantastic? No, what is most striking, even shocking on one level, is the predominance of female characters. Indeed, if one's knowledge of anime is based exclusively on *Akira*, one hasn't seen the majority of anime by any stretch of the imagination.

Urusei Yatsura, *Dirty Pair*, and *Bubblegum Crisis* all have female characters in the leading roles, as does another popular series, *Sailor Moon* (a show which was geared to children and is apparently on Canadian TV in a children's time slot, but which has broken into the adolescent fan market). *Urusei Yatsura* also has a male character of importance, but other shows in which the male character is supposed to dominate make the female characters prominent and, I'd suggest, more the objects of cult following and identification: *All Purpose Cultural Cat Girl Nuku Nuku* (a title to be reckoned with!) and *Oh! My Goddess!* come to mind in this category. An almost all-female cast of characters is the object of attention in a popular stand-alone anime, *Angel of Darkness*, which invokes issues of lesbian sexuality and adolescent male identification; and it's worth pointing out another anime, with which I'm not otherwise familiar, called *Bronze Cathexis*, "a 1994 installment in the tradition of *shojo anime* (girls' cartoons) featuring the homoerotic exploits of beautiful boys."[16] Here, then, is an anime directed at adolescent girls in the throes of gender definitions and being attracted to boys who look like girls (though I imagine such a premise might not win much following among boys). Discussions of individual shows, movies or series will bring this out more clearly.

Akira

There can be little doubt that *Akira* is the best-known example of anime in the west. A hit breakout into the realm of the international art film, *Akira* derives, as is well-known, from a manga, but it was a manga geared toward the male youth market.[17] Its complex animation, its post-apocalyptic setting, its SF and horror elements, and its focus on a male protagonist earmarked it for cult status among the then-emerging anime fans. Indeed, it may very well be the case that *Akira* was the catalyst for the anime fan cults in the west. Its images of Tokyo, "the archetype of the cyberpunk metropolis, the glitzy consumer capital of the world,"[18] must have seemed familiar to Western audiences in the wake of *Blade Runner*. Similarly its themes of rebellious youths breaking free of authority yet pursued by it, of banding together for protection and a sense of family, and of the adolescent allegory of transformation seen through the process of morphing, found a receptive audience here.

Relying on definitions of the postmodern as put forth by Fredric Jameson, Freiberg calls *Akira* a postmodern text by virtue of its reliance on pastiche and schizophrenia. I take exception to the notion of "pastiche" in Jameson and to *Akira* as pastiche. Calling *Akira* "pastiche" because its source is a comic book (and not an original script) and because the comic book itself "appropriates elements from scifi [sic] fiction and movies . . . the horror movie . . . the disaster movie . . . the teen pic . . . and the suspense action"[19] is to miss the point about genre. SF, horror, disaster and the teen pic, combined together and done in a suspenseful way with lots of action, has been the watchword of movie-making since the 1950s. The temptation to over-generalization should be resisted. It is simply too easy to label the success of anime as part of the postmodern condition. Yes, anime does belong to the modern and contemporary, and if we want to call the modern and contemporary "postmodern" we may do so, but at the expense of a certain exactitude.

However, Freiberg is quite right that the film is schizophrenic: "There are a bewildering number of characters, incidents, spatial and temporal leaps, that make the narrative difficult to follow and render it well-nigh incomprehensible on a first viewing."[20] But *Akira* has links to numerous Japanese literary and oral traditions of circumlocution, complexity, evasiveness, the covert, the implied, etc. From *The Tale of Genji* to *rakugo*, Japanese storytelling is frankly quite allusive, not to mention often elusive. Let us think, after all, of the cinematic context, and recall the films of Ozu Yasujiro. He is a favorite of many Western scholars precisely for these "postmodern" qualities of ellipses, temporal leaps, characters whose relation to the plot (such as it is) is either vague at the time of their introduction or vague by the time the film has ended, and spatial confusion and playfulness. Yet surely we cannot in good faith call a director whose last film was made in 1962 "postmodern," anymore than we could claim an 11th century literary classic is postmodern. I would also point to the case of the popular Hong Kong cinema, the films of, say, Tsui Hark and John Woo, where incomprehensibility of plot has been a hallmark since the 1970s. As I've indicated, Hong Kong cinema is part of the same fan culture which includes anime. Is Hong Kong cinema postmodern? Many think so, I will admit.

Yet *Akira* is, as Freiberg has it, quite postmodern. It is a direct outgrowth of war and postwar experiences: from the atomic bombings to the economic miracle to Japan's rise as a major economic power in the world, to overcrowding and over-achieving, *Akira* clearly speaks to a young generation in Japan. Freiberg quotes one critic as saying that, "apart from the experience of the atomic bomb,. . . the Japanese nation's 'collective psyche' has endured . . . [the] pressure of living in a high-tech, collectivist but commercial society; the nation's lack of natural resources; the over-crowded living conditions; and the ever-present threat of earthquake, typhoon and fire."[21] I would also point out the pressures of the nuclear family on Japanese youth and the omnipresence of the mother in particular. Freiberg notes with great insight the absence of the Japanese family in *Akira* (though this is not an absence ubiquitous in anime by any means). And it is not just the family that is absent, but specifically the mother. This lack of the traditional family is common in anime and substitute families predominate. But even when there is one parent around, it is more often than not the father. Breaking away from family in general and from mother in specific is one hallmark in the move from childhood to adolescence and from adolescence to adulthood. It is a universal phenomenon, but it takes on particular poignancy in Japan which is so mother-centered.

The break away from families is often contrasted to and compared with a burgeoning interest in sexuality and gender. Here it is important to note the typical stance SF takes toward sexuality: Vivian Sobchack has argued that "space travel replaces sexual exploration in the science fiction film, which is notably short on sexually active women and sexual activity generally."[22] This is to say, following the important work of Ilsa J. Bick, that SF is as often torn between latency and adolescence as it is between adolescence and adulthood.[23]

Ranma 1/2

A more typical example of anime, and the best example I can think of to demonstrate that anime's fans are attracted to the form's allegorizations of gender identity and gender confusion, is surely *Ranma 1/2*. This is the story of a teenage boy who, when doused with cold water, turns into a teenage girl. That the boy's father, when similarly exposed to cold water turns not into a woman (not into the mother, that is) but into a panda, is surely an absence, a lack, to be noted. For Newitz, *Ranma 1/2* may be allegorical of all of anime: "While quite racially mixed as a group, otaku are overwhelmingly male, particularly in the U.S. For this reason, it is important to understand that what is at stake for Americans watching anime is certainly bound up with gender identity, especially masculine identity." In the subgenre (of the large genre she calls "romantic comedy") of magical girls, the men "are young, bewildered, and sexually inexperienced." This subgenre "features women who are simultaneously powerful and traditionally feminine."[24] Ranma, as both a boy and a girl, is a trained martial artist. Similarly, in both incarnations he/she is quite good looking. Ranma is, it should be noted, in early adolescence. He seems coded as around 15, I think. And he is attracted to the youngest of three girls in the household in which he has come to reside.

This motif of a magical girl and a young male may be seen in another anime that I think is archetypical: *All Purpose Cultural Cat Girl Nuku Nuku*. The family set-up, as in *Ranma 1/2*, is a father and son, though in *Cat Girl*, the boy's mother is a major character. The boy here is late latency, but with shifts to very early adolescence. But since he is a primary school student, he can be no more than 11 or so, and thus should be a latency-aged male. Still, in the first episode the boy befriends a girl student who is his age, but who seems remarkably well developed. The predominate character, however, is the cat girl—an android with the brain of a cat, but who can for whatever reason—probably the plot itself—speak. The young boy's reliance on her is clearly as an all-powerful mother. Ironically or not, it protects him from his actual mother and from other women in her service. Because she is not his mother, however, Nuku Nuku can be eroticized, though not as often for him as for the audience. I would suggest that the audience for this anime, as for many others, can identify with both the boy and the cat girl, especially if we allow the otaku's relative lack of social skills and physical prowess to be seen allegorically in the form of an outsider, the cat girl, who is a super-hero.

For Newitz, *Ranma 1/2*, though presumably other anime as well, has a clear reading: "Quite simply, *Ranma 1/2* demonstrates to the young man who enjoys romantic comedy anime that he is constantly in danger of becoming a girl.... Like Ranma, the male anime fan has a 'feminine half' who enjoys passively consuming animated fantasies about love. His attachment to non-sexual romance might be said to feminize him."[25] I'll amend this a bit however, and point out that non-sexual romance is not necessarily a purely feminine pursuit, though it might be culturally claimed and desired as such. I would say that it is a latency-aged pursuit and not, precisely, an adolescent one. Thus I disagree with her contention, suggestive and insightful though it is, that, "When American fans consume magical girl anime, partly what they enjoy about the genre is its historical incongruence with American mainstream culture. Or, to put it another way: they are enjoying depictions of women which take for granted that women are subordinate to men.... Americans consume magical girl anime as a form of nostalgia for the kind of social situations made possible by traditional gender roles."[26] Instead I would say, in more psychoanalytic terms, that latency or even infantile sexuality is the preferred mode, involving a union with the all-powerful mother, a sense of longing for wholeness, an unwillingness to acknowledge sexual difference, and a fear of the gendered self. *Ranma 1/2*, with its appeal to children as well as adolescents, is closer to an allegory of the transition from latency to adolescence, rather than the transition from adolescence to adulthood. The infantalization of the Japanese man may be the root of this dominant strand in anime, but it is clearly a strand with cultural tendencies across the West, too.

Conclusion

The appeal of anime to a certain segment of a potential audience is not simply a function of infantalization, of a struggle between latency and adolescence, on the part of the boy fans of the genre (though I would insist upon its validity). Anime fans' ability to identify across cultural, racial and gender bounds bespeaks the fluidity of identity within the postmodern context. Similarly, the prevalence of pop cultural intertextuality in anime elicits the same sort of appeal as the works of Quentin Tarantino, an icon for some, but by no means all, of the anime fandom. In disagreement with Newitz, I would say that anime is not an example of "cultural imperialism in reverse," that Americans are not, in fact "being colonized by Japanese pop culture."[27] For Newitz, such colonization makes American fans anxious, makes them feel disempowered and dependent and hence feminized. If this is true, it must mean either that anime fans outside of America in the West—in Canada, Great Britain, and the other places I've mentioned above where anime has found a receptive audience—are similarly experiencing anxieties over cultural imperialism, or else that the issue of Japan vs. America is not a salient one for understanding anime.

In fact, I would remind us all of the dangers, the inability, to formulate a unified "Japanese culture" of the contemporary era (we could barely do it without many qualifications for pre-modern Japanese culture). American popular culture is absolutely ubiquitous in Japan, as well. Thus the dichotomization, Japan/America, will not work. Beyond that, however, is a more important facet: that Japanese youth and American youth share a common culture with worldwide youth, a youth culture often at odds with the official culture of any nation, but especially their own. So I don't quite agree with Newitz when she says that "Whereas anime are mainstream culture in Japan, in America they are still 'alternative culture,' particularly when we start talking about the hard-to-find videos."[28] Anime is not mainstream culture in Japan (though manga are), it is alternative culture, at least youth culture, and it is alternative culture in the West, but not just in the U.S. Anime is an example of a bottom-up cultural movement, a popular culture/mass culture phenomenon of great interest that perhaps scholars should pay attention to; or perhaps not. Let the fans have their way. Teacher, leave those kids alone; the kids are all right.

Notes

[1] There is a bit more on manga, a related cultural phenomenon.

[2] Annalee Newitz, "Magical Girls and Atomic Bomb Sperm," *Film Quarterly* 49: 1 (Fall, 1995), 3.

[3] Ben Crawford, "Emperor Tomato Ketchup: Cartoon Properties from Japan," in Mick Broderick, ed., *Hibakusha Cinema* (London: Kegan, Paul, 1996), 80.

[4] I'm not neglecting adolescent girls as a potent audience segment, but recent evidence reveals that they can't make a hit on their own in mainstream cinema—witness *Now and Then*, say, or *Boys on the Side*. Similarly, in reading the audience which rents anime in video stores, boys are in the majority.

[5] I'll note here that Japanese monster movies have a small cult following in the west, a cult drawn from many of the anime fans as evidenced by many picture books and fanzines devoted to the subject. Similarly, as is quite well known I'm sure, manga have made their way here as well, with a handful of companies producing English-language versions of Japanese originals.

[6] Edward Small, *Japanese Animated Film: A Study of Narrative, Intellectual Montage and Metamorphosis Structures for Semiotic Sequencing*. Unpublished dissertation. The University of Iowa (1972), 73.

DAVID DESSER

[7] The Japanese Ministry of Finance issued a paper in 1957 proclaiming that Japan had succeeded in achieving an "economic miracle" whereby the country had completely recovered from the severe postwar depression.

[8] Small, *Film*, 114-115.

[9] Small, *Film*, 104 and passim.

[10] Small, *Film*, 122.

[11] Crawford, *Ketchup*, 79.

[12] Gunther Nitschke, "The Manga City," in Atsushi Euda, ed.,Miriam Eguchi, trans., *The Electric Geisha: Exploring Japan's Popular Culture* (Tokyo: Kodansha, 1994), 235.

[13] Nitschke, *Geisha*, 231.

[14] Nitschke, *Geisha*, 232-233.

[15] Nitschke, *Geisha*, 237.

[16] Nitschke, *Geisha*, 80.

[17] Freda Freiberg, "*Akira*—and the Postnuclear Sublime," in Broderick, ed., *Hibakusha Cinema*, 94.

[18] Freiberg, "*Akira*," 93.

[19] Freiberg, "*Akira*," 96.

[20] Freiberg, "*Akira*," 96.

[21] Freiberg, "*Akira*," 97.

[22] Quoted in Freiberg, "*Akira*," 100.

[23] Ilsa J. Bick, "Boys in Space: *Star Trek*, Adolescence, Latency and the Neverending Story," *Cinema Journal* 35: 2 (Winter, 1996) 43-60.

[24] Newitz, "Magical Girls," 4.

[25] Newitz, "Magical Girls," 6.

[26] Newitz, "Magical Girls," 5.

[27] Newitz, "Magical Girls," 11, 12.

[28] Newitz, "Magical Girls," 3.

KIRBY FARRELL

Making a Killing in Post-Traumatic *True Romance*

True Romance (1993) projects an equivocal young hero who is at once a romantic bumpkin (comically named "Clarence") and a cunning antisocial killer. The film uses trauma to explain how the harmless loser can become a triumphal survivor. As a trope, trauma justifies the hero's aggression by implying a social and psychic economy in which overwhelming victimization has made all customary constraints moot. I read the film's use of trauma against four contemporary contexts: the Menendez brothers' murders of their parents; the post-traumatic aftershock of the Vietnam War; the economic injustices of the 1990s; and finally the environmental apocalypse insinuated in the solar fireball that closes the film.

In August 1989, at 722 North Elm Drive in Beverly Hills, Lyle and Erik Menendez murdered their parents in such a frenzy of shotgun fire that the bodies were nearly unrecognizable. This excess resembles the ecstatic rage of traumatized soldiers that psychiatrists call "berserking." In combat, berserking is a reaction to an overwhelming sense of helplessness, victimization, and death-anxiety. While the frenzy lasts, soldiers feel indestructible, slaughtering enemies and sometimes, as at My Lai, women and children.[1]

At first glance the comparison seems bizarre. The Menendez brothers planned the assassination of their unarmed parents, a Hollywood executive and wife, and inherited a fortune. Yet the brothers were apparently thinking in terms of trauma, since in their defense they claimed their father Jose had been sexually abusing them over a "lifetime of terror, [a] lifetime of threats."[2] Supposedly Jose had made his son Erik a sex slave, and in Orlando Patterson's trenchant phrase, slavery is "social death."[3]

In the brothers' scenario the victims were monsters, while the murderous sons are meek and suffering heroic victims who deserve to inherit the earth. But given that the brothers lived in a scriptwriting culture, and that Erik had earlier written a play in which a son murders his father for his money, it would not be difficult to imagine that Lyle and Erik devised the story of their innocence out of their own deep feelings and their sense of what an audience would want to hear. While awaiting trial, they read Paul Mones's book *When a Child Kills: Abused Children Who Kill Their Parents,* "a study of true cases and how they were defended in court."[4] For them, traumatic violence was an emotional reality but also a strategic script.

The prosecution's story depicted Lyle and Erik as parasites and failures. Princeton had expelled Lyle for cheating and at one point the brothers were in trouble for burglarizing affluent family friends. In the trial dramas, these stories of guilt and desperate innocence clashed in a literal life and death struggle for credibility. Each of the stories in its way had the power to turn reality inside out and point to fabulous motives invisible in everyday life. Taken together, the clash of stories makes a sort of Greek tragedy of monstrous ambition and family collapse. But it also tells us something about economic strife and generational antagonism in the 1990s.

One way to get at the fantasies implied in that clash of stories is to read the Menendez murders against Tony Scott's *True Romance.* The film opens in decayed industrial Detroit, where unemployed men are warming their hands over a fire in a waste barrel. This cityscape evokes the poverty in Cuba that Jose Menendez escaped by struggling to the top in executive Hollywood. The dying city suggests the punishment awaiting those who fail in the competition for the American dream, and also, for the young, the dead end of post-industrial decline. In a word, the film opens with Lyle and Erik Menendez' worst nightmare.

As "minimum wage kids," store clerk and call girl, the film's young lovers teeter over the economic abyss with the romantic pluck of kids in a Depression-era romantic comedy. When Clarence (Christian Slater) sighs that "The world seems to be collapsing," Alabama (Patricia Arquette) counters spunkily that "sometimes it can go the other way." For the lovers as for the immigrant Jose Menendez, escape lies in the direction of sunny Hollywood.

But in Detroit as in Beverly Hills, fathers seem to control destiny, and as a result sons are dangerously ambivalent. Clarence's feelings are divided among benign or monstrous father-figures: his boss, his girl's pimp; his biological dad, a Mafia godfather. Like Jose Menendez, Clarence's boss sells heroic dreams. He has provided Clarence with a working-class education through his comic book store, a library of superheroes such as Spider Man, who were invented to uplift Depression-era landscapes like the Detroit we see here. In the end the Menendez brothers failed to make it as Ivy League role-models, and they turned to Clarence's shadow world of superheroes and "bad motherfuckers." When they failed to master their father's elite Hollywood, they identified with self-created heroes who thrive by destroying supercriminal father-figures.

The problem with fathers is that sooner or later they weaken and die, and sons have to take their places. Patriarchs traditionally cope with this threat by cultivating symbolic immortality, investing in sons who will carry them into posterity the way Jose Menendez evidently dreamed of establishing a Kennedy-style political dynasty in Florida. But the transition is always precarious. Fathers may make their dreams so grand that sons feel inadequate and resentful. For mediocre sons who have been expelled from Princeton or sell comic books for a living, crime may seem to offer the only plausible way of fulfilling that glory. In *True Romance* as in the polarized 90s, hapless Detroit and fabulous Hollywood are so far apart that only a suitcase full of criminal loot can carry you from one place to the other.

But other dark motives can destabilize coming of age as well. Fathers have as strong an incentive to delay inheritance as sons do to hurry it along. Motives may be fatally mixed. Jose Menendez kept urging his sons to find women and settle down, trying to dictate desires and buy posterity. In *True Romance* Clarence's boss hires a call girl as a birthday surprise for him; when the paid sex turns romantic, the gift inadvertently produces a happy marriage. But such a gift makes a bitter parody of a traditional arranged marriage, since Clarence's "father" is not really willing to share his wealth and name with the next generation. Appropriately, Alabama confesses the birthday sex scheme as they sit on the catwalk of a billboard after making love, caught in the blinding floodlights of commercialism.

The gift unwittingly confirms that father owns everything, including the girl, so that in making love to her the son is actually doing the father's will. In a sense, the son is making love to the father through the prostitute. All the world becomes an expression of the father's will. This sublimated slavery assumes a nightmare face in the Menendez allegations of sexual abuse. In the film it locates an original violation which can explain the son's rebellious urge to go into the underworld and kill the girl's pimp, the vicious surrogate father, lover, and rival Drexl Spivey (Gary Oldman). The symbolic logic of their confrontation is wholly apt. Drexl keeps sneering threats of homosexual dominance with a menacing smile that captures not just the numbness but the emotional disconfirmation of Clarence's childhood world.

At the extreme, in fear or rage, an aging father may turn against his children, trying to devour the child's vitality to replenish his own waning life. As in vampire fantasies, the child becomes the abuser's "creature." In the Menendez sons' courtroom defense, this scenario culminates in Erik's claim that "I thought [my father] was going to kill me that night, and I thought he was going to have sex with me first."[5] In this statement, however fanciful it is, sex and death go together.

This scenario puts the son in a heroic role. The threat of annihilation objectifies his fear of his own weakness and justifies not just self-defense, but heroic, superhuman rage. In confessing the murders to his therapist, Lyle could have been characterizing one of Clarence's superheroes: "What Erik and I did took courage beyond belief. Beyond, beyond strength."[6] But what if the son exaggerates or invents the parental aggression? A child may be tempted to believe himself abused insofar as abuse makes his resentment heroic. The calculating Laius, after all, wanted to have the infant Oedipus put out to die. Much depends on these ambiguities of motive and responsibility. Clarence idolizes not only the noble Spider Man but also the "bad motherfucker." The opposites merge in Clarence's ultimate hero, Elvis (Val Kilmer). At once Elvis is the obedient son who submitted to military service with great fanfare, and the renegade bad boy. At the same time Elvis fuses the roles of son and father, since he is both a rebellious son and also "the king," a hallucinatory father-hero who watches over and advises Clarence at moments of crisis.

Elvis offers a troubled son a gratifying fantasy solution to father-son conflict. The solution imagines antagonism overcome by radical erotic identification with the intimidating power-figure. Though Clarence insists he is not homosexual, he dreams about making love with Elvis. Sexual surrender to "the king" or father entices him because it promises total merger, total approval, direct participation in "the king's" greatness. But the bond is dangerously unstable. Submission can placate the older man's jealousy of the son as a potential rival who is destined to replace him. But sexual surrender also raises the dependent lover's fear of never becoming his own man.[7]

These conflicts help to explain why in fantasy the father tends to split into opposites, and why it may take traumatic violence for sons finally to break away. Clarence's marriage, for example, triggers a fatal reckoning. Where the boss has been benignly manipulating behind the scenes, he now tacitly appears as the vicious pimp who is the lover's "boss." In a hallucinatory encounter, Elvis reinforces Clarence's desire to face down the pimp. "You can count on me to protect you," Clarence pledges to Alabama like a new patriarch. It is easy to forget that in making this promise, Clarence sets up and provokes the film's chain of killings. Supposedly he shoots the pimp in self-defense and "innocently" takes home his wife's suitcase containing a fortune in cocaine. In taking the cocaine, itself stolen from a Mafia godfather, Clarence is wresting an inheritance from evil father-figures, the rightful patrimony that his boss, the deceptively good father, would withhold. In effect, Elvis, the ambiguous son-as-father-"king," authorizes Clarence to destroy the depraved father/pimp. As the pimp exclaims when he learns that "his" whore has wed Clarence, "Then we're just about relations!" The wisecrack implies incestuous abuse between the pimp and "his" girl, but also between the pimp and this upstart rival male. And this fantasy echoes in the Menendez brothers' allegations of abuse and humiliation.

In these on- and offscreen stories ambivalent homosexual feeling surfaces wherever men are struggling together for power and identity—which is to say, virtually everywhere. In a Los Angeles motel room Alabama kills a Mafia hit man named Virgil (James Gandolfini) in an episode of hand-to-hand combat that is as brutal as anything we see in the film. "You have a lot of heart," Virgil says praising her ferocity. At heart, that is, she is tacitly one of the boys. Despite some energetic lovemaking on screen, in the film as in the brothers' stories, the survival struggle between men matters more than tenderness or eros.

As the plot develops, generational stress keeps returning in increasingly grotesque forms. On the run with his new wife and the contraband, Clarence turns for help to his biological father Clifford Worley (Dennis Hopper). Once a cop and an alcoholic, this father abandoned his family and presumably left his son traumatized. Now he is a security guard, living alone, injured but wiser, self-sacrificing and nurturant. Having killed off a selfish incarnation of the father (Drexl), Clarence can be reconciled with a "real" father who is able to say "I love you." Yet almost at once another evil father—the Mafia godfather—emerges. No sooner do the lovers escape to Hollywood than in their wake gangsters come to the father's trailer looking for Clarence and the stolen cocaine. Once again a symbolic father and son are in mortal conflict.

This time the aggressive son, Don Vincenzo Coccotti (Christopher Walken), serves an evil father, the off-scene Mafia godfather. And this time a good father is utterly self-sacrificing to save a son he loves, since Clarence's father provokes his own death so that the gangsters won't torture him into revealing his son's whereabouts. Specifically, he goads the Mafioso "son" into killing him by playing on his racism, shaming the Sicilian by invoking the historical conquest or "penetration" of Sicily by black moors. The moorish "niggers," he taunts, raped ancestral mothers, so that today's Sicilians, including the Mafioso, are racially mixed. This is one more fantasy of the predatory (fore)father, only displaced back into history, and Don Vincenzo reacts with murderous fury.

This historical rape is akin to the aggression of the pimp which has spurred Clarence to murder. Like Clarence reacting to the pimp, and like the Menendez brothers, the Mafiosi are sons outraged by the thought of paternal rape. But there is another dimension to this fantasy as well. Just as the Mafiosi violently deny their "black" origins, so Jose Menendez sought to deny the "black" inferiority of his Cuban origins by founding in the United States a dynasty of sons with Anglo-European names who would go to Princeton and transcend his background. Failure to live up to that dynastic ambition threatened Lyle and Erik not only with a slide into a Detroit-style dead end, but also with a humiliating reminder of the family's lowly origins.[8] The film slyly mocks paternal pretensions to elite purity, even as it covets the supremacy a suitcase full of drugs can buy.

When the lovers flee to Los Angeles, Clarence acts as a sort of dramatist, scripting his caper as he goes along, and his dream of making a fortune by combining acting and crime echoes Erik Menendez' screenwriting and acting aspirations. In this way the plot justifies the drug scam by making Hollywood hopelessly corrupt. Clarence plots to sell the drug stash to a movie producer, Lee Donowitz (Saul Rubinek)—a Hollywood executive as corrupt as Jose Menendez was alleged to be. The producer has clear affinities with the Mafia godfather, as we see when a car cuts him off and he threatens the other driver: "Don't give me the finger or I'll have you killed." That is, the producer is another incarnation of the killer dad. Though he is superficially ingratiating, his tyrannical nature is reflected in the sycophantic, self-abasing behavior of his assistant and surrogate son Elliot Blitzer (Bronson Pinchot). As Clarence gradually cons and bullies Elliot into the drug deal, we are meant to see a cagey independent son overcoming a spineless alter ego.

Picked up accidentally on a drug charge, Elliot Blitzer is forced to betray the producer-father. With Elliot wired to capture incriminating evidence, the police set a trap to catch the producer buying the stolen cocaine. But then the godfather and his soldiers unexpectedly intervene as well. Caught in the middle of the climactic shootout, Clarence slips free with a token wound; but the hapless Elliot dies as punishment for his weakness in betraying the producer-father's drug-lust to the cops. This resembles the Menendez brothers' excuse for not having gone to the police about their years of abuse: supposedly Jose was so powerful he would have had them killed. On another level, as the bugged medium of his boss's incriminating confession, Elliot functions like Hollywood itself, exposing other people's corruption for profit. In putting Elliot to death Hollywood is slyly mocking itself for its profitable exploitation of other people's sins, even as it scorns the self-indulgent producer.

One underlying fantasy is that the film is daringly improvising an exploration of Hollywood's sleazy reality just as Clarence improvises gangster lines so persuasive they draw the naively crooked producer and others into playing parts in "his" play. Faking underworld experience, Clarence is using illusion—Hollywood's tool—to penetrate a shady realm where staggering riches are hidden from the gullible public. The wishful assumption is that everyone is acting, but the imaginative son is a natural actor, an effortless professional, able to use the role of master criminal without being tainted by it. If fathers and godfathers are finally alike, stealing from them is scarcely crime at all. This fantasy has an echo in the Menendez brothers' scheme to be gentleman burglars as well as killers.

Post-Traumatic **True Romance**

In the earlier battles with the pimp and the hit man, Clarence and his girl are caught up in a sudden spasm of violence and kill their adversaries. In the final shootout, however, the crossfire is an all-engulfing and yet sourceless maelstrom. It begins as a standoff. Equally armed and full of lethal suspicion, the respective parties are stunned to find themselves confronting one another in the hotel room. The implicit fantasy is that the moment of supreme tension reveals the deepest motives. Lee Donowitz, the sleazy producer, catches on to Elliot's betrayal. "I treated you like a son!" he screams, launching into a tantrum that triggers the holocaust.

By implication, the sham friendliness of Hollywood masks an underlying tension that resembles the atmosphere in a police state. Surveillance and entrapment are basic modes of operation for all the parties in the drug deal. Not only the police but also the Mafiosi and Clarence are driven by moralistic outrage. Combined with paranoid vigilance, that rage to punish poisons all relationships. Any break in the surface of life triggers rage. Little wonder that Elliot can confide in no one. To survive here, a rebellious son needs to be "cool" like Clarence: meaning wholly dissociated.

The lovers escape with the loot to Brazil, where they romp on the beach, triumphant but alone. They have a son named "Elvis," and they're founding a dynasty as Jose Menendez wished to do. But dominating the closing moments of the film is a setting sun monstrous as an atomic fireball.

•

The final sunset of *True Romance* might evoke Nevil Shute's doomsday scenario *On the Beach,* or even the nightmare shore at the entropic end of time in H.G. Wells's *Time Machine.* In the glib, lurid vocabulary of apocalyptic sci-fi, that furious sun makes this the final couple, chased from a dying civilization like the parents of Superman, bearing in little "Elvis" the eschatological hero. The imagery alludes to environmental catastrophe and sums up earlier hints of cultural crash. But if the raging sun signifies ultimate menace, it also blazons the futility of self-restraint, delayed gratification, and cultural values. In this way the scene deviously reinforces and even inflames assumptions about behavior that have been operating all along. An irrational, hostile, even doomed world demands a capacity for violent assertion and violent enjoyment in the available moment.

The apocalyptic sun makes a striking image of the berserk state. It is emotionally dissociated yet a part of the beach holiday even as rage is a dissociated part of Clarence, the "cool" hero, the new father.

On one level, the berserk state is a trick to bring closure to a screenplay in which late-20th-century conventions of depersonalization and violence are so extreme that no particular action can seem climactic or even authentic. Only losing control, being "cool" in the grip of frenzy, conveys authenticity. In this respect berserking dramatizes an escape from the plasticity of 1990s culture, the glut of interchangeable self-parodic stories that is Hollywood and mass entertainment. If everything is for sale; if computer simulation makes everything possible; then everything is arbitrary and therefore meaningless—which is to say, poisoned by death-anxiety.

On this level, ecstatic violence is a form of terror management. Like drugs, it fills a psychic void with frenzied oblivion. It represents an effort to escape death-anxiety by using death against others, even as the Hiroshima fireball first promised strategists control over the principle of annihilation. It is only a short step to the Vietnam War, which brought berserking to the public eye in accounts of combat trauma and atrocities like the My Lai massacre. This is surely one connotation when the Mafioso calls Clarence's murder of the pimp a "massacre." It is coyly evoked in the sleazy producer's film about the Vietnam War, *Coming Home in a Body Bag,* which Clarence calls his favorite movie of all time, as if the war has been totally commercialized by now like any Kung Fu movie. The producer is working on a sequel, *Body Bag II,* which is in effect this movie, *True Romance.* Like the need for endless movie sequels, berserking represents an effort to impose narrative closure on a war that resists rationalization.[9]

By no accident the extravagant firepower of the industrial post-Hiroshima army evokes slang words for killing, such as "vaporizing." The idea is that methodical excess, as in military fantasies about Vietnam and in the Gulf War, will not simply cripple but actually annihilate the enemy, eliminating the need for negotiation, compromise, and anticlimax. This is the dream of omnipotence lurking in the ideas of nerve gas and the "clean" neutron bomb that would destroy masses of people but leave their property intact like the Jewish apartments Germans took over during the Nazi period.

True Romance implies that social life is war, that the odds are against rational planning and negotiation, and that those who survive do so by abandoning themselves to the berserk state. The underlying conceit is that Clarence is a combat veteran. Among the veterans Robert Jay Lifton treated for post-traumatic stress is one who reported: "The most widely read literature among the guys that return from Vietnam, it's comics. Comic books and adventure stories. You know, Male: you see the picture of some guy killing somebody and the bare-breasted, Vietnamese-type Asian-looking woman.. . . These guys are just living in a dream world."[10]

But combat fantasy is only one association of Hollywood berserking. Another is business. For Clarence as for the Menendez brothers, success is "making a killing." The connection is in berserking, which implies throwing yourself into an action with controlled abandon. In these terms the ultimate deal epitomizes an ethos in which life is a headlong, possibly suicidal, gamble. This is, I think, a subtext that emerged in the Reagan 1980s, when institutional controls over business were relaxed and the buccaneering entrepreneur became a self-aggrandizing, self-declared culture hero. After the murders, the Menendez brothers began buying up businesses with their legacy.

What I want to suggest is that berserking operates to inflate and to excuse ugly, predatory economic motives that look back to the vicious Social Darwinism of the 1890s and to the new post-Soviet world. If traditional business safeguards are compromised, decisions are risky and fellow businessmen can't be trusted. "Berserking" objectifies that anxiety about lost control and offers some relief from the exacerbated tension of "the deal." In "innocently" stealing the cocaine, Clarence dramatizes the assumption that the corporate muscle that destroyed Detroit and owns everything is akin to Mafia. In effect, berserking is the only technique left to the little guy in his revolt against vicious fathers. To further excuse Clarence, the screenplay also makes him a folk-type, the trickster, who fools enemies into destroying one another. It goes without saying that the trickster/business hero is cousin to the Hollywood illusionist and myth-maker, whose story we are in fact beholding on screen.

The apocalyptic sun and the businessman-trickster may seem poles apart. But in fact berserking bridges that gap. And this may explain why the Menendez sons killed in a frenzy—because in split focus they under- and overestimated their parents. Behind their pretensions, Jose and Kitty were contemptibly small, even as their power over their sons seemed so vast that the sons felt only superhuman violence could kill them. I would argue that the brothers operated in a force field of images and assumptions very like those which carry Clarence and Alabama and nominal little Elvis to that utopian beach at the end of livable life.

In its self-involvement, this cluster of images is a tricky mix of nihilism and posturing. The fireball-sun expresses a fear of not being able to get back into the safety of conventional roles after traumatic disenchantment with everyday culture. Life is then like combat, the individual caught between an enemy Other and punishing fathers.[11] But the survivor's reaction is rage against all the rest of the world: everybody else dies. The screenplay makes Alabama say that if Clarence had been killed, she would have wanted to die too—implicitly dooming her baby. This seems to be more the screenplay than a young mother speaking. The apocalyptic wish is related to the exterminatory rage implicit in matter-of-fact Cold War plans for Mutual Assured Destruction, itself an outgrowth of the Nazi death camps and the terror bombing of World War II.[12] At the same time, Alabama is an elfin, sentimental lass, who can gush, "You're so cool."

Like true Hollywood, *True Romance* is both opportunistic and equivocal, and like the hung juries in the first Menendez trials, the film is acutely ambivalent. It sympathizes with victimized youth while reinforcing the media's self-fulfilling prophecies that they are "superpredators" who will "take violence to a new level."[13] Through its hyped-up rhetoric—the verbal equivalent of berserking—the film "wipes out" the problem it attacks, tacitly apologizing for injustice and privilege in the status quo. The Brazilian beach is a cop-out, if only because in compensating for death-anxiety, the fantasy of being supreme survivors is exactly what drives the cruelty and injustices of the dead world the survivors have fled.

The film challenges itself on a number of levels, but mostly in order to protect the core values it most needs to move beyond. The proof of this, I think, is not so much what *True Romance* includes as what it leaves out—what it can't think about. The obsession with berserking and "popular" apocalypse tacitly nullifies mother and child, nurture and desire, and in this way recreates and justifies the sort of brutal family that triggered the first killings on screen and also in the Menendez living room. Read this way, the film unwittingly dramatizes a cultural *system*. And the crucial question we need to ask is a systemic question—an ethological question: how to open up a cultural obsession as confining as the ruthless business frenzy that makes killers of young men like the Menendez brothers and their counterparts in the film.

Notes

[1] See Jonathan Shay's account in *Achilles in Vietnam: Combat Trauma and the Undoing of Character* (New York: Atheneum, 1994).

[2] Dominick Dunne, "Menendez Justice," *Vanity Fair,* March, 1994, 114.

[3] Orlando Patterson, *Slavery and Social Death: A Comparative Study* (Cambridge MA: Harvard University Press, 1982).

[4] Dunne, 112. He is referring to Paul A. Mones, *When a Child Kills: Abused Children Who Kill Their Parents* (New York: Pocket Books, 1991).

[5] Dunne, 117.

[6] Dunne, 119.

[7] These issues pervade American culture in the 1990s, as in a *New Yorker* cartoon in which one king says to another, "No, I wasn't abused but I cut off my father's head anyway."

[8] The father's murder, it is worth noting, involves a direct blast to the face the way the brothers annihilated their mother. The violence dramatizes an effort to obliterate personal (mortal) origins.

[9] See, e.g., Kali Tal, *Worlds of Hurt: Reading the Literatures of Trauma* (New York: Cambridge University Press, 1996), 64.

[10] Robert Jay Lifton, *Home from the War* (New York: Simon & Schuster, 1973), 204. The comic book hero is acting out a poignantly crude form of traumatic rescue fantasy.

[11] See the Rambo films in which the betrayed son is trapped between evil Asian and treacherous American "fathers" who threaten death either way.

[12] See Tom Engelhardt, *The End of Victory Culture* (New York: Basic Books, 1995), 54-58.

[13] Peter Annin, "Superpredators Arrive: Should we cage the new breed of vicious kids?" *Newsweek,* January 12, 1996, 57. For an assessment of the revived myth of vicious youth, see Michael Males, *The Scapegoat Generation* (Monroe ME: Common Courage Press, 1996).

MURRAY FORMAN

The 'Hood Took Me Under: Urban Geographies of Danger in New Black Cinema

Now I'm of age and living in the projects
getting paid off the clucks and the county cheques
I'm telling ya, fresh out of high school, never did I wonder
that the motherfucking 'hood would take me under
MC Eiht, "Streiht Up Menace"

Teen Violence: Wild in the Streets. Murder and mayhem, guns and gangs:
a teenage generation grows up dangerous — and scared.
Newsweek, August 2, 1993

In a recent interview, Richard Price, author of the novel *Clockers* and, with Spike Lee, co-writer of the screenplay for its cinematic adaptation, addresses the social basis upon which black youths are represented in the film:

> The reality is that these kids don't give a fuck about stuff like preying on your own people. They don't think of themselves as political or sociological.. . . They are thinking about how to get visible. Plus they are teenagers, and teenagers think of nothing but themselves, not whether they are black or white or rich or poor.[1]

Despite his observation, there remains substantial evidence to contradict this notion of black youth, identity, and collective cultural awareness. In practice, prevailing institutional forces make it difficult for many black and Latino teenagers to ignore either their racial or their class-based status. In contrast to Price's thinking, these

45

teen groups are continually isolated as visible minorities and are subsequently demonized as a mobile threat, leading Henry Giroux to note that "the racial code of violence is especially powerful and pervasive in its association of crime with black youth."[2]

In the 1990s economy of danger, black teens are inordinately wealthy and they have a deathly concise comprehension of how they are perceived by the parent culture in their daily circulation through the urban landscape. Take, for example, a conversation I overheard while leaving a suburban American cineplex after a screening of F. Gary Gray's film *Friday* (1995), starring the popular rap star Ice Cube. The film was not a blockbuster advertised with the accompanying slogan, "on screens everywhere." It was shown in select locations in and around the city, mainly in neighborhoods with high density working-class minority populations. As the crowd of mostly black and Latino teenagers shuffled out of the cineplex one young brother mentioned that "the 'hood films" are always screened in the same theater, closest to the place's entrance/exit. His understanding of this practice was based on the belief that the management was uncomfortable with the idea of a crowd of minority youth traversing the full length of the lobby and potentially intimidating other paying customers.

On several subsequent occasions this was corroborated, as the films which tended to draw a predominantly black teen audience from the surrounding neighborhoods were, in fact, consistently situated close to the doors. The additional presence of a rent-a-cop in the lobby when such films as Nick Gomez' *New Jersey Drive* (1995) were shown further confirmed his observation. The practice of selective exhibition and segregation in theater spaces is nothing particularly new, yet today it is common practice to single out and isolate those films that are thematically focused on the lives and experiences of contemporary black youth from the 'hood.[3]

And what, or more precisely where, is the 'hood? Differentiated from the displaced construct of the ghetto which formed the dominant spatial configuration of such early 1970s "Blaxploitation" films as *Shaft* (1971), *Superfly* (1972) or *The Mack* (1973), the 'hood offers a generational variant on "inner city" regions and the landscapes of urban oppression that prevail there. In the Blaxploitation film, ghetto space is often rendered as a vast, abstract expanse of urban dilapidation. Its topography functions mainly as background, providing a setting of urban decay in which action unfolds. In this sense, the ghetto is a rusty container to be filled by the cinematic exploits of John Shaft, Youngblood Priest, Goldy, Foxy Brown or Cleopatra Jones. The ghetto hasn't disappeared (i.e., the economic and social forces that negatively affect many urban black and Latino communities have not abated), but with the rise of hip hop culture, the range of images and terms through which it was traditionally defined has been superceded by the alternate youth discourse of the 'hood.

In contrast to earlier representations of the ghetto, the 'hood is a more compressed construct, more tightly bounded and closely demarcated as a place. It emerges in the late 1980s as a spatial effect of increasingly common social patterns of localization and particularity which are in contrast with concurrent trends toward globalization and transnationalism. Kevin Robins consequently refers to an emergent tension occurring within "a global-local nexus," and entailing the formation of "placed identities for placeless times."[4] Similarly, Akhil Gupta and James Ferguson describe emergent trends whereby "territoriality is reinscribed at just the point that it threatens to be erased."[5] This suggests that the 'hood is an expression of social scale that is situated along a spectrum of relations spanning the local, regional, and global. Scale is thus a representational determinant in the visual and narrative portrayal of the 'hood (although it is important to stress that it is a scale which is inscribed by the interrelations of internal and external social dynamics—dynamics of "here" and "there"—that can lead to hierarchies of difference through representational practices of spatial othering[6]).

The 'hood is simultaneously a general or abstract conceptual space; an actually existing site of sociological and historical significance; and a product of a particular state of mind or sensibility that has unique and important resonance within the hip hop culture. As a discursive construct, the 'hood is everywhere, taking shape in and through the artistic work of the young members of the hip hop culture who "express themselves" (as N.W.A. suggest in one song) through the popular recording, film, and video media. Crucially, the 'hood is coded and communicated in rap and contemporary black cinema as a zone of chronic danger and risk which delineates the practices that occur within its representational landscapes. It is the primacy of this spatial logic locating black urban youth experience within an environment of continual proximate danger that largely defines "the 'hood film."

Paula Massood asserts that it was director John Singleton who, with *Boyz N the Hood* in 1991, "first mapped the 'hood onto the terrain and into the vocabulary of the popular imagination,"[7] but the release of the song "Boyz N the Hood" in 1986 (Ruthless/Macola Records) by Eazy E and the core members of what eventually became the rap group N.W.A. was influential in establishing "the 'hood" as an emergent term in the spatial discourse of young urban blacks and Latinos (and eventually other youths as well) across North America. The song vividly portrays the 'hood as a space of violence and confrontation, a zone of indiscriminate aggression where threat and danger are commonplace, even banal. With the subsequent release of the album Straight Outta Compton (1988, Ruthless/Priority), N.W.A. consolidated the stereotypical association of black male youth, the drug trade, gang-banging, gun violence, and routine police harassment with the place names Compton and South Central L.A. Their pioneering album, as well as early recordings by Ice T, introduced a situated "place-image"[8] of danger that characterizes the subgenre of west coast gangsta rap and that is a literal presence in *Menace II Society* (1993) and *Boyz N the Hood*.

With the co-emergence of gangsta rap and 'hood films, previously marginal urban geographies were repositioned at the centre of civic attention and public debate as the musical representations of the 'hood space conferred reputations of danger upon what are almost exclusively black and Latino neighborhoods. Understood as a process of "spatial labeling" whereby "sites and zones associated with particular activities become characterized as being appropriate for exactly those kinds of activities,"[9] gangsta rap's narrative diffusion of highly particular, spatially determined styles, argot, and practices elevated the national profile of these urban regions.

The general conjunction between rap and new black cinema can be seen in *Menace II Society*, in which rap artist MC Eiht is cast as A-Wax, a street hustler and O.G. (original gangsta) in his early twenties who is described as being slightly older and more battle-worn than the teenaged members of his crew. The character is "down for the 'hood," a tested street soldier who scrapes by with his wits and a gun, selling crack to hapless "cluckheads" and doling out retribution to adversaries who cross him and his posse—a role not at all unlike that adopted off the screen by MC Eiht since the age of thirteen.[10] Adding his rapping skills to the soundtrack with the song "Streiht Up Menace," Eiht recounts and elaborates on scenes from the film, emphasizing the progression of threat, violence, and danger that forms the basis of what many rappers refer to unproblematically as the "reality" of "Growing Up in the 'Hood"—which is also the title of the contribution to the *Boyz N the Hood* soundtrack by Compton's Most Wanted, featuring MC Eiht (1991, Sony Music). It is productive—even necessary—to maintain a sense of this crossover influence between rap and the 'hood film as the two media maintain a relationship of cross-pollination and mutual invigoration extending beyond the range of narrative and visual imagery to include the enhanced public exposure of rap artists on the movie screen (most notably Ice T, Ice Cube, and Tupac Shakur) and the influence of commercial success with soundtrack recordings on the careers of rap artists (as well as in the overall earning power of these films).[11]

Gangsta rap's graphic description of space, place, and danger has its correlative in contemporary 'hood films, as is evident in *Menace II Society*'s opening narration by the central protagonist, Caine (Tyrin Turner):

> Went into the store just to get a beer. Came out an accessory to mur-

der and armed robbery. It was funny like that in the 'hood sometimes. You never knew what was gonna happen or when. After that,
I knew it was gonna be a long summer.

The 'hood is the informing space in which the narrative action is framed and the
film's timeline follows the evolution of that "long summer," beginning with Caine's
high school graduation and ending with his violent death in a drive-by shooting as
he, his girlfriend and her young son prepare their departure from South Central
L.A.'s mean streets. His trajectory throughout the film is not linear, however, as he
swerves between the roles of victim and victimizer, in one instance getting car-
jacked and shot in the shoulder, in another pointing a gun at the head of an unfortunate teenager whose gold wheel rims he covets. In the end, his summer sun is
blotted out in a final act of payback and one-upmanship when he is shot dead in
response to his vicious beating of a teen from another 'hood who has encroached on
his home environment. The elements of risk and surprise are fused in his statement,
"You never knew what was gonna happen or when," and the narrative reinforces a
sense of the 'hood's capacity for imminent danger through a gradual escalation of
random incidents of violence that also emphasize the centrality of turf and bordered
enclaves within the social systems of the 'hood in urban Southern California.

As a core element of both rap lyrics and contemporary black cinematic narratives,
youth and danger are conflated with life in the 'hood. As Manthia Diawara explains,
this often follows a geo-socially specific coming-of-age theme:

> Just as in real life the youth are pulled between hip hop life style,
> gang life, and education, we see in the films neighborhoods that are
> pulled between gang members, rappers, and education-prone kids.
> For the black youth, the passage into manhood is also a dangerous
> enterprise which leads to death both in reality and in film.[12]

Youth is represented as a heterogeneous formation and its highly stratified composition is emphasized with distinctions between juvenile and twentysomething status
playing a decisive role in character construction and plot. Films such as *Menace II
Society*, *Boyz N the Hood*, and, more recently, *Fresh* (1995) and *Clockers* (1995) successfully portray the often subtle differences that separate and complicate the lives of
youths in the 13-24-year-old demographic, at the same time as they show a range of
reactions and responses to the dangers that young black men routinely confront. In
Boyz N the Hood, when the pre-adolescent Tre (Cuba Gooding, Jr.), Doughboy (Ice
Cube), and Ricky (Morris Chestnut) wander the periphery of their 'hood and
encounter a gang of older teenage thugs, they cross the railroad tracks into a rela-

tively hostile danger zone. There, they dispassionately stare at a decomposing human corpse; then moments later when the teenagers steal their football, Doughboy is beaten for trying to retrieve it. The spatial construction of danger in the scene is consequently organized within accompanying age boundaries that indicate a pattern of interlocking constraints which define the 'hood for children. The processes by which youth negotiate localized neighborhood space and its associated dangers at different stages of their development, alluded to by Diawara, are vitally central for an understanding of the narrative core of the 'hood film.

The spatial logic informing representations of the 'hood also intervenes in the process of identity formation inherent in the nexus of youth and race and present as an underlying current in *Clockers*. Within a system of place-based values, the 'hood is fetishized as the unqualified site of "nigga authenticity" which, as R.A.T. Judy explains, is an existential and ontological conundrum confronting black youth today.[13] The "real nigga" of the 1990s is, in the perception of many black teens as well as older, middle- and upper-class mainstream Americans, young and "deadly dangerous."[14] For example, in the opening sequence Strike and his drug-slinging cohorts debate the danger quotient of various rap artists, discussing their "hardness" and, consequently, their legitimacy in terms of whether or not they have ever killed anyone. The rise of a discourse locating the danger-ridden 'hood as a realm of authentic black identity and experience also invalidates a substantial segment of black culture and black experience that exists in other rural and suburban locales and cultural milieux. Suburban and middle-class black constituencies are frequently reviled or dismissed within a discourse of the 'hood on the basis of their fundamental disconnectedness from the 'hood itself as the privileged space of authentic blackness. Whereas John Jeffries writes that "In black popular culture, the city is hip. It's the locale of cool. In order to be 'with it,' you must be in the city, or at a minimum, urban culture must be transplanted, simulated, or replicated outside of the city wherever possible,"[15] it is more precisely the extreme inner-city, or the 'hood, that is the primary locale of cool for teenagers.

Just as the demographic subset "youth" should not be conceived in singular terms, neither should the 'hood be approached as a homogeneous space or unified geo-cultural terrain. Paul Gilroy's critical interrogation suggests that, while the discourse of the 'hood has emerged as socio-spatially dominant for black teens, in its implied localism it problematizes the potential for expansive diasporic identification and collective political movement among black youth:

> It's important that the 'hood stands in opposition to foreign things ...
> if the 'hood is the essence of where blackness can now be found,
> which 'hood are we talking about? How do we weigh the achieve-

ments of one 'hood against the achievements of another? How is black life in one 'hood connected to life in others?[16]

The distinctions between this 'hood and that 'hood have crucial, often life-threatening consequences for those who inhabit them and live in and by their territorial codes. By extension, however, the cinematic representation of different 'hoods and of different modes of habitation also allows for an elaborated understanding of what the 'hood is in American society and how its social dimensions are constructed.

For example, while Massood compellingly examines the means through which contemporary black filmmakers "map the 'hood" as a previously concealed space on the American cityscape, her exclusive focus on films set in South Central Los Angeles does little to illuminate the manner in which the 'hood is represented in films set elsewhere. As a reminder of the implications involved, Jeffries has noted:

> In thinking about what the urban is, we have some preconceptions.. . . For those of us living on the East Coast, especially considering the way L.A., with its urban conflict and gangs, has been described to us in the newspapers, some of the images that were most shocking in *Boyz N the Hood* were the shots of low-density housing. Many of us in East Coast audiences either subconsciously or unconsciously asked, "Where's the city?"[17]

Set in New York's high-rise housing projects and their adjoining neighborhoods,[18] *Straight Out of Brooklyn* (1991), with its title harking back to N.W.A.'s "Straight Outta Compton," *Juice* (1992), and *Clockers* portray a different kind of 'hood that is constructed much more vertically than California's horizontal 'hood with its wide boulevards, neat single-family homes, and low-rise public housing units. In these films, the sense of danger is intensified by a pervasive spatial compression that fuels the stress and tension of the various characters. The twin elements of constraint and restricted mobility (to name two points that Massood sensibly foregrounds) are signified through a visual tightness that is only rarely alleviated, as in the scenes where geographic distance and cultural difference are communicated in *Straight Out of Brooklyn* through Dennis's (Lawrence Gilliard, Jr.) wistful gaze across the river toward the towers of lower Manhattan.

In *Juice*, the four protagonists—led by Tupac Shakur as the rapidly unravelling Bishop (whose name suggests a nod towards Ron O'Neal's character Youngblood Priest in *Superfly*) and Omar Epps as the optimistic hip hop DJ Quincy (or "Q")—are continually framed against buildings and brick exteriors. Theirs is a world of architectural height and institutional might that contrastingly diminishes their own stature as black teenagers in the city. Throughout the film they are defensively positioned against the multifaceted dangers of the city: a rival gang, the school truancy cop, the police; and, in the end, one another as Bishop's fear and paranoia turn to desperation and he hunts his friends down. Both before and after committing their murderous crime in what is supposed to be a straightforward robbery of the local Asian-owned corner store, they are shown scurrying through derelict buildings, alleys and back streets. Here, the narrow and constricting architectural contours of the city evoke a danger that lurks around the corners as *Juice* confronts the navigational dilemmas of avoiding violence and death in the 'hood.

Despite Spike Lee's denial that *Clockers* is a 'hood film, it fails to fully escape its allegiances to the genre, maintaining a narrowly bounded spatial perimeter within which the central protagonist Strike (Mekhi Phifer) operates as a street-level drug dealer in the projects. According to Lee:

> Hood films are kind of over. This was one of the reasons I was hesitant about doing it. Audiences, black and white, are getting pretty fatigued of that genre. Rightly so, they want to see some different stories coming out of black culture besides a shoot-em-up hip-hop film.. . . I thought we could transcend the hood genre and make something greater.[19]

In *Clockers*, the 'hood is portrayed as a space of extreme limitations, constructed as a profile of density which is nonetheless replete with human intercourse that thrives and falters in an intense proximity. Lee's construction of the 'hood fully acknowledges the magnification of danger under such tight conditions and the inherent threat engendered in the stratified arrangement of power, authority, and territorial contestation. Unlike most films in the 'hood genre, however, he leavens his assessment of the 'hood by encompassing positive, even liberating images of hope that also inform the experience of urban existence.[20]

Lee's New York setting constructs Strike's zone of operation meiotically: his landscape is cramped and circumscribed in ways that correspondingly amplify the dangers that inform his actions and options. Strike is constantly under surveillance, watched by competing forces (primarily the police and his criminal mentor), effectively frozen in place on the bench at the center of the low-rent housing complex where he lives with his mother. Yet spatial compression increases the intensity of relations among the primary characters, particularly Strike and the various males (a local drug entrepreneur, a police detective, a beat cop, and an elder brother) who inflect his sense of self and identity; whose push and pull combine to produce a hybrid composite replacing an absent father-figure. The transcendent element Lee refers to may inhere in the unique means through which danger is narratively structured, for it is not solely the danger of inner city violence that Strike must overcome but also the danger of failure in the eyes of those whose respect he most desires. Complexities of identity and respect function as crucial codes of the street. They must be renegotiated through ceaseless attention to profile, status, and reputation.

If, as is often suggested, parody is the ultimate tribute, then *Friday* offers a tribute to the 'hood genre by humorously exemplifying the dangers of the place. Co-written by Ice Cube and DJ Pooh, *Friday* affirms the bonds between 'hood and home environment in a display of exaggeration and camp excess. The spatial construct of the 'hood comprises the film's core but the screenplay simultaneously sustains conventions of the 'hood film while exposing them to irreverent critique. Ice Cube plays Craig, a teenager facing a personal employment deficit, who with his blunted neighbor Smokey (Chris Tucker), spends the day sitting on the front porch of his family home. The compression and constraint that is common to the 'hood film is reduced to an absurd scale of minimal mobility with Craig and Smokey never wandering more than one or two houses away from their roost. Yet, their stasis resonates with non-comedy films such as *Do The Right Thing* (1989), *Menace II Society*, and especially *Boyz N the Hood* with its porch posse scenes (starring Ice Cube in a central role), all of which feature images of men of various ages sitting idly and bantering as they survey the 'hood around them.

The unmoving site of action provides an amusing motivation for the film's narrative flow as various characters circulate through the 'hood, coming and going from the front porch where the boys sit. Their vantage offers them a window on their small world. For all its limitations, it is a rich and full world of drama and suspense. Danger is encountered in the menacing character of Deebo (Tiny "Zeus" Lister, Jr.), a slightly cross-eyed and slow-witted bully. Deebo's approach is announced by music similar to that which heralded the shark attacks in *Jaws* (1975). Undercutting this intertextuality, however, is the accompanying sound of his squeaking bicycle which neutralizes the threat he presents by infantilizing him. Where other 'hood films portray vicious car-jackings, *Friday* portrays the neighborhood thug stealing a bike. In another scene depicting a drive-by shooting, the bravado and machismo that imbue the male characters in most 'hood films are parodied as Smokey quivers and cries in total fear. *Friday* consequently remains true to the conventions of the 'hood film by foregrounding the ever-present risk and dangers that arise for young blacks, but by inverting and exposing them to exaggeration and humorous critique it situates itself uniquely in relation to other 'hood films.[21]

This essay began with a description of spatial segregation and the exhibition of 'hood films that discriminates against young minority audiences. However, the incidents of real violence that have erupted in the past at movie theaters screening black films including *New Jack City* (1991) and *Boyz N the Hood* make it difficult to ignore or dismiss the concerns of theater managers and the police. As a series of precedent-setting occurrences, this violence seems to validate the association of danger with 'hood films. In its multivariegated character as a discursive construct, as a representational/cinematic space, and as an array of actually existing places, the 'hood is constitutive of a powerful image-idea of young urban black experience. At the same time, the 'hood is constituted by the multiple ways these images and experiences are merged and rearticulated daily within North America's urban geographies. Understood from this perspective, the portrayal of ubiquitous danger in the 'hood film also forces society to reconsider the means through which representation and reality often bleed together.

Notes

[1] Leonard Quart and Albert Auster, "A Novelist and Screenwriter Eyeballs the Inner City: An Interview with Richard Price," *Cineaste* 22:1 (1996), 16.

[2] Henry Giroux, *Fugitive Cultures: Race, Violence and Youth* (New York: Routledge, 1996), 67.

[3] For example, in a *Newsweek* cover story entitled "Black Movies: Renaissance or Ripoff?" (Oct. 23, 1972) the construction of a distinctly black, urban audience is discussed at length. More recently, director Matty Rich criticizes the ways that black movies are marketed primarily to black audiences, targetting exhibition spaces in black neighborhoods. (*Village Voice* [May 21, 1996]).

[4] Kevin Robins, "Tradition and Translation: National Culture in its Global Context," in John Corner and Sylvia Harvey, eds., *Enterprise and Heritage: Crosscurrents of National Culture* (London: Routledge, 1991), 41.

[5] Akhil Gupta and James Ferguson, "Beyond 'Culture': Space, Identity, and the Politics of Difference," *Cultural Anthropology* 7:1 (Feb. 1992), 11.

[6] The concept of *spatial othering* emerges as a recurrent theme within the field of critical cultural geography. As such, it generally corresponds with Michael Keith and Steve Pile's statement that "Space can now be recognized as an active constitutive component of hegemonic power: an element in the fragmentation, dislocation and weakening of class power, both the medium and message of domination and subordination. It tells you where you are and it puts you there." ["Introduction: The Politics of Place," in *Place and the Politics of Identity* (London: Routledge, 1993), 37]

[7] Paula Massood, "Mapping the Hood: The Genealogy of City Space in *Boyz N the Hood* and *Menace II Society*," *Cinema Journal* 35:2 (Winter 1996), 90.

[8] Rob Shields, *Places on the Margin: Alternative Geographies of Modernity* (New York: Routledge, 1991).

[9] Shields, *Places*, 60.

[10] *The Source* (June, 1994), 67.

[11] As an example of the interrelations between gangsta rap and 'hood films, DJ Quik's "Jus Lyke Compton" (Profile Records, 1992) refers to the nation-wide proliferation of Southern California gang structures and the enmity between Crips and Bloods as being partially influenced by the films *Colors* (1988) and *Boyz N the Hood*. Furthermore, regular

Urban Geographies of Danger in New Black Cinema

cameo appearances by rap artists such as EPMD (who appear briefly in Ernest Dickerson's *Juice*), Too Short (*Menace II Society*), Onyx's Neva and Sticky Fingaz (*Clockers*), and Yo Yo (*Boyz N the Hood* and *Menace II Society*) strengthen the bonds between hip hop music and film.

[12] Manthia Diawara, "Black American Cinema: The New Realism," in Manthia Diawara, ed., *Black American Cinema* (New York: Routledge, 1993), 25.

[13] R.A.T. Judy, "On the Question of Nigga Authenticity," *Boundary 2* 21:3 (1994).

[14] As an example of the conflation of youth, race, and danger, see the cover of the Canadian news magazine *Maclean's* (May 18, 1992) which, in the aftermath of urban riots relating to the acquittal of California police officers in the beating of Rodney King, pictured a black male teenager wearing a hooded sweater under the headline "Young, Black and Angry."

[15] John Jeffries, "Toward a Redefinition of the Urban: The Collision of Culture," in Gina Dent, ed., *Black Popular Culture* (Seattle: Bay Press, 1992), 159.

[16] Paul Gilroy, "It's A Family Affair," in Dent, ed., *Black Popular Culture*, 308.

[17] Jeffries, "Redefinition," 213.

[18] In the case of *Straight Out of Brooklyn*, this is the specific locale of the Red Hook housing projects, home to director Matty Rich. The projects depicted in *Juice* remain anonymous although the city is clearly New York and the locale is representative of Harlem or the Bronx.

[19] Michele Wallace, "Doin' the Right Thing," *The Village Voice* (May 21, 1996), 12.

[20] For example, Strike is not portrayed as a menacing gangster figure but as a teenager who, by virtue of his social positioning, is subjected to the magnetic pull of "the street." His hustler image is diluted by a closeted fascination with trains which, as Richard Price observes, is "a symbol of mobility and the desire to break out." (Quart & Auster, "Novelist," 17)

[21] The conventions of the 'hood film have also been scathingly parodied in *Don't Be a Menace to South Central While Drinking Your Juice in the Hood* (1996) which failed to capitalize on the 'hood film market and subsequently fared poorly at the box office.

EDWARD A. GAMARRA, JR.

Generation X and Neurasthenia: Cultural Pathology in *Reality Bites, Singles,* and *Spanking the Monkey*

We are the New Victorians.
H.W. Janson, 1991

Twentysomethings and their cinematic counterparts, the characters of Generation X films, suffer from a host of social problems similar to those which plagued a generation of neurasthenics one hundred years ago. Their behavior reveals a symptomatology congruent with a previous form of cultural pathology known to have affected the United States and, ostensibly, the rest of Western civilization. Characters from seminal Generation X films such as *Singles* (1992), *Reality Bites* (1994), and *Spanking the Monkey* (1994) all manifest the defining morbid signs. This discussion of the parallels between neurasthenia and slacking will address contrasts between notions on the aetiology of this neurosis held by George Beard, the inventor of neurasthenia, and those held by Sigmund Freud. Beard's writings, which strongly argued that modern American civilization caused the disease, were embraced so enthusiastically, from the 1880s until as late as the 1930s, that the language of neurasthenia was subsumed into Victorian popular culture and could be found in art, literature, and advertising.[1] Freud countered Beard's popular environmental explanation with a physiological one that restructured the nosology of neuroses, desocialized the disease, and led to the dismissal of the disease in general. Throughout his writings on neurasthenia, Freud concluded that masturbation was the primary cause. This paper calls upon Generation X films to support a rejection of Freud's theory that neurasthenia was sexual or somatogenic in nature. The recommendation is made to reinstate the term with the understanding that it is less a disorder of the person than a social malady, a pathology for a culture of slackers.

In the last 25 years, some have described our society as pathological. Historian Christopher Lasch describes this pathology as an "escape from emotion."[2] Postmodern theorist Fredric Jameson calls it a "waning of affect."[3] Their similar observations correlate with the 1990s mass media's observations of a burnt out generation of youth who are said to have lowered expectations, a lack of faith, tempered ideals, and distrust of social structures. Cultural theory, as developed by Lasch and Jameson, looks to socio-psychological phenomena such as "late" capitalism, the increased pace of living due to advances in technology, and other factors including rising divorce rates, the AIDS epidemic, rampant drug abuse, government corruption, the abatement of religious belief, and continually strained race relations. Cultural traumas affecting youth also include isolated moments of violence such as the Challenger explosion and the Kennedy, King and Malcolm X assassinations. Together these problems have caused a pathological condition, one noted for its feelinglessness.

In 1979, Lasch characterized our culture as narcissistic. More recently, Jameson offers a diagnosis of schizophrenia. This current cultural pathology might be better labelled neurasthenia. All three labels share symptomatology, but of the three, neurasthenia best captures the slacker's essence. During the Victorian era, George Beard wrote about this disease as being marked by fatigue, lack of motivation, low self-esteem and a variety of physical problems including dyspepsia. According to Beard, the neural exhaustion debilitating his countrymen was strictly modern and limited to the United States. Considered to impair the professional class and intelligentsia, the disease was readily accepted by both the medical community and society at large. But the same environmental forces of urbanization, industrialization, and modernity which Beard felt caused the American disorder of the 1880s and 1890s have been observed afflicting us during the last twenty-five years. A comparison of Generation X texts and the literature of neurasthenia reveals a parallel between the modern and postmodern eras.

Neurasthenia has reemerged as Chronic Fatigue Syndrome or CFS, evoking an article *Time* ran in 1900, under the heading, "The Government tries to find the cause of a devastating fatigue." Although the disease remains a mystery to researchers, many view it as some malfunction of the immune system triggered by stress. One important issue is brought to light in recent re-examinations of both neurasthenia and CFS: how, if at all, class works to produce cultural pathology. What was once, in the late 1980s, short-sightedly called a "yuppie disease" with symptoms of sluggishness, fever, headaches and depression, is now seen to affect "people of all ages and from all walks of life,"[4] according to Walter Gunn of the Center for Disease Control's Viral Disease Division. In his reexamination of the literature of neurasthenia, Tom Lutz points out that the same short-sighted class bias was present in the discourse of the disease. His research shatters the myth that only white collar workers fell victim to chronic fatigue. According to his analysis, everyone from country folk to students, from manual laborers to brain workers, could be afflicted.[5] Both diseases were understood in terms of class, but contemporary research demonstrates that anyone can fall victim. The knowledge that neurasthenia and its modern day counterpart are to be viewed as undiscriminating disorders provides us with a reliable clinical perspective before we attempt to illuminate congruent symptomatology through textual analysis of Gen X films.

Abraham Myerson's landmark book on neurasthenia, *The Nervous Housewife*, divides the symptom fatigue into three types: fatigue of mind, fatigue of purpose and fatigue of mood.[6] All three types can be found in the common discourse of Gen X. Fatigue of mind is characterized by the sort of short attention span many have seen in today's youth, attributing it to the effect of MTV. Shirking from responsibility marks the second type—fatigue of purpose; that this generation does not want to work is a point of contention, but older people typically believe this to be true of younger ones. As one father in Ben Stiller's *Reality Bites* remarks, "The problem with your generation is that they don't have a work ethic." Fatigue of mood includes mild depression and a lack of enthusiasm. One character from Joel Schumacher's *St. Elmo's Fire* (1985), the defining film for older Gen Xers, comments, "I never thought I'd be so tired at twenty-two." Blind Melon sings, "I don't understand why I sleep all day." Pop culture bears witness to the enervation of a new generation.

Jameson states that alienation was the primary psychological problem affecting modern society.[7] Discourses of Generation X similarly emphasize this symptom's primacy. Jason Cohen and Michael Krugman, authors of *Generation Ecch!*, describe youth today as "an age group united by nothing more than alienation."[8] A *Psychology Today* article blames the dangerous increases in "America's collective stress level" for the anomie felt by Generation Xers.[9] Sarah Dunn's *The Official Slacker Handbook* lists alienation as one of the hot thematic trends in modern music.[10] Slacking, or the avoidance of work, is a defensive reaction to our collective stress. While there are different ways to slack, a typical method is to remove oneself entirely from social structures like the office or campus. The result is a self-imposed alienation from others. Representation of this process is found throughout Generation X cinema.

Cameron Crowe's *Singles* opens with a woman in her mid-twenties describing how, for the first time in her life, she has a space of her own. Linda Powell (Kyra Sedgwick) is "alone" and "happy." After a rapid series of life-altering events, Linda decides to take a research job. "I should just be out somewhere in the middle of the ocean. Alone." Linda needs time away from life in Seattle to collect her thoughts. Alienation is her escape. Upon her return, she and Steve Dunne (Campbell Scott), her lover, conclude that they are no longer what they once were. As a result of the break-up and a failed work project, Steve begins his own self-imposed exile. He cannot take the pressure any more. A slowly rotating overhead shot shows him lying vitiated among beer cans and Chinese food containers. Janet Livermore (Bridget Fonda), an ex-girlfriend and neighbor, stops by to check up on him. He asks her, "Do you realize in modern day society there is almost no need to leave the house at all." "Steve, you're wiggin'." She tries to convince him to reconnect with his fellow humans. She herself is an expert on the matter of loneliness. Indeed, she knows alienation when she sees it. Her boyfriend Cliff (Matt Dillon) tells her that "Not everyone needs to be someone. My music is all the juice I need. I'm a self-contained unit. I'm a solo artist." Janet tries to justify her sense of loneliness, which is caused by the inequity in their relationship, by rationalization: "Being alone, there's a certain dignity to it."

The citizens of Crowe's Seattle are really no different than those in Houston, Texas, home for the characters of Ben Stiller's *Reality Bites*. *Reality Bites* also features a group of friends united by their alienation. Lelaina Pierce (Winona Ryder) is torn between two men and has neither job, nor money, nor support from her parents. Like Steve, she turns into a slacker. She sits in front of the TV for days, never moving. Vickie Miner (Janeane Garofalo), Lelaina's roommate and friend, finally complains about Lelaina's behavior; the fact that she doesn't interact with the outside world. While Vickie does not literally remove herself from the real world as Lelaina does, she feels estranged from it nevertheless. Vickie fears she has AIDS. A dreadful and overpowering feeling of loneliness accompanies this fear. Although she does not yet know the results of her HIV test, Vickie states she already feels like an AIDS patient; that she has to teach people it is okay to touch her, that it is okay to be near her. These characters either act like hermits or feel like lepers.

Along with alienation, fear has been designated as a defining quality of both Generation X and neurasthenics. Fear comes in many forms and includes "the worry over the life situation in general," fear of responsibility, fear of society, fear of being alone, fear of everything, fear of death, fear of the future.[11] In a 1990 *Time*/CNN poll of 18-to-29-year-olds, 53% said they were "worried about the future."[12] These worries are manifest in Lelaina and Vickie of *Reality Bites*, the latter worrying constantly about finding a job and paying the rent, about sexuality and dying of AIDS. In *Singles*, Linda and Steve worry constantly about relationships, pregnancy, marriage, and parenthood. These characters suffer from the same kind of general worry, from the same free-floating anxiety noted by Myerson.

Generation X suffers from low self-esteem, a pre-eminent symptom of neurasthenia in Freud's diagnosis;[13] yet about a hundred years later Dunn's slacker handbook describes the 90s as "a decade of shame and self-loathing."[14] *Singles'* Steve exemplifies this low self-regard as he insults himself when Janet stops by to visit him in his exile. In a sarcastic tone he states, "I went with my gut feelings which were wrong, the opposite of right." Wallowing in a pit of self-despair, he feels that every important choice he has made has backfired. His life is a shambles, and he blames no one but himself. Poor self-image links the nervous disorder and the Gen X character type.

David Gross and Sophronia Scott comment that the twentysomething generation has trouble making decisions.[15] Similarly Beard includes in his list of symptoms of neurasthenia the "lack of decision in trifling matters."[16] Gen X films take moments of decision-making and inflate their importance. In *Singles*, Linda's balk at purchasing a new garage door opener has significant ramifications. In this scene, Linda listens to the salesman's spiel as the camera looks over the selection. Rather than making a choice valuing one specific model over another, she leaves the decision up to the salesman. "Just give me the best." She does not want to determine for herself which is the best. This conflict lies at the heart of her neurosis. Such insignificant choices one makes everyday—where to eat or what to wear—become central to the psychological make-up of the characters and the development of their relationships.

One problem many professionals and brain-workers faced in Beard's time was over-work and the resulting burn-out or nerve exhaustion. The pressure to succeed and excel wore down a person's constitution. In *Reality Bites*, Lelaina worked at a TV studio assisting a talk-show host (John Mahoney), and spent her nights in the editing room laboring over her video documentary. When her boyfriend, Michael Grates (Ben Stiller), helps destroy her documentary by making it more commercial, she breaks down completely. "I worked so hard on it," she sobs. While separated, Steve and Linda of *Singles* found themselves wholly dedicated to and excelling in their careers. Raymond Aibelli (Jeremy Davies) of *Spanking the Monkey* desperately wants a prestigious internship with the Surgeon General's office and spends late hours researching and writing about AIDS. These characters demonstrate that productivity is as valued now as it was in the late 1800s.

While many symptoms could signal a case of neurasthenia, masturbation, more than any other symptom, took on paramount importance in Freud's nosologically revisionist writings in the 1890s. Although it is true that Beard and his colleagues felt assured they had a case of neurasthenia once a patient admitted he or she masturbated, Beard considered the disease to be the explicit result of modern civilization. A look at the civilization one hundred years later reveals that masturbation has taken a prominent role in pop culture. Our culture's openness to masturbation can be explained, at least in part, as a response to the AIDS crisis. Author Judith Krantz comments, "From the time of the Pill to Rock Hudson's death, people had a sense of freedom. That's gone."[17] People have struggled to regain this sense of freedom through other forms of sexual expression. The current mainstream acknowledgment of "alternative" sexual behaviors such as homosexuality, cybersex, voyeurism, S/M, transvestitism, and fetishism, results in a proliferation of sexual choices. For a generation known for its inability to make decisions, such decorous proliferation only complicates the problem.

Masturbation is the one alternative sexual activity to have gained the greatest level of acceptance within the prevailing cultural discourse of sexuality. Censorship standards have loosened over the last few decades, allowing for depiction of auto-eroticism to move from innuendo to explicitness, as demonstrated in movies like *Fast Times at Ridgemont High* (1982), *Risky Business* (1983) and *Ace Ventura: When Nature Calls* (1995). The Divinyls' "I Touch Myself" was a number one hit in the early 1990s. The prominence of masturbation brings us to Freud who in the 1890s argued that actual neuroses—anxiety neurosis and neurasthenia—were due to contemporaneous physiological causes, like *coitus interruptus* and masturbation. Freud believed that his discovery of the somatogenic nature of these disorders was a "monumental step"[18] in the evolution of his theories, but abandoned his study of neurasthenia. In his "Autobiographical Study," Freud laments having abandoned the issue of neurasthenia, but reasserts his opinion that the disease and its symptoms (such as fatigue) were caused solely by the depletion of nerve force by inappropriate sexual behavior, i.e. non-heterosexual intercourse. Even to the end of his career, Freud never discarded his neurological training and its biases that privileged the somatic over the psychic. He still attributed a disorder caused by environmental forces to physiological problems. James Strachey points out that when Freud first started writing about actual neuroses he was "at a half-way stage in the process of moving from a physiological to psychological explanation of psychopathological states"[19] like neurasthenia. While Freud's theories of neuroses and sexuality may have grown more psychological over the years, Freud never let go of his notions about neurasthenia's somatic origins. He dismissed the overwhelming evidence for environmental causes, causes evident even in his own writings.

In "A Case of Successful Treatment by Hypnotism" (1893) Freud described a "typical case" of neurasthenia:

> Starting originally with a good constitution, the patient is haunted by the usual sexual difficulties at puberty; there follow years of overwork as a student, preparation for examinations, and an attack of gonorrhea, followed by a sudden onset of dyspepsia accompanied by obstinate and inexplicable constipation. After some months the con-

stipation is replaced by intracraniel pressure, depression and incapacity for work. Thenceforward the patient grows increasingly self-centered and his character more and more restricted, till he becomes a torment to his family.[20]

Freud's description, which calls attention to both physical and environmental factors, is an accurate summary of Raymond's life in *Spanking the Monkey*. At first, his life seems fine, but then it slowly spirals downward. Like the average straight male teenager, he feels anxious about being physically intimate with females. His coursework at MIT is demanding enough, but he pushes himself ever harder to get a prestigious internship. He begins to grow short-tempered and increasingly frustrated by the fact that he has to take care of his disabled mother (Alberta Watson) and can no longer accept the internship. Raymond gets into a fight over a lewd remark about his "red hot" mother and, as the film goes on, his life is further complicated as his sexual anxieties leak into his relationship with his mother. Ultimately he sleeps with her. Afterward, he grows so tense he explodes at his Aunt Helen (Judette Jones). When home, Raymond's father treats the dog with more kindness than his own son. As his life comes crashing down around him, Raymond repeatedly goes off to masturbate during moments of conflict.

Despite the correspondence to Freud's account, *Spanking the Monkey* is very explicitly the story of a Beardian neurasthenic. Raymond's masturbation is not the cause of his condition. It is a result of the pathogenic environmental forces working against him. Masturbation is Raymond's coping strategy. When something bad happens to him, he goes to the bathroom to relieve himself. The fact that Raymond's efforts are always thwarted further aggravates the matter. He can never complete the task in hand. He never effectively discharges that energy. While these events may seem to support Freud's construction of the disease's sexual/somatic aetiology, one must instead view Raymond's unsuccessful attempts at sexual activity, either alone or with his neighbor Toni (Carla Gallo), as contributing factors to the "environmental stress" from which he knowingly suffers. Rather than being the solitary determining causes of actual neuroses, masturbation and unfulfilled sexual encounters are part of the snowballing quality of the neurasthenic's life. Even if Raymond had had intercourse with Toni, it would not have alleviated the pressures of school, work, or his parents' inevitable divorce.

Peter Gay suggests that Draft B of Freud's "The Aetiology of the Neuroses," demonstrates Freud's tendency to think of himself as a "physician for society,"[21] and yet Freud held fast to his belief that despite its social causes neurasthenia was primarily the literal result of a weak nervous system due to inadequate discharge of libidinal energy. In his effort to finesse the definition of neurasthenia by strictly attributing it to a single physical process, Freud essentially de-socialized a social disease. Eventually, neither psychoanalysts nor general practitioners could view the collection of symptoms previously covered by the umbrella term "neurasthenia" as a single disease. The result was the disappearance of the term from the psychiatric lexicon. The body of symptoms can now be found under different, supposedly more descriptive titles like Stress and Chronic Fatigue Syndrome.

When art historian H.W. Janson compared contemporary culture to the Victorian era,[22] it is unlikely he was commenting on the re-emergence of neurasthenia; that affliction must be appraised anew, at least in light of what has been suggested here. The psychiatric community must break away from the Freudian tradition of neurological and somatic aetiology. It must stop misreading the medical signifiers; falling victim to the "dizzying reversibility between signifier and signified."[23] The symptoms are not the disease, nor the cause. As the cinematic discourse of Generation X demonstrates, neurasthenia is best understood as a reaction to the social pressures and cultural demands which plague life at this postmodern *fin-de-siècle*. That neurasthenia is a psychological disorder and not a physiological one, a social disease and not an individual one, explains why it is best the *Diagnostic & Statistical Manual-IV* does not include the disease in its listings.

At the microscopic level of case studies and individual patients, the diagnosis of neurasthenia may not be as useful or practical as CFS, Stress, Depression or other such labels. Nevertheless, the correlations between this disease and social forces have passed the test of time. For over a hundred years, cultural theorists and social psychologists have been noticing the same phenomenon. Perhaps rather than continuing to view Raymond's masturbation, Vickie's proclivity for self-diagnosis, and the singles' self-loathing as triggers of an ineffable and hidden spiritual malfunction, we should see self-involvement as a way out of intolerable fear, loneliness, and strain induced by a highly problematic society. Perhaps for clues to CFS, researchers should look beyond their own field and towards cinema studies.

Notes

[1] Tom Lutz, *American Nervousness, 1903: An Anecdotal History* (Ithaca NY: Cornell University Press, 1991), 2.

[2] *The Culture of Narcissism* (New York: W. W. Norton, 1979), 201.

[3] *Postmodernism, or, The Cultural Logic of Late Capitalism* (Durham NC: Duke University Press, 1991), 15.

[4] Linda Williams, "The Government tries to find the cause of a devastating fatigue," *Time Almanac CD-ROM* (May 14, 1990).

[5] Lutz, *American Nervousness*. Note, too, that CFS and the slacker stereotype are even linked chronologically, both having emerged in the early 1990s.

[6] (Boston: Little, Brown, 1920), 20.

[7] *Postmodernism*, 11.

[8] (New York: Simon & Schuster, 1994), 9.

[9] Cohen and Krugman, *Ecch!*, 14.

[10] (New York: Warner Books, 1994), 96.

[11] Myerson, *Housewife*, 23.

[12] David Gross and Sophronia Scott, "Preceding with caution," *Time Almanac CD-ROM* (July 16, 1990).

[13] Freud writes of "*status nervosus* in general—we have to assume that there exists a *primary* tendency to depression and to a lowering of self-confidence." "A Case of Successful Treatment by Hypnotism," (1892), in James Strachey, ed. and trans., *The Standard Edition of the Complete Psychological Works of Sigmund Freud* Vol. I (London: Hogarth Press and The Institute of Psycho-analysis, 1966), 39.

[14] Dunn, *Handbook*, xi.

[15] Gross and Scott, *Almanac*.

[16] George Beard, *American Nervousness: Its Causes and Consequences* (New York: Putnam, 1881).

[17] Philip Elmer-Dewitt, "Now for the Truth about Americans and Sex," *Time Almanac CD-ROM* (October 17, 1994).

[18] Sigmund Freud, "An Autobiographical Study," (1925), in Peter Gay, ed., *The Freud Reader* (New York: W. W. Norton, 1989), 24.

[19] James Strachey, introduction to "Studies on Hysteria," in Strachey, ed. and trans., *The Standard Edition of the Complete Psychological Works of Sigmund Freud*, Vol. II (London: Hogarth Press and The Institute of Psycho-analysis, 1966), xxiv.

[20] Freud, "Hypnotism," 118.

[21] Peter Gay, *Freud: A Life for Our Times* (New York: Doubleday, 1988), 63.

[22] H. W. Janson, *History of Art*, rev. and exp., Anthony Janson (New York: Harry N. Abrams, Inc., 1991), 754

[23] Lutz, *American Nervousness*, 23.

BARRY KEITH GRANT

Once More Without Feeling: The Disaffection of Contemporary Youth

The imagination of the protagonist of Walker Percy's 1961 *The Movie-goer*, a novel of course much admired by *cinéastes*, is largely shaped by films. But Percy's character clearly sees the disparity between his own life and the movies: as he observes, "Other people, so I have read, treasure memorable moments in their lives: the time one climbed the Parthenon at sunrise, the summer night one met a lonely girl in Central Park and achieved with her a sweet and natural relationship, as they say in books. I, too, once met a girl in Central Park, but it is not much to remember. What I remember is the time John Wayne killed three men with a carbine as he was falling to the dusty street in *Stagecoach*."[1] This narrator prefers the masculine ego ideal constructed by Hollywood, yet although his own identity may suffer by comparison, it is still distinct—as, importantly, is the reader's ability to distinguish between the narrator's imagination and the diegetic reality he narrates.

Thirty years later, in the postmodern era, this distinction between the real and the representation collapses. As Patrick Bateman, the narrator of Brett Easton Ellis's controversial 1991 novel *American Psycho*, also about the influence of media on the imagination, says when describing one of his sexual encounters, "I am so used to imagining everything happening the way it occurs in movies, visualizing things falling somehow into the shape of events on a screen, that I almost hear the swelling of an orchestra, can almost hallucinate the camera panning low around us, fireworks bursting in slow motion overhead, the 70 mm image of her lips parting and the subsequent murmur of 'I want you' in Dolby sound."[2]

By the time we get to the late chapter "Chase, Manhattan," a slam-bang, shoot-em-up passage in the mold of the contemporary hyberbolic action movie wherein Bateman is almost caught by the police, we aren't sure whether we are inside a pulp fiction fantasy on his part or not. Like the science fiction blockbuster *Total Recall* (1990), *American Psycho* situates us within a Baudrillardian dilemma, a postmodern nightmare of the simulacrum which, because we cannot distinguish the narrator's fantasy from his reality, simulates the condition it describes in our very experience of reading it. Ellis's Bateman, a psychotic mass murderer, as evil as he may be, is himself a victim, possessed by the monster Jean Baudrillard would call "the evil demon of images."

Indeed, in the world of *American Psycho* everyone is superficial, concerned with, and ultimately reduced to, mere image. Every time a character enters the scene Bateman gives us a lengthy description devoted to his or her apparel, complete with brand names, what shops the items come from, and sometimes the retail price. One of the book's ongoing jokes—in a prolonged black comedy of errors—is that while Bateman gives us such details, neither he nor any of his friends are able to correctly identify their acquaintances by name. Ironically, nobody notices the missing people Bateman has killed because they are virtually interchangeable, all wearing the same trendy upscale fashionwear and mouthing the same inane banter—"clucking their thick tongues oh so delicately," as *Psycho*'s Norman Bates would say.

One might regard him as Steven Shaviro does Drew Barrymore's infernal teenager in *Poison Ivy* (1992): her crime, Shaviro writes, "is finally just that she overinvests in the glamorous images of familial togetherness, paternal authority, and suburban affluence that have proliferated so abundantly and so sickeningly in post-Reagan America. She simply takes these media images 'at their word,' enacting them in her own flesh, on the level of lived reality."[3] Similarly, Bateman, as Robin Wood says of the significance of cannibalism in the modern horror film, is merely a horrifying literalization of "the logical end of human relations under capitalism."[4] His horrifyingly violent treatment of women is a result of the fact that his sexuality, like everything else in the book, is thoroughly determined by consumer culture. Bateman is nothing more or less than a complete product of popular culture, his imagination both limited and shaped by it. So he moves without a transition from discussing scenarios of porn videos to remarks about the new Stephen Bishop CD, from masturbating while fantasizing about real women he knows to thinking of "a near-naked model in a halter top I saw today in a Calvin Klein advertisement"; it is all product for consumption.

But the book's ultimate dark joke is that our tedium in reading its many consumer catalogues is relieved only when something—that is to say, something violent—happens. This response only implicates us further in Bateman's heinous acts, so that we become Bateman's "accomplices"; for we are made to confront the not infrequent loathesomeness of the popular culture into which we frequently, and fervently,

The Disaffection of Contemporary Youth

escape. In other words, Bateman victimizes women because the myriad forms of popular culture do so consistently and routinely. The book is written in a flat, disaffected style because, in the end, it is a flat, disaffected document in a flat, disaffected world. It is a demonstration case of Fredric Jameson's "waning of affect"[5] characteristic of postmodernism, and predictably, it was precisely this quality that informed the book's general condemnation in the popular press. In Bateman, desire has been completely molded, commodified, by the media.

Since everyone else in the book is, like Bateman himself, an image, there is a sense in which to do violence to another person is merely to enter the televisual flow, with yourself as star in a narrative world and others cast in supporting roles as victims. Bateman videotapes some of his murders, his unfortunate victims in the process becoming—to use Paul Bernardo's description of the young girls he killed[6]—mere "props" in his scenarios. In "The Metapsychology of Endless Consumption," Beverle Houston argues that while cinema sutures its viewer with a dream of plenitude, television "insists upon the [constant] reformulation of desire."[7] Because the televisual flow lurches back and forth between different kinds of narrative and spectatorial address—between shows, commercials, and that abject category, infomercials— desire is repeatedly interrupted, blocked, and renewed. As Houston puts it, the particular nature of televisual flow repeatedly opens "the gap of desire" for consumption of yet more flow. The result, in short, is that the televisual subject becomes a "serial viewer."

Thus video, with its ability to insert us immediately into that flow, is now perhaps more a graphic proof of our postmodern fragmentation than a technology of grassroots political liberation, as it was once heralded to be. In a culture where interior life is at every turn diminished and disparaged, where the physical is everywhere privileged over the spiritual, watching ourselves in home videos—seeing our images out there, on the television set, itself a palpable thing occupying space—confirms, from without and as essentially a visual site/sight, our sense of presence, our being in the world. As many postmodern theorists would argue, video is the theater where identity becomes performance. It provides us with a stage on which we may strut and fret—or whatever gets us through the night. It offers us a technological schizophrenia wherein we may identify with ourselves, creating a narcissistic feedback loop that cancels out other subjectivities, who become mere bit players whose purpose is "to die for."

The deadly accuracy of Ellis's characterization of Bateman is confirmed by Annalee Newitz, who argues in a recent discussion of real serial killers that many of them are motivated by a desire for media fame. She claims that "they kill precisely in order to see themselves mass produced as simulations in the newspapers and television reports about them."[8] It is no surprise, then, that in many recent serial killer movies video figures centrally, especially during sequences of violence. *Natural Born Killers* (1994), for example, is structured around video, in form as well as content. Some of the shots are done in "home video" style (hand held camera, "amateur" framing, jump cuts), and even the protagonists' consciousness is rendered as video—Mallory "remembers" meeting Mickey as if in a sickly sit-com.

In the most chilling sequence in *Henry: Portrait of a Serial Killer* (1990), Henry and his accomplice Otis arbitrarily break into a family home and kill the family members while videotaping their actions, which are "choreographed" for the camera. Like them, we see the event as video, which they compulsively watch over and over again, replaying the "good parts" that, amazingly, have not been edited for video release. In these movies video is the most pervasive signifier of postmodern alienation, and it is no coincidence that movies like *Henry* employ a "zero-degree" tone similar to that of *American Psycho*. Through this rhetorical trope, of course, cinema may be valorizing itself at the expense of video, but this trope also reinforces the treatment of violence as ultimately meaningless.

It has been said that in British detective fiction death is depicted as a violent intrusion into the quotidian world, a shock perfectly captured by the striking image of a blood stain on the expensive drawing-room carpet. Today, however, the stain on the carpet is no longer a horrifying reminder of the fragility of civilization, but rather, as one of the grisly trio says about Hugo's corpse in the Scottish thriller *Shallow Grave* (1995), simply a matter of logistics. Now we laugh at the sight of blood—not to mention brains—as it is splattered on two hapless hit men in *Pulp Fiction* (1994). Indeed, the new tone of violence is less shock than bemused detachment—a recognition of insignificance, not consequence.

Violence is now commonly represented as brute fact rather than important deed. Of course, such a reaction may not be entirely surprising in an age of drive-by shootings and random terrorist attacks, or when bomber pilots tell CNN that watching their payload exploding over Iraqi civilians is like being at Disneyland. Frequently now, our works of popular culture dealing with serial or multiple murderers focus on the seemingly "inexplicable" actions of apparently normal folks who suddenly engage in paroxysms of mass carnage—violent variations of what André Gide called *l'acte gratuit*. Bateman expresses this absurdist view perfectly in his thoughts about a woman who has survived a date with him: "She's lucky," he muses, "even though there is no real reasoning behind the luck.. . . Maybe the glass of Scharffenberger has deadened my impulse or maybe it's simply that I don't want to ruin this particular Alexander Julian suit by having the bitch spray her blood all over it. Whatever happens, the useless fact remains: Patricia will stay alive, and this victory requires no

The Disaffection of Contemporary Youth

skill, no leaps of the imagination, no ingenuity on anyone's part. This is simply how the world, my world, moves."[9]

In January, 1979, Brenda Spencer, a 17-year-old San Diego girl, randomly shot 11 passersby, killing 2. Her "reason," she said, was that "I don't like Mondays." For Bob Geldof and the Boomtown Rats, this rather inadequate explanation became a metaphor of the stultifying banality of contemporary bourgeois life; Spencer, in the group's song entitled "I Don't Like Mondays," is a late 20th century Richard Cory whose vague, amorphous dissatisfaction has caused her to put bullets through the heads of others rather than her own. In many popular representations, even when a "reason" is offered for violence, its banality and the absurdity of its context tend to be emphasized.

This is clearly the fundamental appeal and discursive logic of many of the various series of True Crime trading cards. For example, as one card in the "True Crime #5: Strange Crime Stories" series tells us, Joseph Fallet, age 61, of Harrison City, Pa., one day in August, 1992, killed his wife of twenty years, stabbing her 161 times, because he had become suddenly enraged by her habit of putting the fresh vegetables in front of the milk on the refrigerator shelf. The implication is that the violence on Fallet's part was incommensurate with its cause—inexplicably excessive—and so "incomprehensible" as a response to his wife's relatively trivial domestic habits.

Like *American Psycho*, many recent movies treat violence by similarly "flattening" it: since violence in our culture is no longer remarkable, it is presented unremarkably. This tone characterizes such recent movies as, for example, *River's Edge* (1989), *Kids* (1995), *Juice* (1992), and *Menace II Society* (1993). All of these share a depiction of young people responding to violence with an indifference that infects the films' very style. *River's Edge*, with its factually-based story of a group of teenagers who respond without concern to the death of one of their number, her body left stretched out on the grass of the town's river bank, is most explicitly about the failure today of blood on the carpet to shock.

Because violence is no longer a privileged moment within narrative, it is no longer redemptive or cathartic. But it is almost as if such "senseless," "meaningless" violence now seems most meaningful to us. The fact that so many of these movies focus on young people underscores Hollywood's sense that this is a psychological situation. Interestingly, as if to compensate for the meaningless worlds they envision, serial killer narratives are often full of overdetermined meanings. The recent *Seven* (1995) pushes this tendency to the extreme: every action and object becomes a potential signifier of the deadly sins motif meticulously constructed by Jonathan Doe, fiendish cipher though he is. Many serial killers, both real and fictional, consider their actions to be loaded with meaning, but their views remain private visions, demonic cosmologies rather than communal, utopian aspirations. Both *Virtuosity* (1995) and *Copycat* (1995) rely on knowledge of the *modus operandae* of previous serial killers in order to "decode" the insane logic of their serial killers, thus further enclosing their meaning within a layer of self-referential "trivia."

It is no wonder that the first sentence of *American Psycho* is "Abandon all hope, ye who enter here."[10] In such a world as these works depict, action—in sharp distinction to both traditional American fiction and classic Hollywood cinema—can be neither truly heroic nor moral, because nothing is especially meaningful, nothing more real or important than anything else. The contemporary hyperbolic action movie is merely the other side of the same coin—full of the stuff of heroic action, but performed by undifferentiated Steven Seagals, Chuck Norrises, and Jean-Claude Van Dammes; they present heroic violence without character, action reduced to merely the gestures of heroism.

Literary critic Marius Bewley once observed that in Fenimore Cooper's *Leatherstocking Tales* action serves as "the intensified motion of life in which the spiritual and moral faculties of men are no less engaged than their physical selves."[11] In other words, the characters' physical, often violent, doings were always the concrete expression of an ethical vision. "First be sure you're right, then go ahead," in the words of Disney's Davy Crockett, icon of 50s America. This embodiment of ethics in the physical world is the informing principle of what Richard Chase calls the American form of Romance, and is embodied, most famously, in the virtuous "code" of the Western hero. When the guns of the classic western hero spoke, the action was never arbitrary or impulsive: it was always for a reason, one that in the end served communal goals, and we inevitably felt a righteous identification with the hero. This is hardly commensurate with the philosophy of the teenage killer John in *River's Edge*, who opines: "You do shit, it's done, and then you die."

Significantly, in Quentin Tarantino's *Pulp Fiction*—a movie which in many ways defines the sensibility of the contemporary action movie—the narrative structure is a fractured one, offering the spectator no stable position of identification. In the (in)famous scene alluded to above, Tarantino puts us in the back seat of the hit men's car along with their captive at the moment when he is accidentally shot point blank in the face by Travolta's gun. In this one moment splatter becomes emblematic of the postmodern condition, translating our eroded subjectivity into the graphics of the fractured head. The scene's emphasis on the stain rather than death's pain further signifies, once again without feeling, the logical end of human relations under capitalism.

Droogie Alex of *A Clockwork Orange* would describe such works as *Pulp Fiction*, *Henry*, *Natural Born Killers*, *American Psycho*, and so on, as "real horrorshow." Of course, he would mean this as a compliment, a frightening opinion that, in itself, we would find the true horror. (As we approach the millenium, the extrapolative accuracy of Anthony Burgess's "speculative" novel and Kubrick's film adaptation seems epiphanic.) Yet it might be argued that these works of "ultra-violence" are progressive to the extent that, in making violence mundane, they demythify it, revealing it for the inglorious, brute fact that it always is. For John Fraser, the artistic use of violence involves the mobilization of our emotions in order to provide a shock of recognition, as in Artaud's *théâtre de la cruauté*. The ultimate aim of these works I have discussed here is a moral one in such a view, because they do seek to shock us—but they do it precisely by (shockingly) not shocking us where we would expect to be shocked. Theoretically, a gap is created between our consciousness and that of the characters, and we thereby attain some sort of insight into the human capacity for violence.

Bruce Kawin has argued that "A good horror film takes you down into the depths and shows you something about the landscape."[12] Yet as Martin Rubin notes, "The interrelated discourses of liberal humanism, scientific rationalism, and expressive realism, though appropriate for the postwar problem film were . . . inadequate to convey the emerging popular mythology of modern multiple murder."[13] These works certainly do not make Kawin's journey of revelation a smooth ride. Nevertheless, as readers and viewers, we have to find new strategies for negotiating the new violence. To simply dismiss it, or to respond with knee-jerk moral outrage, does not help us very much to truly reach, or return from, the depths. Without confronting these representations head on, we shall remain trapped, like Forrest Gump, in a world we cannot really understand. And unless we do, the last words of *American Psycho*—"THIS IS NOT AN EXIT"[14]—will undoubtedly prove prophetic.

Notes

[1] Walker Percy, *The Movie-goer* (Harmondsworth: Penguin, 1961), 12.

[2] Brett Easton Ellis, *American Psycho* (New York: Vintage, 1991), 265.

[3] Steven Shaviro, *The Cinematic Body* (Minneapolis: University of Minnesota Press, 1993), 263.

[4] Robin Wood, "An Introduction to the American Horror Film," in Robin Wood and Richard Lippe, eds., *American Nightmare: Essays on the Horror Film* (Toronto: Festival of Festivals, 1979), 21.

[5] Fredric Jameson, *Postmodernism, or, The Cultural Logic of Late Capitalism* (Durham NC: Duke University Press, 1991).

[6] Paul Bernardo became an infamous figure in Canadian crime when he was arrested, charged, and convicted in the abduction, torture, mutilation and murder of two teenage girls in St. Catharines, Ontario. He videotaped his sexual

humiliations and torture of these two young women, and the tapes were used as evidence in the trial. The details of the crimes were apparently so horrifying that, by court order, details of the trial were not allowed to be discussed by the media (this, interestingly enough, happening at the same time as the media circus surrounding the O. J. Simpson case in the United States). Bernardo was also convicted of an earlier series of rapes committed in Scarborough, a suburb of Toronto.

[7] Beverle Houston, "Viewing Television: The Metapsychology of Endless Consumption," in Nick Browne, ed., *American Television: New Directions in History and Theory* (Switzerland: Harwood Academic Publishing, 1994), 81.

[8] Annalee Newitz, "Serial Killers, True Crime, and Economic Performance Anxiety," *CineAction!* 38 (1995), 45.

[9] Ellis, *Psycho*, 77.

[10] Ellis, *Psycho*, 3.

[11] Marius Bewley, *The Eccentric Design: Form in the Classic American Novel* (New York: Columbia University Press, 1963), 73.

[12] Bruce Kawin, "Children of the Light," in Barry Keith Grant, ed., *Film Genre Reader II* (Austin: University of Texas Press, 1995), 237.

[13] Martin Rubin, "The Grayness of Darkness: *The Honeymoon Killers* and Its Impact on Psychokiller Cinema," *Velvet Light Trap* 30 (Fall 1992), 50.

[14] Ellis, *Psycho*, 399.

The Disaffection of Contemporary Youth

KEITH C. HAMPSON

Authenticity, Music, Television

Authenticity, in its most basic sense, constitutes a core value through which fans and critics make sense of and evaluate popular music. What constitutes the authentic and, conversely the inauthentic, is variable over time but is always organized according to a number of distinctions which work to position artists, music and audiences on one side of the authentic-inauthentic dichotomy or the other.

These distinctions have traditionally, although not exclusively, revolved around the broader distinction between music as a unique and meaningful art form, autonomously authored by a creative individual,; and music as a commercial product with commercial purposes. In short, this is the traditional contraposition between genuine expression and commercial imperative. In practice though, this distinction involves more specific concerns such as the presence and particular use of technology; the main audience for the artist; the degree of commercial success achieved by the performer; the metatextual identity of the act; the lyrical content; and the career trajectory of the act [did they "pay their dues," or are they simply the product of clever record company management?].

A further clarification essential to the social definition of "authentic" is constructed in terms of a narrative, what has been described as "The Rock Myth."[1] The Rock Myth suggests that definitions of the authentic typically follow a particular chronology and trajectory. "Authentic musical performance" emerges from a context outside the mainstream popular music industry to (a) publicly communicate the privately held values and emotions of a community of fans, and/or (b) express a unique and meaningful artistic vision. With the rise of commercial success and a broader public support for the performer, the authentic quality of the artist declines. Either the pressures of the profit-oriented and artistically-ruinous commercial music industry or the artist's own inability to resist "selling out" lead to this downfall. The story is complete when the artist is reduced to producing formulaic "product," a kind of pap which makes him unfit for the appetite of serious, mature and discriminating fans.

The emergence of music television as a key source of rock culture has, not surprisingly, intensified the interest in this debate. The most common distinctions made in terms of music television and its relationship to authenticity are (a) between television and youth rock culture—"Television corrupts the purity of real rock"; and (b) between the visual and the aural—"Glitzy images corrupt the purity of real sound." As Will Straw has noted, these discourses are not only about the fear of what the visual component of television might do "to" music, but also about the cultural and political matter of discriminating what "is" music from what "is" television.[2] Popular music is deeply embedded in conceptions of youth and counter-culture: it is, at least potentially, an authentic form of expression. Television, on the other hand, is culturally framed as familial, mainstream, and fundamentally commercial. It is, bar none, *the* inauthentic medium of our time.

The development of these distinctions in music video provides a useful illustration of how definitions of authenticity are linked to social and economic contexts. Paul Attallah suggests that the social distinctions between rock youth culture and television are largely a result of the different ways in which these forms were originally made available to their audiences.[3] The cost of television sets dictated that they were a "family" purchase. Also, the television was typically positioned within the family- or living-room and thus subject to influences of the familial context. Well into the sixties, television content (adventure series, family-based sitcoms, game shows, and variety programming) was produced in order to appeal to an undifferentiated "family" audience.

In contrast, rock music was typically made available to its audience in such a way as to define itself as youth culture and, significantly, in opposition to parental and mainstream culture. Access to popular music required a relatively small investment: the purchase of a radio, a record player, or coins for the jukebox. It was consumed in physical spaces beyond parental control, such as the beach, restaurants, night clubs, the bedroom, and cars. Moreover, musical content, radio programming and marketing stressed the difference of rock music, not only from parental and mainstream culture but also from other types of music and their respective fans.

As a result of these different modes of distribution and consumption, popular music "rapidly came to be understood as the particular idiom of youth and as having a special bond with its young audience whereas television easily let itself be understood as a big business aimed at a big audience. Consequently, to the world of private teenage pleasures and enjoyment which rock music symbolized, stood opposed the world of publicly approved mass entertainment which television instantiated."[4]

But adherence to the authentic-inauthentic distinction can itself be seen as the product of a false and politically regressive romanticism. This view argues that the acceptance of the distinction between authentic and inauthentic music, and the related concepts of autonomous artistry, anti-commercialism and political significance which it celebrates, obscures the fact that all popular music—pop or rock—is implicated to some degree and in some way with the commercial, technological and cultural framework of the music industry. As a result, the myth that rock eventually sells out, or is co-opted by the commercial system is misleading; all acts are always already part of the cultural industries. The artifice of romanticism—rock against "the system"—encourages audiences to lend to popular music a certain social and political value which is based on false pretenses. It is this false romanticism which is rock's regressive element.

Clearly, there is a good deal of evidence to support the view that definitions of authenticity are subject to historical, social, technological and economic conditions. For example, what constitutes too much or inappropriate technology in "serious" rock music is a continually changing specification. Prior to the success of music video, the tactic of lip-synching, today an accepted part of musical performance, was considered by many fans to be grossly inauthentic.[5]

Likewise, the once fundamental distinction made between television and youth-based rock culture is shifting. For contemporary music television viewers—chiefly, those between twelve and twenty-five years of age—television has served as a central source of youth and rock culture. For today's sixteen-year-old, MuchMusic has been available since the age of four, and MTV since the age of one. The emergence of this new relationship disrupts the traditional view of television as a cultural form restricted to the province of mainstream and non-rock culture.

This transformation is due to the existence of music television itself, but more fundamentally, it can be understood as a product of the industry move to narrow-casting of which music television is a prime example. As Paul Attallah has noted, the fragmentation of programming (or narrowcasting) provides television with the capacity to target and address the logic and attitudes of specific audiences, to create relatively private cultural enclaves.[6] Music television—as a case of this fragmentation—provides a site of youth culture which can, and regularly does, define itself against parental, educational, and mainstream culture, all traditionally seen as consistent with television. The introduction in the late 1980s of a wider variety of programming within music television—including news, fashion, politics and fictional programming in addition to the original emphasis on music—has expanded music television's capacity to serve as a comprehensive source of youth culture.

As a result of these corporate and technological shifts, music television can now serve as a legitimate site of authentic music culture to a degree once thought impossible for television. The placement of *The Monkees* within television in the late 1960s determined their fate: they were inauthentic pop because they were on television. Today, however, with their spare, minimalist style, MTV's *Unplugged* and MuchMusic's *Intimate and Interactive*—both of which, interestingly, are defined through their opposition to music video—can serve for many fans as highly authentic presentations.

This first perspective, then, highlighting the fact that the definition of the authentic is subject to shifts in the social, political and economic context of popular music, is consistent with the theoretical directions of early British cultural studies; a key facet of which was the unpacking of exclusionary definitions of authentic, ideal or official culture. It was an attempt to redefine *Culture* as culture. However, this treatment of the authentic is inconsistent with the more recent trajectory of cultural studies which has sought to emphasize the capacity of audiences to create their own meanings and values through their diverse interpretations and uses of the cultural resources imposed upon them; a shift, then, from studying the text to studying the uses of the text. Authenticity, it seems, has been largely immune to this shift.

In this respect, the recent work of David Tetzlaff is significant.[7] Tetzlaff suggests that while the distinctions created by fans and the music industry may be inaccurate, objectively speaking, it is the use of these distinctions by audiences to make sense of their experiences and conditions, to create identities, and to contest social and political conditions, that matters most. I would add that few people—other than cultural critics—have the time or resources to delve into the inaccuracies of the distinctions which they use. The discrimination made between authentic and inauthentic is, despite its inaccuracies, "how people who care about pop music tend to talk about it in the real world."[8]

Tetzlaff wants to understand authenticity as a contested discourse which facilitates a resistance against the oppressive conditions of a fan's life. Authenticity is not just an ideological screen that obscures the workings of capital—although it can be that—but also "a vehicle by which fans and artists have attempted to work against their institutional position."[9] "The Rock Myth," Tetzlaff writes, "is a story about alienation, about how the desires and labors of both producers and consumers are exploited and then frustrated by economic imperatives and the interests of the ruling elites. It is a coded analysis and critique of the facts of subordination. The idea that rock *can* be authentic in spite of all this represents the Utopian belief that the forces of production can be bent to fulfilling non-alienated expression, that the hit-machine can be reclaimed in the name of *soul*."[10]

Tetzlaff's theorization of authenticity as a critical, censorious practice is, I believe, a very useful one. However, he restricts his definition of this critical resistance to an overly simple, class-based politics of resistance: a bottom-up response to top-down power. To adequately address the diverse and complex ways in which constructions of authenticity are organized and utilized in contemporary life, it may be more useful to frame this notion of critical resistance within the processes and strategies of competitive consumer practice.

A critical resistance in consumer practices can certainly serve as a rejection of the values, meanings and social positions which the cultural industries may work to impose, and it can also serve as a demonstration of consumer knowledge and sophistication, and as a means of demarcating social differences between individuals and communities. For example, environmentally friendly shopping—the choice of a "green" lifestyle—can be a sign of opposition to big business. Similarly, the investment by adolescent females in feminist pop music cannot easily be reduced to either critical opposition to patriarchy or a desire to be associated with an appreciation for "serious" music. It may be both in highly variable mixtures. I want to resist the temptation of viewing all non-mainstream behavior as "resistance" and leave open the possibility that it might also be an attempt to express individuality, the management of identity, a hormonal revolt against parental authority, the pursuit of social status, the result of a breakdown in clear value structures, and so on.

Let us employ this last perspective to consider a provocative theory which claims that the value of authenticity is, in fact, increasingly irrelevant to contemporary youth. The key figure in this debate, Lawrence Grossberg, suggests that authenticity is no longer the central measure of value within the consumption of music and music television. Increasingly, youth recognize that all popular culture, all representations, are illusory. Everything is a construction. Music fans are now indifferent to the question of authenticity; to questions of the music's sincerity, its politics, or its degree of popularity. All styles of music, then, are interpreted by fans to be equally serious, equally authentic and, consequently, equally deserving (or undeserving) of being allowed to matter. Authenticity in this cultural context is seen as "just another style."[11] The growing irrelevance of authenticity, once the core of rock's cultural politics, signals for Grossberg the possible end of rock itself: "Rock had a beginning, and it is reasonable to assume, that it may have an end."[12]

The eroding credibility of authenticity has displaced the desire for staking out differences onto a new and postmodern affective logic: what Grossberg calls "ironic nihilism" or "authentic inauthenticity." Cultural practice consistent with this logic renounces its "claim to represent reality."[13] "Authentic inauthenticity," Grossberg writes,

> assumes that since there are no grounds for distinguishing between
> the relative claims of alternatives, one cannot read beyond the fact of

investment. To appropriate, enjoy or invest in a particular style, image or set of images no longer necessarily implies any faith that such investments make a significant (even affective) difference.... If every identity is equally fake, a pose taken, then authentic inauthenticity celebrates the possibilities of poses without denying that is all they are.[14]

By addressing the skeptical disposition of contemporary audiences, and the increasingly common use of self-referential and ironic texts, Grossberg pushes the analysis of authenticity in a new, provocative direction. Indeed, the presence of this ironic aesthetic may be even more common than he suggests. Cultural products from a variety of fields—music, cinema, music videos, situation comedies, and especially advertising—employ ironic strategies which regularly refer to their place within the cultural industries, to their intentions and, ultimately, to the question of authenticity.

But Grossberg's interpretation, while intriguing, may misinterpret the ways in which the value of authenticity and the consumption of music operate within youth culture. The skepticism of audiences towards the possibility of authenticity in popular culture is, as he argues, a growing factor in music consumption. However, in this context, skepticism is better understood as a sign of the importance of the authenticity to fans, rather than as a sign of its irrelevance. A critical distrust of claims to authenticity that are made by artists and other fans is an act of consumer distinction which serves to regulate the distribution of this form of cultural capital. Put simply, if authenticity didn't matter to the audience, it wouldn't demand their attention.

For an intellectual and a member of a differently situated rock audience, ironic nihilism may be a reasonable response to the state of contemporary rock, but I think it may be prudent to consider the possibility that youth, by and large, continue to seek out and distinguish between the authentic and the inauthentic.

We may examine ironic text from a perspective grounded in the purposes and logic of consumer capitalism and consumer culture. This alternate perspective suggests that investments in the ironic can be best understood as not a reflection of the irrelevance of, and indifference to, authenticity but as (a) a critique of a specific version of authenticity, and (b) a means by which consumer capitalism and its consumers can position themselves in opposition to the inauthentic.

In Grossberg's analysis, the foregrounding of the inauthentic nature of the text is a recognition by the performer, song or video that it is, itself, inauthentic. And this is acceptable to its audience because, as Grossberg argues, the value has grown irrelevant. When understood according to the objectives and strategies of consumer marketing and competitive consumer culture, though, this aesthetic practice is best understood as a reference to the inauthenticity of something other than the text or product itself. It is, I would argue, a reference to the inauthentic quality of *other artists, songs, videos or audiences*. The "Other" constructed through the text is inauthentic while the artist, song or video in play is authentic due to its astute recognition of, and critical opposition to, the inauthenticity which it foregrounds. Rather than suggesting that the ironic inauthentic text expresses the idea that "everything is constructed," as Grossberg has, it may be more accurate to characterize this practice as suggesting that "everything *else* is constructed."

Moreover, the ambiguous nature of the ironic text is, in one important sense, a flattering appeal to the cleverness of the viewing audience. Intrinsic to the ironic text is both an appropriate and inappropriate interpretation. The appropriate interpretation requires a certain cultural knowledge and orientation from its audience. And, as Andrew Goodwin argues, it is this ability to recognize and understand the codes employed which is the source of much of the pleasure for the music television audience.[15]

The significance of this type of appeal in terms of consumer culture specifically, is that it serves to form an alliance between the product and certain audiences, and notably, not with other audiences. It situates the audience and the product on the same side of the fence, in a manner of speaking, and defines the audience's difference against other consumer communities or audiences who "don't get it." From both a marketing and consumer differentiation standpoint, then, it defines "us" against "them": it creates in-groups and out-groups.

This is not to suggest that music television involves particularly subtle uses of irony, which limits the pleasure available through the text to a small cultural elite. The irony employed can be such that it is understood by the entire music television audience. The inauthentic "other" constructed in this form of discourse need not be part of the audience at all, and typically, it is not. But whoever and whatever is defined as inauthentic is an "outsider," lacking appropriate cultural knowledge.

Further, the practical demands of the commercial music industry strongly encourage individual acts and their promotional vehicles, such as music videos, to make available images and music which are consistent with the concepts of authenticity and creative individuality. In order to distinguish themselves in the marketplace, groups need to establish a desirable difference from competitors. Repeat sales of artists require the development of a discernible difference from other acts (within the framework of specific styles or genres) in order that financial risk can be minimized and the artist can be resold without expensive start-up costs. A style of ironic inauthenticity can be an earmark.

But if, as has been argued by Grossberg, the inauthenticity was in respect to the text itself then this difference would be, on one level, not a difference at all, as it would invite an interpretation of the artist, song or video as common and conventional—as "just another song or video." A text which is consistent with Grossberg's concept of authentic inauthenticity cannot serve well as a recognizable and marketable product because it is about the very *lack* of difference, the end of creative individuality and the autonomous artist.

It is certainly the case that the desire to create social distinctions according to the authentic-inauthentic dichotomy remains central to the production and consumption of music and music video. Despite the increasing presence of self-conscious cultural forms and practices, the area of music consumption has, by and large, clung to this particular type of social difference. As Andrew Goodwin has suggested, "Pop fans generally appear to want their stars clad in denim, leather, and spandex, not in ironic quotation marks."[16]

Nevertheless, the particular quality of this investment in the authentic-inauthentic distinction points to a considerably more substantive issue. The authenticity that I have described is one which is based predominantly on the rejection of a former, hegemonic notion of authenticity. This in itself is not new or inconsistent with the ideology of authenticity: the rejection of values associated with past generations is an integral component of the ideology of authenticity. However, this new authenticity falls short of completing the traditional cycle of Rise and Fall and Rise Again, by basing itself completely on a rejection of the past and generating nothing for the future. And the unwillingness of youth to construct and invest in a new brand of authenticity which embodies their particular experience and attitudes does reflect, as Grossberg argues, some form of postmodern nihilism, wherein the faith in the possibility of creating something new and meaningful has eroded. And in this respect, it is consistent with aspects of postmodernity. David Harris has noted that modernity was characterized by a continual process of taking from the past in order to construct the future.[17] Postmodernity, on the other hand, simply steals from the past with no misconceptions about creating something new.

I do not interpret this skepticism as a total collapse of faith resulting in an indifference to the question of authenticity. The increasingly common appearance of cultural texts which question or reject the claim of authenticity reflects, instead, (a) the recognition by some audiences of the increasing (but not complete) impossibility of authentic culture and, (b) the subsequent *increased* value of those moments, sites, and entities—"Just another plagiaristic bar band," Kurt Cobain called himself and his musical friends in Nirvana[18]—where authenticity is believed to reside still. The process of questioning the claims of authenticity acts to control, limit and channel the exchange of a cultural value that has become increasingly scarce and precious.

Notes

[1] David Tetzlaff, "Music for Meaning: Reading the Discourse of Authenticity in Rock," *Journal of Communication Inquiry* 18 (1994), 95-117.

[2] Will Straw, "Music Video in its Contexts: Popular Music and Postmodernism in the 1980s," *Popular Music* 7, (1988).

[3] Paul Attallah, "Music Television," in Working *Papers in Communication* (Montreal: McGill University, 1986).

[4] Attallah, "Music Television," 3.

[5] Andrew Goodwin, *Dancing in the Distraction Factory: Music Television and Popular Culture* (Minneapolis, University of Minnesota Press, 1992).

[6] Attallah, "Music Television," 18.

[7] Tetzlaff, "Music."

[8] Tetzlaff, "Music," 103.

[9] Tetzlaff, "Music," 113.

[10] Tetzlaff, "Music," 113.

[11] Lawrence Grossberg, "The Media Economy of Rock Culture: Cinema, Post-Modernity and Authenticity," in Simon Frith and Andrew Goodwin, eds., *Sound and Vision* (New York, Routledge, 1993), 203.

[12] Grossberg, "Economy," 198.

[13] Grossberg, "Economy," 224.

[14] Grossberg, "Economy," 225.

[15] Goodwin, *Dancing*.

[16] Andrew Goodwin, "Sample and Hold: Pop Music in the Digital Age of Reproduction," in Simon Frith and Andrew Goodwin , eds., *On Record: Rock, Pop, And the Written Word* (New York, Pantheon, 1988), 78.

[17] David Harris, *A Society of Signs* (New York, Routledge, 1996).

[18] Posting on TAML (Teenage Angst Mailing List).

MICHAEL HOECHSMANN

I am White, Male and Middle-Class in a Global Era: Marketing (to) Generation X

> I am not a target market.
> Douglas Coupland, *Generation X* [1]

> Now [the media is] waking up to the discovery of 46 million people
> which is like all of a sudden noticing France.
> Bob Guccione, Jr., editor of *Spin* [2]

When Douglas Coupland published his first novel, *Generation X* in 1991, he could hardly have predicted the reception it would get. *Generation X* is not simply a popular book; rather it has been adopted into the canon of North American cultural literacy as the definitive statement for the habitus of a new generation. The term "generation x" has slipped smoothly into common parlance, nudging out *Time* magazine's 'twentysomethings' and Richard Linklater's 'slackers' as the moniker of choice for the post-boomer generation. The book *Generation X*, with its catalogue of witty aphorisms in the margins of each page, has been afforded an unusual opportunity to infiltrate the North American lexicon at a rate far outstripping its actual readership. Like the *Bible, The Communist Manifesto,* or *The Closing of the American Mind,* you do not have to read *Generation X* to know it.

Given the astounding reception accorded to *Generation X*, it comes as no surprise that John Fraser, the editor of *Saturday Night* magazine, recently referred to Coupland as "The Dalai Lama of Generation X."[3] While not wishing to diminish the impact upon North American popular culture of Coupland, who is regularly solicited to write for youth market magazines such as *Wired* and *Shift*, it would seem premature to deify him as the beacon voice of a generation. The coupling between

Generation X and Coupland, while understandable, overestimates the role of the author of a tract whose time had come. Lose the title and the marginal aphorisms, and Coupland is the author of a witty novel of contemporary youth anomie, a sort of *Shampoo Planet*, Volume 1. To his credit, however, Coupland (and/or his publisher) showed great market sense by plugging his anti-commodity narrative into a sleek commodity form. This hitchhiker's guide to the new generational world view offers the type of sound bite wisdom which marketers require to ply their trade, mixed with an irreverent challenge sure to wake up the slumbering giant of commodity culture: "We are not a target market."

On February 1, 1993, the trade magazine *Advertising Age* ran an article entitled "The Media Wakes Up to Generation X" which warned that "if the media didn't do a better job of courting twentysomethings . . . they risked alienating a group ready to overtake [baby] boomers as the primary market for nearly every product category."[4] Boasting approximately $125 billion in annual disposable income, these new pilgrims to the temple of consumption are not naive. As advertising executive Natalie Perkins (Trone Advertising, Greensboro, NC) states, "You've got to work hard to get in under the radar with these people. As soon as they think you're trying to sell them something, they turn off and walk away."[5] The solution to GenX consumer cynicism, so the argument goes, is to create a fast-paced, self-reflexive genre of advertising which parodies traditional 'mom and apple pie' ads while offering up a range of irreverent non-sequiturs, sound bites of a new world wisdom stolen from GenX lore. "Life is good," mumbles a cartoon dog named Leonard for Acura Integra, "Mondo good."

Examples of this new advertising aesthetic abound: Burger King featured the popular MTV veejay Dan Cortese frenetically hawking burgers; Pepsi ran a high-energy campaign for its *Mountain Dew* beverage; Nike bounced televisions off a floor like basketballs; and Subaru attempted to market its *Impreza* model by casting a Christian Slater look-alike who intoned, "This car is like punk rock." In a major campaign targeted for this generation, Molson Canadian adopted the aesthetic and attitude of GenX ads into its *I Am Canadian* campaign for its *Canadian* brand of lager. The television ads string together a fast-paced montage of images which show young people engaged in leisure activities such as sports, parties and travel. The print ads develop the leisure theme in relation to an aversion to work. For example, a bored youth faxes a photocopied picture of his face to a friend and a group of muddied youth cavort in a mosh pit with the by-line: "Sorry I can't work this weekend. I'm helping friends move."

While *Generation X* offered an intriguing *entrée* into the contradictory position in which North American youth find themselves as emergent consumers in a period of economic decline, the rapid and voracious appropriation of the concept of 'Generation X' by the advertising industry suggests a perceived need to corral these self-described renegade shoppers. Thus, there are two versions of Generation X. One is unnamed; it is the habitus of a displaced generation. The other is unashamedly displayed; it is the dream of marketers.

The epochal, ruptural shifts in the global economy are being lived by North American youth in contradictory ways. On the one hand, the global realignment of industrial production away from the nations of the global North[6] has created the conditions where, for the first time in the post-war era, young people in North America must face diminishing economic expectations. On the other hand, the increasing centrality of consumption as the motor of domestic economic growth in the nations of the global North, interpellates these same young people as a powerful new consumer force. For theorists, activists and educators, this period of rapid change presents a unique challenge and opportunity. While the walls of a manufacturing empire crumble around us and the nation state loses its sovereign distinctiveness, our attention must be firmly fixed upon the emergence of new ways of life.

Certainly, the globalizing economy—or what some writers are calling post-Fordism[7]—is having direct impacts on North America. The central assumption of post-Fordism is that there has been a major shift of the mode of production in the global North involving "just-in-time" production, the consolidation of global markets, the increased mobility of international capital and the diminishing power of the nation state. In geopolitical terms, this has resulted in the transfer of the ("Fordist") manufacturing industries to the global South and the development at home of an "information society" with an ever-increasing service sector. So-called "competition" from low-wage sweat-shop sectors around the world, facilitated by the shrinking costs of the circulation both of marketing information and of goods, has made it irresistibly profitable to mothball North American factories and to import consumer goods from abroad.

While transnational capital is having its day in an increasingly deregulated world, the domestic economies of North America are taking a beating. For North American youth, the likelihood of reaching, let alone surpassing, their parents' standard of living is very low. The *Globe & Mail,* Canada's "national" newspaper, has taken to referring to youth as the "lost generation."[8] Unemployment for youth—those aged 15 to 24—is 16.6% in Canada, 8% higher than the population at large. Furthermore, Statistics Canada has shown that youth make up a disproportionate percentage of the underemployed in Canada who are not calculated into the official unemployment rate. The underemployed include "discouraged workers"—or, in Richard Linklater's term, slackers, who have given up looking for work; and part-timers, who would prefer to work full-time. The number of underemployed youth has ballooned in the past ten years; if the workforce participation for youth were the same as in 1986, the official youth unemployment rate would be a staggering 26.6%.[9]

Another significant feature of youth employment patterns in the growing service economy is the "McJob" syndrome, another Coupland aphorism that has taken on a life of its own. A McJob, according to Coupland, is "a low-pay, low-prestige, low-dignity, low-benefit, no-future job in the service sector."[10] In *Good Jobs, Bad Jobs,* a statement by the Economic Council of Canada,[11] it was reported that 70% of Canadian workers now work in the service industries. This research document distinguished between upper- and lower-tier service jobs (good jobs, bad jobs) in order to discover what percentage of those employed in the service sector have (bad) "McJobs." This report found that one-third of those in the service economy hold "McJobs," roughly three million workers among whom women and youth are overrepresented.

Many young people are overqualified for these jobs, a problem which raises major questions about the validity and appropriateness of education as it was conceived in the modern era. While in 1989 49% of young people were in full-time studies in Canada, by 1993 this figure had ballooned to 56%. However, Lars Osberg, a Canadian economist, states that, "Going back to school only delays the problem. It doesn't actually solve it."[12] The concern is that if young people are not given adequate opportunities in good jobs, they are unlikely to be prepared to take those jobs on if and when they are available again. Rather, they risk becoming the lost generation when the boomer's kids come of age at the turn of the millenium.

In this period of profound social and economic flux, the so-called Generation X is positioned uniquely to observe the mutually determining character of economy and culture. The American century is over. Theorists of post-Fordism have pointed to 1973, the year of the OPEC crisis, as the watershed date which marked the end of the Fordist era. Since that time the influence of the U.S. has been in the wane, and Canada, which has historically pinned its economic fortunes on its southern neighbor, has shared in the decline. North American youth, those born between 1968 and 1978, who have arrived at the dinner table of an unprecedented age of affluence just as the candles are going out, are confused and bitter. Adding to the confusion is the perception that the American Empire has not yet crumbled. Rambo still flexes his muscles across New World borders, Mickey Mouse and his cronies still monopolize the global media and *Coca-Cola* still flows into the world's consumer appetites. With all the excitement, however, Scrooge McDuck has fallen into crippling debt, and his last progeny, the baby boomers (who would be, to extend the metaphor, Huey, Duey and Luey) are smugly ensconced in the cultural mainstream, hogging all the jobs.

The Gap, a company which has evolved into a clothing empire on the backs of Generation X, ran the following slogan in a recent ad campaign: *For every generation there's a gap.* Resentment of the boomers, what Coupland calls "boomer envy," runs high. Boomers are perceived to have transformed from hippies to yuppies, leaving a shattered economy and environmental degradation in their wake. A cover story in *The Atlantic*, "The New Generation Gap," reported that the boomer generation, now experiencing its second generation gap, is again monopolizing the moral high ground. This article, written by Neil Howe and Bill Strauss, two boomer Xer wannabes, refers to the new generation as thirteeners, the thirteenth generation since the U.S. Independence. Thirteeners, according to Howe and Strauss, make up "a generation weaned on minimal expectations and gifted in the game of life . . . now avoiding meaning in a cumbersome society that, as they see it, offers them little."

The Christian Slater character, Mark, in the movie *Pump Up the Volume* (1990) captures well the purported historical despair of North American youth:

> There's nothing to do anymore. Everything decent's been done. All the good themes have been used up and turned into themeparks. So I don't find it cheerful to live in the middle of a totally exhausted decade when there's nothing to look forward to and no one to look up to.

While Mark is not a bona fide slacker, preferring to change his conditions by orchestrating his fellow high school students to rebel against the oppressiveness of their school, Richard Linklater's *Slacker* (1991), a group of white youth living in the late 1980s, epitomize the new spirit of a lost generation. The narrative of the film lazily wanders from one youth to another. Along the way, the viewer is treated to a mix of random insights which do little to explain the contemporary conditions of youth, but rather reveal pessimism and disdain:

> Same old same old . . . just lollygagging around. Still unemployed. I'm in this band . . . We're the Ultimate Losers now. And, ah, the singer's still a jerk.[13]

The problem with *Slacker*, *Generation X*, and *13th GEN*, to name a few of the most influential renderings of the North American post-Fordist generation, is that they substitute anthropological and literary insight for historical rigor. According to them, the conditions which young people face today are simply there. It's a bummer, but— hey—that's just the way it is. Henry Giroux argues that an important opportunity to discuss social change might be missed if these texts carry the day. States Giroux:

What in fact should be seen as a social commentary about "dead-end capitalism" emerges simply as a celebration of refusal dressed up in a rhetoric of aesthetics, style, fashion, and solipsistic protests.[14]

While Gen Xers are in a unique position to reconsider the down sides of capitalism—and arguably they are doing so—what is taken up by the media celebrates what Giroux calls "slacking off" while leaving aside the thorny question of just who will be spending the $125 billion a year which Generation X purportedly controls.

While "generation X" has taken on a life of its own, the fallout of *Generation X* spawned a small publishing "boom" in 1994, targeted principally to a youth audience. *The GenX Reader*, edited by Douglas Rushkoff, is the most comprehensive volume of GenX lore for one-stop shoppers. Rushkoff has assembled a collection of fiction and non-fiction pieces, including canonical tracts by writers such as Coupland and Richard Linklater, and excerpts from both mainstream (ie. *Elle, Rolling Stone* and *Newsweek*) and alternative (ie. *bOING! bOING!* and the *I Hate Brenda Newsletter*) publications. To get an overview of 'generation X' as discourse, *The GenX Reader* serves as a good starting point.

But the most critical rendering of the "generation X" phenomenon is *Generation Ecch! The Backlash Starts Here* by Jason Cohen and Michael Krugman.[15] What Cohen and Krugman share with Xer luminaries such as Coupland and Linklater is a wry and irreverent sense of humor, but they focus their analysis on the very texts of "generation X." Cohen and Krugman point out that the texts of "generation X," which "seem to validate conservative old fart Allan Bloom's bellyaching about the accelerating vapidity of post-TV youth and their complete lack of depth, smarts, feeling or history," serve to support contemporary moral panics about youth. While their Xer tone grows wearisome, Cohen and Krugman use their encyclopedic knowledge of GenX pop culture texts to provide sharp critical analysis.

A clue to the problem of generalizing X is given in one of the many provocative essays in *Next: Young American Writers on the Next Generation*, edited by Eric Liu.[16] In "Trash that Baby Boom," Ian Williams argues that "the only people willing to burn the calories to bitch in public about the perils of being directionless and apathetic possess far too much direction and gumption to come close to representing the kind they call their own." Liu's collection is wide-ranging and eclectic, with a focus on contradictory political positions and identities-in-process. Given that most GenX literature is really about the contemporary ethos of white middle-class males, this collection, which is split along gender and race lines, is remarkably representative.

In his contribution to this volume, "Generation Mex," Lalo Lopez argues that there is a tendency in the white middle-class cultural mainstream to speak in universal terms about things which are ultimately culturally and ethnically specific. States Lopez:

> For the Gringorder, there's gotta be baby boomers and thirtysome-things, Generation Xers and slackers. I'd like to be a slacker, but my family would kick my ass. A poor Mexican worrying about esoteric emotions like angst? Get a job, "mijo."[17]

Of course, the term 'generation' is imprecise at the best of times. Issues of difference, whether in terms of class, race, gender or sexuality, are systematically excluded by this generalizing term which puts everybody in the same boat. It is important to discuss the absences in Generation X. What is not said, but is amply apparent in the texts of GenX, is that Generation X is lily white. While the occasional faces of people of color show up in GenX texts, this is due more to the ever-broadening use of the term which is mushrooming out of control. By ignoring questions of difference, the problems of disaffected white males can monopolize the cultural mainstream. On the other hand, if *Slacker* and *Generation X* are seen precisely as texts about disaffected white boys, if issues of difference are foregrounded, they can be taken as starting points for some productive analyses. Perhaps it is simply the case that the loud, protracted whine of 'generation X' is an ethos shared by young white males, those very people who were socialized to expect social power and privilege to come easily.

One of the most significant contributions to the generational lament of white youth—and one which reveals the gender bias of GenX lore—is *Late Bloomers: Coming of Age in Today's America: The Right Place at the Wrong Time*, by David Lipsky and Alexander Abrams.[18] Perhaps the comment on the dust cover, that this book offers "constructive, non-confrontational analysis," and the pictures of two clean-cut young white suits, should offer a warning, but nothing would quite prepare a reader for this: "Didn't we imagine that we'd have money, and houses, and families of our own, as we approached the end of our twenties? Didn't we imagine we'd be easy in our lives—that life would be an affair of lawns and washed cars and coming in through the front doors of our houses?" Despite the theme of lament for privilege lost, this book is loaded with research data on the new hard times for youth; but these two go-getters, worried as they are about the relative costs of a new Mustang and university tuition, could hardly seem to be affected by it.

Two other energetic white boys, Rob Nelson and Jon Cowan, teamed up to write *Revolution X: A Survival Guide for Our Generation*. Nelson and Cowan, founders of the grassroots, "nonpartisan" Lead . . . *Or Leave* network, defy the GenX stereotypes of fatalistic slackerdom to promote political engagement on the part of U.S. youth. They take aim at important social issues of the day such as the environment, crime, and the debt (which they attribute to U.S. military spending, tax breaks to the rich and "middle-class welfare"). They espouse a contradictory politics congruent with a middle-class lifestyle that buys into the material benefits of mainstream culture without completely selling itself out:

> No fire hoses, tear gas, police dogs, or riots. Let's face it: Most of us aren't looking for unnecessary confrontation. A generation that reads *Details* and *Spin,* watches *Melrose Place, Seinfeld,* and *The Simpsons,* and waits in line for the *StairMaster* after work is probably not going to be taking to the streets with guns or Molotov cocktails anytime soon. And why should we? Just because we're not prepared to die to eliminate the national debt or wipe out poverty doesn't mean we can't get involved in changing the country and protecting our future.[19]

Their book offers an extensive resource list for political action including addresses and phone numbers of advocacy groups, politicians, and both mainstream and alternative media. Unfortunately, though it is hipper and more streetwise than *Late Bloomers,* it is cut from the same cloth. While Lipsky and Abrams might vote Republican, Nelson and Cowan's "post-partisan" revolution is content to get youth out to the ballot box, presumably to vote Democrat.

If the New York publishers, who unleashed a small "generation X" publishing boom, feared they had missed the boat, they didn't let on. *The GenX Reader, Generation Ecch!, Next, Late Bloomers* and *Revolution X* arrived and departed quietly from bookstore shelves. Despite its bring-back-the-eighties ethos of individualism and greed, it was *Late Bloomers* that attracted some critical attention thanks to a prepublication excerpt in *Harper's.*[20] Lipsky and Abrams presented some media analysis which showed that, until 1990, major newspapers and magazines had portrayed youth as confident, ambitious, determined, fiercely self-reliant and even "older than they used to be." Suddenly, in 1990, this all changed. *Time* published a cover story entitled "Proceeding With Caution" which characterized youth as paralyzed shirkers, who were "overly sensitive at best and lazy at worst" and for whom "second best seems just fine." *Fortune,* which had lauded young people in the late eighties, promptly adopted this same tone. To explain this editorial shift, Lipsky and Abrams point out that one million jobs were lost to youth between May 1990 and May 1991. Somewhat tongue-in-cheek, Lipsky and Abrams ask whether the new editorial stance on youth was an act of unconscious kindness: "after all, if we had never cared about careers and material success, it would be less disturbing for us—and for the country—when we didn't achieve them."

While Lipsky and Abrams perceptively demonstrate in *Harper's* the impact of a changing economy on youth in general and on the discourse about youth in particular, their book shows that they are principally concerned about how that changing economy would squelch their own material aspirations. Nonetheless, to begin to answer the question of what was "generation X," the impact of a changing economy on youth must be foregrounded. Given the malleability of the term "youth," and given the gender and ethnicity of most of the GenX pundits, the next question which follows is, whose "youth" are we talking about? As Leslie Savan writes in the *Village Voice:* "There's no Malcolm X in Generation X—except when an ad is deliberately 'multi-cultural,' the X of the media mind means almost entirely grungy white youth."[21] To test this hypothesis, one needs only take a look at the current Molson *I Am Canadian* campaign which borrows all the elements of U.S. GenX ads.

The *I Am Canadian* campaign celebrates white, male middle-class identity in an era of diminishing returns. Like many beer commercials, these ads feature young white middle-class males enjoying leisure pursuits congruent with economic privilege. Outdoor sports, parties and travel provide the narrative backdrop for the pursuit of pleasure. These narratives of pleasure denied by the new economic conditions are resolved in the ongoing pursuit of heterosexual desire. Young women are cast as part of the pleasure spectacle, compliant participants who serve to vindicate male economic impotence in the reproduction of gender privilege. People of color, if cast at all, are simply assimilated others, bystanders to this cathartic display of white male middle-class identity. While these ads highlight the last gasp representations of white male middle-class privilege, they assert a notion of nation, of national identity, bereft of conflicting claims to power, a spectacle of the "great white north" where the boys socialized to expect class privilege continue to have their way despite the real economic conditions which mitigate against this.

While exploring questions of difference may provide a clearer image of the so-called "lost generation," advertisers are more interested in looking for ways to sell their products to middle-class white youth. As MTV tells its advertisers, "Buy this 24-year-old and get all his friends absolutely free . . . He heads up a pack. What he eats, his friends eat. What he wears, they wear. What he likes, they like. And what he's never heard of . . . well . . . you get the idea."[22] If only life were so simple for the marketers. Pepsi's *Mountain Dew* campaign was moderately successful but the Burger King ad campaign with Dan Cortese and Subaru's "This car is like punk rock" ad both failed miserably.

Thus, as the 90s wear on, "generation X" appears to be falling into disfavor. If there was ever a subcultural moment associated with it, its *bricoleurs* have moved on to new, more fertile terrain. To his credit, Coupland won't answer a question with the words 'generation X' in it. And advertising executives, ever the perceptive ethnographers, are searching for new answers. Already in the spring of 1994, a Coca-Cola marketing executive, Sergio Zyman, asserted that "Generation X came. It took a few breaths. And it went. Generation X doesn't exist—and barely ever did."[23] As if to punctuate the end of an era, the news emerged barely three weeks later that "generation X" had a martyr, Kurt Cobain, who left behind him a legacy of pain and torment.

Generation X, as a cultural phenomenon, corresponded to a great extent to a period of mourning of young white males who had been socialized to expect easy access to privilege and power, even if only for a middle-class American Dream which today seems almost unattainable. While the economic conditions which gave rise to "generation X" are shared by all youth, the public spokespersons and the dominant characters of fictional accounts were predominantly young, white and male. The texts which they created or represented reflect that fact. While GenXers are in a unique position to reconsider the down sides of "free-market" capitalism, their spokespersons have rushed to characterize them as shallow, apathetic social drop-outs. The fall-out of this new mythos has been a string of lamentable movies, the appropriation by the music, television and fashion industries of grunge rock and fashion as a kind of *ur*-moment of the whole phenomenon, the emergence of Seattle as a new cultural mecca—a San Francisco of the 90s—and a number of aggressive fast-paced ad campaigns produced by an industry bewildered by Coupland's claim that "We are not a target market." The more things change, it appears, the more they stay the same.

Notes

[1] Generation X: Tales for an Accelerated Culture 3(New York: St. Martins Press, 1991), 17.

[2] Quoted in Scott Donaton, "The Media Wakes Up to Generation X," *Advertising Age* (February 1, 1993), 16.

[3] John Fraser, "The Dalai Lama of Generation X," *Saturday Night* (March, 1994), 8-9.

[4] Donaton, "Media," 16.

[5] Quoted in Donaton, "Media," 17.

[6] Willy Brandt, *North-South: A Programme for Survival* (Cambridge MA: MIT Press, 1980).

[7] See, for example, Stuart Hall, "Brave New World," *Marxism Today* (October 1988); and David Harvey, *The Condition of Postmodernity* (Oxford: Basil Blackwell, 1989).

[8] Barrie McKenna, "Rough Road Ahead for Unemployed Youth," *Globe & Mail* (January 14, 1993), B1 and B6. See as well Alanna Mitchell, "Future is Bleak for Youth, Study Says," *Globe & Mail* (March 3, 1994), A1-A2.

[9] "Time to Emphasize Youth Employment," *The Toronto Star* (July 11, 1996), A22.

[10] *Generation X*, 5.

[11] Economic Council of Canada, *Good Jobs, Bad Jobs: Employment in the Service Economy* (Ottawa: Minister of Supply and Services Canada, 1990).

[12] Quoted in Mitchell, "Future," A2.

[13] Richard Linklater, "Slacker," in Rushkoff, ed., *The GenX Reader* (New York: Ballantine Books, 1994), 40-43.

[14] Henry Giroux, *Fugitive Cultures: Race, Violence & Youth* (New York: Routledge, 1996), 38.

[15] (New York: Fireside Books, 1994).

[16] (New York: W. W. Norton & Co., 1994).

[17] In Liu, ed., *Next*, 134.

[18] (New York: Times Books, 1994).

[19] (New York: Penguin Books, 1994), 8.

[20] David Lipsky and Alexander Abrams, "The Packaging (and Re-Packaging) of a Generation," *Harper's* (July, 1994), 20-22.

[21] Leslie Savan, "Generation X-Force," *Village Voice* (August 24, 1993), 51.

[22] Savan, "X-Force," 51.

[23] Reuter News Agency, "There's No Generation X, Marketing Expert Says," *The Toronto Star* (March 21, 1994), E1.

MARY CELESTE KEARNEY

Girls Just Want to Have *Fun*?: Female Avengers in '90s Teenpics

These two are different, you mark my words.
Madame Danzard in *Sister My Sister*

In 1983 Cindy Lauper released a song that has permeated our popular culture and collective consciousness to such an extent that it now functions as a cliché of teenage girlhood. The song was, of course, "Girls Just Want to Have Fun." Though Lauper's song clearly attempts to represent a liberated and contemporary view of adolescent femininity, the music video created for it (by Ed Griles)—replete with Lauper's all-night phone conversations and dress-up games with her girlfriends, as well as an omnipresent atmosphere of heterosexual romance which climaxes with a kiss from her boyfriend—ultimately reproduces the same sugar-coated version of teenage girlhood we have been force-fed since Gidget hit the big screen.

More than ten years later, Rafael Zelinsky has attempted to show us just how myopic this notion that "girls just want to have fun" really is by focusing his most recent film on two teenage girls who meet each other hitchhiking, bond over shared dissatisfaction with childhood, and become co-conspirators in a frenzied day of adolescent mayhem. Unlike Lauper's video which ends with a wild co-ed dance party in her bedroom, the climax of Zelinsky's film *Fun* (1995) occurs when the two girls, Bonnie (Alicia Witt) and Hillary (Renee Humphrey), brutally murder an elderly woman in her suburban home. When asked later by a prison psychologist why they did it, Bonnie states emphatically, "I told you a million times: Hillary and I killed the old lady just . . . for . . . *fun*." While it is not entirely clear what these two girls mean by "fun," we can be fairly certain that their definition is not the same as Lauper's.

In his review of Zelinsky's film, *Los Angeles Times* film critic Kevin Thomas argues that *Fun* "doesn't tell us anything new about disaffected youth."[1] In turn, Janet Maslin notes that *Fun* doesn't deviate from the cliché of teen killers in film: "The murderers were in love when they committed their crimes. The day of the mayhem was the best day of their young lives. They slept like babies after their heinous deeds were done."[2]

If Thomas and Maslin are right that films like *Fun* show us nothing new about adolescence, then what are we to make of two other films released around the same time—*Heavenly Creatures* (1994) and *Sister My Sister* (1995)—which also broke out of Hollywood's obsession with blonde clueless mall-rats to explore the "darker side" of teenage girlhood? Like *Fun*, a low-budget and relatively unknown independent film adapted from James Bosley's play based on the true story of two high school girls who murdered a total stranger apparently "just for the fun of it," *Sister My Sister* is a film adaptation of Wendy Kesselman's play based on the infamous story of two French sisters who brutally murdered their mistress and her daughter in the 1930s. Similar in theme and content, *Heavenly Creatures* is a cinematic dramatization based on the lives of two adolescent girls in New Zealand in the 1950s who killed one of their mothers to avenge their separation from one another.

Since the narratives of *Fun*, *Heavenly Creatures*, and *Sister My Sister* are taken from actual historical events and depict a pair of adolescent girls who ruthlessly kill older women, these films are easily distinguishable from the fictional stories of teen girls mass-produced by Hollywood each year. Moving far beyond Lauper's happy-go-lightly heterosexual notion of feminine adolescence, *Fun*, *Heavenly Creatures*, and *Sister My Sister* are not your typical teenpics, and the girls in these films, young lesbians who will do anything in order to remain together, are not your typical movie teens.

What might films like *Fun*, *Heavenly Creatures*, and *Sister My Sister* tell us about the nature of feminine adolescence and female homosexuality, the causes of female delinquency and crime, and the fragility of mother/daughter relationships? Do these narratives about young lesbian killers merely reproduce the "lesbian as monster" narrative we have seen in so many previous films, or are they celebrations of the discovery and fulfillment of lesbian desire? Are these representations of female violence connected in some way to the popularization of the feminist and queer ideologies of empowerment, or are they part of the ongoing backlash against feminism and homosexuality which holds both responsible for the decrease in stay-at-home mothers and the disintegration of traditional family values? In short, how do these films deconstruct the myth that "girls just want to have fun"?

To explore how these films offer new and provocative depictions of feminine adolescence, female friendships, and lesbian desire we may focus on two issues. First, there is their relationship to the horror genre and the activation of powerful, aggressive female adolescent bodies in contemporary cinema. Secondly, there is the disturbing inclusion of matricide in narratives whose primary focus is the homoerotic bonds formed by teenage girls who are victims of child neglect, sexual abuse, and psychological torment. Both of these issues are related to the changing face of gender and sexual politics in recent years. Let us begin with the "horror" of feminine adolescence.

In her study of contemporary horror film, *Men, Women, and Chain Saws*, Carol Clover traces the transformation of the female adolescent body in horror film from its earlier use to connote pure victimization to its more recent function in troubling feminine and masculine attributes. She notes that in more recent horror films female adolescents occupy two of the primary positions necessary in such stories, that is, victim and hero. Although Clover's main concern is to understand how strong female characters can appeal to predominantly male adolescent audiences, her theories offer provocative insights on the activation of female adolescent bodies in contemporary cinema.

For example, Clover notes that the slasher formula has undergone a distinct transformation with the emergence of the Final Girl figure in the mid-1970s. Unlike previous films in which females functioned predominantly as victims, the Final Girls who appear in films such as *Halloween* (1978) and *Slumber Party Massacre* (1982) progress from a feminized state of passivity and fear to a fully phallicized state of aggression and control so as to become the films' sole survivors and heroes—a progression she attributes to a "one sex" model of sexuality which was displaced in the 18th century by the "two sex" model we are more familiar with today.[3] I would argue that we might also understand representations of masculinized female adolescent bodies as related to the specific socio-historical context of the 1970s and '80s, wherein female success in a male-dominated society was thought (especially by liberal feminists) to require the incorporation of the two logics of gender into one body. As liberating as these figures appear, however, Clover cautions that reading the Final Girl as a sign of feminist progression in cinema is "a particularly grotesque expression of wishful thinking" given that the slasher genre is fully implicated in patriarchal ideology and discourse.[4]

Having written her thesis about slasher films in the mid-1980s, and being confined to the movies on hand at that time, Clover asserts that "female killers are few and their reasons for killing significantly different from men's.... They show no gender confusion. Nor is their motive overtly psychosexual; their anger derives in most cases not from childhood experience but from specific moments in their adult lives in which they have been abandoned or cheated on by men."[5] The anger reaches a kind of apotheosis in *Fun, Heavenly Creatures*, and *Sister My Sister*, in which female adolescents fully inhabit the roles of not just the victim and the hero but also the monster whose wrath is distinctly related to a dysfunctional childhood.

While Clover's theories about the girls in slasher films provide some means for exploring the cinematic activation of the female adolescent body, her discussion, in texts such as these, of rape victims who retaliate against their oppressors in rape-revenge films is perhaps more helpful for understanding the abuse-matricide narratives we find here.[6] Clover notes that rape-revenge narratives underwent considerable transformation during the 1970s, shifting from rape as a small sequence in larger narratives to rape as the subject of full length rape-revenge films; from the depiction of rape as primarily sexual in nature to its representation as a violent crime; from the portrayal of the rapist as a psychopath to his depiction as a "typical" male; and, most importantly, from the depiction of rape as a male-centered action to that of a female-centered experience.[7]

If, as Clover argues, rape-revenge narratives of the 1970s were grounded on the feminist premise that we live in a "rape culture," in which all men are—at least in part—complicit in the violent oppression of women; and if we take those narratives as emerging from a feminist insistence on categorizing and punishing rape as a violent crime (rather than a sexual act); then *Fun, Heavenly Creatures*, and *Sister My Sister*, films of the 1990s, seem to represent a new political focus, away from the concerns of adult women to those of female adolescents. And this move can be seen to have been initiated in large part by young women and girls. Instead of rape alone as the impetus of these three filmic narratives, we have child neglect, sexual repression, and psychological abuse. Instead of men violating women, we have maternal authority figures who oppress their daughters. And instead of the singular adult rape victim on a rampage of revenge, we have pairs of adolescent lesbians as the bold avengers of their abuse.

In her analysis of Brian De Palma's *Carrie* (1976), Vivian Sobchak contextualizes the wrath the female protagonist inflicts on her abusers as "a response to a comprehensible betrayal," an outrage "as 'justifiable' as it is frightening."[8] While *Fun, Heavenly Creatures*, and *Sister My Sister* are profound departures from "abused girl as witch" narratives found in films such as *Carrie*—wherein power is not a quality inherent in girls but something that visits them in the form of possession—we might still understand the crimes committed by the girls in these more recent films as an outrageous yet justifiable response to a "comprehensible betrayal." Just as Carrie's mother is presented as colluding in her own demise by virtue of a religious fanaticism which results in the sexual repression of her daughter, the mother figures in

Female Avengers in '90s Teenpics

Fun, *Heavenly Creatures*, and *Sister My Sister* are implicated in their own brutal deaths by virtue of their complicity in attempting to reproduce the normative development of heterosexual femininity in the girls for whom they are responsible. While none of these women (with the possible exception of the mistress in *Sister My Sister*) approach the level of monstrosity we see in Carrie's mother, each of them is presented as partially responsible for the monstrous acts committed against them.

In *Fun*, Bonnie and Hillary are portrayed as two loners who meet by chance while hitchhiking. Hillary is on her way home from a counselling session and Bonnie is running away, or so she tells her new-found friend. As they spend the day together involved in minor adolescent mischief, the girls open up to one another and reveal the difficult experiences each has faced growing up in a family that is anything but nurturing. For example, when Hillary tells Bonnie about the sexual abuse she suffered from her father, she relates that her mother not only failed to intervene, but, in focusing more on her own needs and those of her boyfriend after her divorce, virtually abandoned her. Similarly, we learn that Bonnie's mother failed to protect her daughter from her husband's violent outbursts, a problem that became more severe when she finally abandoned her family.

While the anger of the two girls towards their neglectful mothers is patently clear, it is not so obvious why an elderly woman completely unrelated to them becomes the object of their outrage. Zelinsky's film, however, provides us with some information from which we might infer a rationale. For example, when Hillary tells Bonnie about being sexually abused by her father, she also relates that her grandmother, in an obvious instance of "blaming the victim," thought that Hillary was "asking for it." And when Hillary was sent to a foster home after her father was convicted of raping her, her foster mother thought she was a tease coming on to her husband. In an attempt to help Hillary avenge her mistreatment by this couple, Bonnie encourages her new friend to go to their house and cuss them out. Not thwarted when the foster parents fail to answer their door, Hillary and Bonnie simply inflect their verbal abuse on other unsuspecting adults in the neighborhood. Feeling elated by their assertiveness and the chance to finally retaliate against adults, the girls decide to rob one of the neighbors so that they can run away together. However, once the girls are inside their victim's house, events do not proceed as planned.

Mrs. Farmer, the elderly woman who invites the girls into her home, is a frightful reminder of what Bonnie and Hillary repeatedly assert they don't want to become: "pussies," boring women who don't stand up for themselves. Coded as fully feminized through her passivity and acquiescence, as well as fully maternalized through her placement within a suburban home and her nurturing, sympathetic treatment of the girls, Mrs. Farmer is portrayed as the classic horror victim (femininely passive), the antithesis of Hillary and Bonnie. As Clover might argue, Hillary and Bonnie function as the film's "victim-heroes," their monstrosity unleashed only in their attempt to avenge the multiple oppressions and rejections they have endured while growing up.

Like Zelinsky's film, Peter Jackson's *Heavenly Creatures* uses brilliant, highly-saturated colors to depict the intensity of the relationship between its two female adolescent leads—Juliet Hulme (Kate Winslet) and Pauline Parker (Melanie Lynskey)—who bond over their similar histories of childhood illness, their lack of friends, and their frustrations with their families. At first, Pauline and Juliet's whimsical literary creations of "The Fourth World" and "Borovnia" provide some means of escape from their families and schoolwork. However, their imaginative fantasy life cannot prevent the girls' eventual separation from one another when Juliet's parents decide to move their family from New Zealand; so Pauline, challenging the controlling power of her mother, makes plans to go along. But Pauline's mother, Mrs. Rieper (Sarah Peirse) sees the girls' close ties as abnormal and forbids Pauline to associate with Juliet. Pauline accordingly devises a plan—to which Juliet later assents—that will remove the main obstacle to their perpetual union: her mother. Pauline's scheme to kill her mother is seen as the only act which will both free her and erase her working-class roots, ensuring an opportunity for the girls' complete identification with one another.

Both Juliet's and Pauline's mothers are presented as problematic maternal figures: Mrs. Hulme (Diana Kent) is not only a career woman but an adulteress who often leaves Juliet behind while she travels; while Mrs. Rieper is a harridan who dominates her husband as well as her children. But while *Heavenly Creatures* is disturbing in its implication that matricide is somehow a necessary step in the development of female homosexuality, and that violence and death are the only possible outcomes of lesbian desire, it is, like *Fun*, less about the brutal killing of a mother than about the increasing interdependence and love between two girls. As Luisa Ribiero appropriately argues in her review, the murder of Pauline's mother is not "a crime *of* passion,. . . [but] a crime *for* passion."[9]

Of the three films I am concerned with here, *Sister My Sister* remains distinct, and not merely because it is the only film which was both written and directed by a woman. Though similar to both *Fun* and *Heavenly Creatures* in its abuse-matricide narrative, unlike these other films it presents a world which is occupied solely by females: with the exception of the disembodied male voices of a photographer and the narrator at the film's end, there are no men here. Therefore, *Sister My Sister* is able to depict a broad range of feminine emotion and behavior, a range which is inflected not just by gender, age, and sexuality but also, and perhaps more importantly, by class. Indeed, unlike the girls in *Fun* and *Heavenly Creatures*, the two female protagonists—Christine (Joely Richardson) and Lea (Jodhi May)—are not middle-class schoolmates but impoverished sisters who work as maidservants for an overly-domineering wealthy widow, Madame Danzard (Julie Walters), and her daughter, Isabelle (Sophie Thursfield).

Neither of the women who experience death at the hands of the girls is their mother, though she does figure strongly in the narrative. As we learn through conversations between the sisters, Lea, the younger, was always the mother's favorite, receiving all of the mother's attention while Christine was left to fend for herself from an early age. While Lea maintains a relationship with her mother through letters, weekly trips home, and the sharing of her meager wages, Christine, jealous, finally convinces her younger sister to break her affectionate ties with their mother and to save her money for their future escape from Madame Danzard's claustrophobic household.

Like the narratives of *Heavenly Creatures* and *Fun*, it is just after the sisters' acknowledgment of mutual devotion that they are confronted with the choice of separation from one another or the removal of the obstacle that blocks their shared path. And like Bonnie and Hillary and Pauline and Juliet, Christine and Lea choose the option that they believe will cause the least harm to their relationship. Their attempt at liberation is a desperate act which ultimately brings about the disintegration of their union. Finally driven to the point of desperation in the overly-disciplined, oppressive environment created by their mistress, the sisters kill the older woman and her daughter and then viciously mutilate their bodies.

Adolescent girls like Christine, Lea, Pauline, Juliet, Bonnie and Hillary also provide an effective means by which to represent the complex and fluid nature of female homosexuality. Because the concept of feminine adolescence operates liminally, challenging both the adultist view of femininity and the masculinist understanding of youth and, thus, the boundaries upon which patriarchal heterosexuality is structured and ordered, adolescent girls are signally unlike adult women (whose very bodies remain trapped in the gendered logic of heterosexuality that predominates in our culture). Attempting to find a way out of the traditional heterocentric psychoanalytic paradigms which structure and contain female homosexuality by describing such identification and desire in heterosexual and gendered terms, Monique Wittig has emphatically asserted that "lesbians are not women."[10] *Fun, Heavenly Creatures*, and *Sister My Sister* may offer an alternative to the conventional heterosexual and gendered formulation of homosexuality by using female adolescents, rather than adult women, as their protagonists.

The girls in these three films do not become more phallicized as their narratives progress; they are represented from the very start as possessing qualities that are both masculine and feminine, active and passive, aggressive and submissive. Thus, while other recent horror films with aggressive female adolescents as protagonists remain fixed in a distinctly heterosexual and patriarchal world by employing them as a feint for stories about masculinity in crisis (e.g., *The Crush* [1993]); or by putting female aggressiveness in the service of preserving patriarchal law and order (e.g., *Buffy the Vampire Slayer* [1992]); *Fun, Heavenly Creatures*, and *Sister My Sister* balance their unrestrained depictions of horrific murders committed by phallicized female adolescents with sensitive portrayals of the girls' growing feminine affections for one another. It is the ambiguity of both the girls' gender and their sexuality which makes these films so intriguing and so troubling for those unwilling to think beyond the gendered binarism that makes the concept of "killer girls" seem so paradoxical.

One could read the matricidal acts of *Fun, Heavenly Creatures*, and *Sister My Sister*, therefore, as not only the girls' revenge upon those women who have abused and neglected them, but also their opposition to the generative, reproductive function of female bodies demanded by patriarchal heterosexuality. Another way we might understand the logic of these murders is to analyze the mothers in these films who are *not* killed. Indeed, it is important to remember that, in spite of these abuse-matricide narratives, the mothers of Hillary, Bonnie, Juliet, Christine, and Lea are all spared the full extent of their daughters' wrath. As the films tell us, despite their representations as "bad mothers," each of these women has already broken free of the familial, patriarchal logic of heterosexuality by relinquishing their roles as mothers and wives through adultery and divorce. In relation to these films' reliance on the genre of horror, it is important to consider Alex Doty's point that "the central conventions of horror . . . actually encourage queer positioning as they exploit the spectacle of heterosexual romance, straight domesticity, and traditional gender roles gone awry."[11]

In their attempts to explode the boundaries which circumscribe their existence and their desires, the lesbian youth in these three films function as what Doty calls "binary outlaws,"[12] demonstrating the queer refusal of the structures, systems, and roles which normally contain desire, fantasy, and identification within a patriarchal heterosexual paradigm. Indeed, the films' shifting, dynamic depictions of gender, generation, and sexuality, their refusal to adopt a singular, moral position on homosexuality and violence, their play with narrative structure and temporality, and their "slidingness"[13] between different cinematic genres and modes of representation subvert the same heterocentrist paradigms against which the girls within their narratives are battling.

Although these lesbian adolescents portrayed in *Fun, Heavenly Creatures*, and *Sister My Sister* are ultimately reminded that for them, as members of a predominantly bigendered heterosexual culture, there is no true escape, the fact that the greater part of each film is focused not on the horrors of murder but on the representation of the girls' growing devotion to one another remains an important progression in the depiction of both feminine adolescence and female homosexuality. In turn, though each of these films portrays the nature of the girls' relationships as intense and their acts to protect their union as desperate, the films do not ultimately treat the pursuit of lesbian fulfillment as inherently evil, abnormal, or deviant. Because the film-makers never succumb to the "lesbian as monster" narrative Hollywood has relied upon in so many of its films, these texts are able to more fully depict the intense bond of female friendship and the merging of lovers' identities, as well as how the potential destruction of such a bond, and severance of such merger, can lead to bold, even deadly, acts of vengeance.

Notes

[1] Kevin Thomas, "*Fun* Aims to Make Sense of the Senseless," *Los Angeles Times* (September 15, 1995), F19.

[2] Janet Maslin, "Just Youngsters Having a Drop-Dead Good Time," *The New York Times* (April 12, 1995), C16.

[3] Carol Clover, *Men, Women, and Chain Saws: Gender in the Modern Horror Film* (Princeton: Princeton University Press, 1992), 21.

[4] Clover, *Chain Saws*, 53.

[5] Clover, *Chain Saws*, 29.

[6] Though Clover slips back and forth between the use of "woman" and "girl" to describe the rape victims in pre-1990s films, the characters in the films she is analyzing are distinctly independent adult women. Thus, her theory on the activation of the female *adolescent* body in horror films does not hold up here. Films such as *Fun, Heavenly Creatures,* and *Sister My Sister* call for a rethinking of her theories in relation to generation.

[7] Clover, *Chain Saws*, 138-140.

[8] Vivian Sobchak, "Child/Alien/Father: Patriarchal Crisis and Generic Exchange," *Camera Obscura* 15 (1986), 13.

[9] Luisa Ribiero, "Heavenly Creatures," *Film Quarterly* 49:1 (Fall 1995), 37.

[10] Monique Wittig, "The Straight Mind," in Russell Ferguson, Martha Gever, Trinh T. Minh-ha and Cornel West, eds., *Out There: Marginalization and Contemporary Cultures* (Cambridge: MIT Press, 1990), 57. I am thinking here specifically of Sigmund Freud's theorization of normal female sexuality as predicated on the separation of girls from their mothers and Jacques Lacan's theory of the mirror stage (formulated after his analysis of the two Papin sisters who are represented in *Sister My Sister*), as well as Nancy Chodorow's theory of feminine subjectivity as grounded in the inseparability of mothers and daughters by virtue of their mutual "desire to mother."

[11] Alex Doty, *Making Things Perfectly Queer: Interpreting Mass Culture* (Minneapolis: University of Minnesota Press, 1993), 15.

[12] Doty, *Making*, xvi.

[13] Clover, *Chain Saws*, 15-16.

James C. McKelly

Youth Cinema and the Culture of Rebellion: *Heathers* and the *Rebel* Archetype

Writing from an Italian prison during the Mussolini regime, the socialist cultural critic Antonio Gramsci articulated an idea which would profoundly influence the social, psychiatric, and literary theory of the second half of the twentieth century. In his *Prison Notebooks*, Gramsci identifies "hegemony" as a kind of pervasive cultural consensus regarding a particular set of social values, which in turn privileges, promotes, and protects itself through the establishment of analogous political, cultural, and social structures.[1] According to Gramsci, because of the permeating quality of its consensus, true hegemony need never assert itself through violence; rather, it secures its ascendancy by representing itself as a "natural" order. In so doing, it presents as "natural" an arbitrary and constructed socio-political hierarchy for culture and a particular socio-economic and psychological "identity" for the subject existing within that culture. Through hegemony, ideology is naturalized as history, beauty, order, "common sense," and, on the level of psychology, sanity and maturity.

This naturalization, this latent and vaguely pleasurable dissemination of dominant ideology throughout the social, is accomplished through the agency of culture itself, in all of its formations. In his 1957 work *Mythologies*, Roland Barthes identifies as "mythic" any cultural artifact that in its structure, style, narrative, or thematic implication serves to effect such a naturalization.[2] In this sense, film exerts a profoundly mythological function, contributing to the symbolic order images of the values and behaviors endorsed through hegemony, and facilitating frame by frame the self-identification of the subject within that order.

In one of the myriad ironies of commodity culture, however, film has also functioned as a vehicle by means of which cultural alterity and counter-hegemonic dissent—in short, rebellion—have achieved "projection." As is manifestly evident in the critical discourse, it is a moot point whether the capitalist symbolic order "always already" contains such images of delinquency merely by virtue of the fact that they find representation and commodification in it, or whether it yields to the subversive power of these projections of difference, which carve out for rebellion new symbolic space free of the oblique insinuations of hegemony.

What is not a question of debate is that these mythologies of rebellion symbolically situate the delinquent subject within what Jean-François Lyotard has termed the *"grands recits,"*[3] the hegemonic metanarratives of knowledge, morality, aesthetics, and social progress that wheel above our culture like the constellations of the night sky—those eternal, predictable, "natural," clockwork metonyms of divine order, according to whose positions we orient ourselves, navigate our chaos, measure our "progress," tell our time, chart our destination, and foretell our destiny. During the first planetarium scene in Nicholas Ray's *Rebel Without a Cause* (1955), Jim Stark (James Dean) and his classmates watch these constellations explode and hear humankind's fleeting presence in the universe declared "an episode of little consequence." This simulacrum of apocalypse provides a first cinematic image of youth culture's introduction to what Lyotard identifies as the postmodern condition, and what Douglas Coupland has since termed "life after God"[4]: the legitimating certitude of these *grands recits* of meaning and order has been torched; in the subsequent crisis in value, institutions conventionally viewed as vehicles of social and psychological stability—church, state, school, family—have been disclosed as irrelevant, insufficient, and delusory. With this scene the film presents itself as an archetypic mythology in Barthes' sense of the term—an inaugural cinematic artifact of a postmodern culture of rebellion, which anticipates a radical moral, relational, and psychological disorientation for youth culture, and investigates the forms of responsivity with which youth culture might both express and negotiate this condition.

The diegetic structure of *Rebel* is built around an inquiry into the possible meanings of the figure "honor" in the symbolic order of a culture suffused with cowardice, apathy, denial, self-interest, pragmatism, and hypocrisy. Jim is the precariously situated protagonist trying to Do The Right Thing in facing the twofold moral challenge issued to him in the idiom of a twofold self-destructive threat—physical and social. At its outset the film configures Buzz Gunderson (Corey Allen), the catalyst of both dimensions of this challenge, as an unproblematically assaultive nemesis driven by testosterone and ruthless insecurity. However, at the Millertown Bluff, where Jim responds to the first part of the challenge to his "honor" by meeting Buzz in the suicidal "chickie run," the film makes clear in a famous exchange the affinity between these two delinquents: at the edge of the precipice, Buzz admits, "I like you." Jim pauses, and asks, "Then why do we do this?" Buzz replies, "We gotta do something!" Their shared self-destructive risk is a way of cultivating "honor" despite the boredom and morally enervating affluence of their environment. Ray here makes it apparent that even in his role as nemesis Buzz is, like Jim, Judy (Natalie Wood), and Plato (Sal Mineo), a victim of hegemony, driven by self-destructive frustration, sent hurtling toward the literal edge of culture. His fate at the bluff foregrounds the concrete danger of a contrived attempt to construct value on the margins. In Buzz's own words, "It's a crazy game, man!"

Buzz's death precipitates the second, more exacting, dimension of Jim's moral challenge regarding "honor." The Millertown Bluff scene functions as the apogee of the film's depiction of the physical and psychological consequences of marginalization at the hands of hegemony: death or exclusion. The moment just after the crash, in which Jim extends his hand to Judy and pulls her back from the edge, marks a turning point in the film's thematic interest. If the first half of *Rebel* concerns itself with examining the lacerating contradictions which hegemony visits upon youth through the agency of parents—the key indication of which is Jim's oft-imitated howl, "You're tearing me apart!"—the second half of the film chronicles Jim's decision to return to the conventional order, but on his own terms. He wants to accept responsibility for his role in the violence the social order has precipitated—"For once in my life I want to do something right!" he says—but also to insist on the culpability of hegemonic consensus in the tragedy: "We are all involved!" The scene in the abandoned mansion, wherein Jim, Judy, and Plato "play house," represents the imaginative exploration of both the hypocrisies and possibilities of conventional order; Jim's leaving the scene of Plato's death *in a police car with his parents* vividly represents his inclusion in that order.

There is an ambiguity in this reconciliation with hegemony effected by Ray. On the one hand, it confirms Jon Lewis's assertion in *Road to Romance and Ruin* that *Rebel* is "a very conservative film"[5] exemplifying a "thinly veiled search for authority"[6] that permeates American youth culture. When Jim enters that police car, he capitulates to a dominant order responsible, directly in the case of Plato and indirectly in the case of Buzz, for the deaths of these two fellow outsiders. From this perspective, the film constitutes an opera of tragic, coercive rehabilitation. On the other hand, the final reconciliation enacts the assertion that "rebellion," that volatile combination of exclusion and dissent, can introduce itself as a new term in the symbolic order without compromising its critique of that order. In short, Jim's reconciliation with hegemony makes a rebel "honor" possible by virtue of its own authority, unimpaired by psychosis, alienation, or a romanticized futility. "Honor" becomes more than just "a crazy game."

But no matter how you read the ambiguity at play in its protagonist's movement toward moral orientation, it is ironic that the film very unironically addresses its postmodern issues in a naive, straightforward, unambiguously "modern" idiom. The film presents itself as remedial, therapeutic, and redemptive; its title notwithstanding, *Rebel Without a Cause* identifies causes, explains symptoms, and implies cures. This is what gives the film its earnest, somewhat clumsy "sociological" tone, something Ray inherited from his mentor Elia Kazan. We see evidence of it in the film's comically Oedipal family portraits: Jim's mother (Ann Doran) screaming, "You want to kill your own father!"; Plato lamenting to Jim, "If only *you'd* been my dad!"; and Judy telling her emotionally repressed father (William Hopper), "I didn't *want* to stop [kissing you]!" The film's assumptions are grounded in the Enlightenment-fueled, social-realist moral and aesthetic imagination: though there is a complex problem, yet it is empirically identifiable; the sociologically adventurous artist can suss it out (here we see the significance of Ray's naming his insightful Juvenile Officer "Ray"); and, most importantly, a socially attentive, stylistically realist art can (1) accurately represent it and (2) transmit its enlightening and salvific message to culture. Although the film anticipates the thematization of the postmodern one can see in many of its generic progeny—*Rumble Fish* (1983), *River's Edge* (1987) and *Heathers* (1988) all come to mind—its stylistic expression of this condition remains locked in the grammar of modernity.

Michael Lehman's *Heathers* tropes on the postmodern culture of rebellion as defined by the *Rebel* archetype, in so many ways that a comparison is inevitable. There are the more superficial associations: the story's antagonist (Christian Slater) is named "J.D.," short for Jason Dean (that the full name conflates America's favorite rebel with America's favorite hockey-masked, cleaver-wielding, machete-brandishing, chainsaw-swinging, pitchfork-poking, speargun-toting, murderous adolescent psychotic is a significance not to be overlooked); like Jim Stark, J.D. has just transferred to a new school from out of state, and has a history of social disruption and subsequent dislocation ("7 schools in 7 states and the only thing in common is my locker combination"); his entrance provokes the jealous, aggressive attention of the alpha males of the school's ruling clique and the romantic attention of one of its leading women, he reciprocally engaging both forms of attention; and he and the leading woman together participate directly in the "crazy game" that leads to the death of the clique's big cheese and catalyzes the narrative drama of the film.

Other associations lead to telling distinctions. As with *Rebel*, the diegetic structure of *Heathers* is built around an inquiry into the possible meanings of a particular figure of moral orientation in the symbolic order of a culture suffused with cowardice, apathy, denial, self-interest, pragmatism, and hypocrisy. As we have seen, in *Rebel* that figure is "honor" informed, adversarially, by a conscience desiring social inclusion; in *Heathers*, it is "honor" as well—but an honor informed, consonantly, by a conscience desiring social justice, and linked, due to the protagonist's prominent position in the dominant order, to a form of *ex*clusion.

This difference is signalled by *Heathers'* inversion of *Rebel's* narrative point of view. We experience *Rebel* almost exclusively from the perspective of Jim Stark, a male outsider seeking affiliation; our witness of the effects of his agency vis-à-vis the social is unmediated. In this way, the film coerces our sympathetic identification. *Heathers* on the other hand problematizes the agency of J.D., its explicitly Starkesque outsider, by virtue of its introspective, first-person voice-over narration by Veronica Sawyer (Winona Ryder), a female insider who seeks not affiliation but difference. Veronica's narration mediates our experience of J.D., disrupting our naive identification and forcing us, to borrow Slavoj Zizek's expression, to "look awry"[7] at his influence. Furthermore, if we understand J.D. as a Harley-humping synecdoche of the Rebel genre *in toto*, the hermeneutic distance implied in Veronica's narration interrogates not only the central figure of that genre, but the genre itself. *Heathers'* Veronica is *Rebel's* Judy empowered by ascesis and the narrative authority with which to express it; Veronica is Judy with a monocle and a pen, reconfiguring for us the significances comprised by the culture of rebellion as represented by the conventions of the Rebel genre.

Heathers accelerates the *Rebel* archetype in other ways as well. Like Jim, Veronica is a precariously situated protagonist trying to Do The Right Thing in facing a twofold moral challenge issued to her in the idiom of a twofold self-destructive threat. The first part of Veronica's challenge results from her realization that as a member of the Heathers clique, she is contributing to the establishment of cruelty as the self-destructive social currency of Westerburg High. "I am allowed an understanding that [others] have chosen to ignore," she says. "I must stop Heather." As we have noticed, in *Rebel*, Jim's challenge is conditioned by the desire to belong, on his own terms, to a hegemonic order from which he is exiled: "For once in my life I want to do something right." The Gunderson nemesis is just as marginalized by hegemony as Jim is. In *Heathers*, Veronica's challenge is conditioned by a desire to extricate herself from a hegemonic order in which she is not only included, but privileged with executive influence. And unlike Buzz, the Heathers nemesis is not victimized by hegemony; it constitutes hegemony.

Indeed, from the first line of Veronica's narration—"Heather told me she teaches real life"—the Heathers embody hegemony's naturalization of a particular set of social locations as "real life." The Orwellian imperative of the clique's kingpin, Heather Chandler (Kim Walker)—"Don't think"—neatly summarizes the importance to the dominant order of the inertia of consensus over the possibility of an activist, counter-hegemonic critique. And her elegantly succinct *précis* of her ascendancy—"They all want me as a friend or a fuck"—demonstrates the degree to which that ascendancy is insinuated into the psychology of the subject, which desires intercourse with the dominant despite the coercive character of that relation. Ironically, hegemony thrives on the complicit desire of the subject. To paraphrase J.D. late in the film, "People are going to look at the ashes of Westerburg and say, it self-destructed not because society corrupted the school, but because the school was society!" Therefore, for Veronica, "doing something right" doesn't just mean taking a firm moral stance; it means attempting to subvert the dominant order at the risk of utter expulsion. As Heather Chandler puts it, "Transfer to Washington, transfer to Jefferson—no one at Westerburg is going to let you play in their little reindeer games."

Heathers also operates as an uncanny deconstructive critique of the self-congratulatory "sociological" presumptions deployed by the Rebel genre generally, and by *Rebel Without a Cause* in particular. As we have seen, *Rebel* implies that like Jim, Judy, and Plato, Buzz Gunderson is a victim of failed bourgeois social institutions, particularly that of the family, which the film critiques straightforwardly with "modern" analytic certitude. And through its figure of institutional enlightenment, Officer Ray Fremick (Edward Platt), *Rebel* suggests that psychology offers the key to averting this victimization. *Heathers* mocks the very idiom of social-scientific analysis and its grounding in experiential cause-and-effect, parodies the rhetoric of dysfunction, and destabilizes the therapeutic pretense of the socially "redemptive" institution. *Rebel* represents redemption as opera; *Heathers* represents redemption as Oprah.

This Oprahfication is accomplished stylistically through the film's increasingly surrealistic treatment of the institutional response to the non-suicides. Particularly exemplary is the funeral service of Ram Sweeney (Patrick Labyorteaux) and Kurt Kelly (Lance Fenton), during which the two deceased jocks, killed in what J.D. has staged as a "repressed homosexual suicide pact," sport their team helmets and cradle footballs in state. The minister, Father Ripper (Glenn Shadix), an unsavory amalgam of Jim Baker, Jerry Springer, and Wavy Gravy decked out in a tie-died cassock, testifies that Jesus is "the righteous dude who can solve your problems." As Kurt's tearful father (Mark Carlton) stands over the casket poignantly fondling his son's funereal football, he addresses the corpse: "I don't care that you really were some . . . pansy. You're my own flesh and blood, and well, you made me proud." In the best trash-tv tradition, he then weepily declares to the congregation, "My son is a homosexual. I love my dead gay son!" Ms. Flemming (Penelope Milford), the psycho-babbling baby-boomer put in charge of Westerburg High's official response, sublimates self-destruction into evidence of authenticity, extolling the "pathetic beauty" of Heather Chandler's non-suicide as "an example of the profound sensitivity of the human animal," and turning the grieving process into a big-top custom-pitched for the media circus she cultivates. "Whether or not to commit suicide is one of the most important decisions a teenager can make," she intones. Profoundly self-annihilating psychosis is not only naturalized, but celebrated, as one of the normative conditions of adolescent development.

The second aspect of Veronica's challenge comes with the realization that J.D., the revolutionary principle which originally had empowered her own anger—which gave, as she writes in her diary, her "teen-angst bullshit . . . a body-count"—has become as enchanted with violent, deceptive coercion as the Heathers had been with hegemonic coercion-as-consensus. "Chaos is great!" he says. "We scared people into not being assholes." *Heathers* brings Veronica face to face not only with her physical complicity in the murders, but also with her psychological complicity—her retributive anger, self-justifying and suppressed, the amoral unleashing of which J.D. functions as the symbolic avatar. The denouement of *Rebel*—Jim's attempt to protect Plato, the innocent traumatized by the effects of hegemony—is represented as an act of mediation with an element of physical risk. The denouement of *Heathers* is represented as a ruthless confrontation in which not only the fate of the innocent is at stake—shots of students cheering at the pep rally are intercut with those of the struggle—but also both the physical and psychological fate of Veronica herself. Earlier she had called J.D. on his Starkesque pretense: "Rebel? You think you're a rebel? You're not a rebel! You're fucking psychotic!" He replies, "You say to-may-to, I say to-mah-to!" At the end of Jim's story, he emerges unscathed save by the deaths of two of his culturally delinquent peers. The Rebel is embraced by a dominant order the hypocritical agents of which—his parents, the police—have understood their failures. At the end of her story, Veronica, on the edge of her own Millertown Bluff between rebellion and psychosis, is responsible for pulling herself back, for forcing the amoral manifestation of her revolutionary anger to self-destruct, and for living with the several deaths for which she is, in a certain psychological sense, directly culpable.

As with Jim Stark's reconciliation with hegemony, there is an ambiguity in Veronica Sawyer's final declaration that "there's a new sheriff in town" as she assumes the Heathers' scarlet mantle—or, rather, the scarlet "scrunchie"—of power. Is the film another instance of Jon Lewis's "search for authority" thesis—meet the new boss, same as the old boss—or is it a myth of morally informed revolution resulting in psychological as well as material liberation? Whatever the case, *Heathers*' expression of a postmodern culture of rebellion serves to liberate the Rebel genre from the grammar of modernity as naturalized by the *Rebel* archetype. In constructing the images and language of this new idiom, Veronica and *Heathers* make the myth of rebellion, of which Jimmy Dean/Jim Stark is the dominant star, burn again.

Notes

[1] Antonio Gramsci, *The Prison Notebooks* (New York: Columbia University Press, 1991).

[2] Roland Barthes, *Mythologies*, trans. Annette Lavers (New York: Hill and Wang, 1972), 129-49.

[3] Jean-François Lyotard, *The Postmodern Condition: A Report on Knowledge* (Minneapolis: University of Minnesota Press, 1984).

[4] Douglas Coupland, *Life After God* (New York: Pocket Books, 1994).

[5] Jon Lewis, *The Road to Romance and Ruin* (New York: Routledge, 1992), 30.

[6] Lewis, *Road*, 37.

[7] Slavoj Zizek, *Looking Awry: An Introduction to Jacques Lacan Through Popular Culture* (Cambridge: October Books, 1991), 9-12.

E. GRAHAM McKINLEY

In the Back of Your Head: *Beverly Hills, 90210, Friends,* and the Discursive Construction of Identity

In the fifth century B.C., Plato worried about the stories to which children were exposed. In the 1990s, this same concern seems finally to have reached its highest position ever as western society increasingly focuses on the way television and movies portray gender roles, race relations, moral issues, commercialism, youth violence and rebellion, homosexuality, even the meaning of youth itself.

For those of us concerned with youth and media, the issue extends beyond the reach of the clumsy hand of legislation, which clutches at solutions through such unwieldy methods as audience suitability ratings, V chips, and parental warnings. We are concerned here with issues that cut to the heart of who we are: as individuals, as members of a culture, as denizens of the global village—as human beings. Can our concern over violence really be boiled down to number of gunshots or number of seconds of on screen blood per episode? Can the tensions of race and gender relations be boiled down to number of times blacks are shown getting arrested or number of times women are shown in the kitchen? Before we can suggest solutions that will really work to improve the media representations that claim to reflect us, more needs to be known about the process of watching television, about what happens when individual viewers interact with what Fiske[1] has called the polysemic television text, with its rich and multiple meanings.

We can begin by focussing on the links between a popular television show, *Beverly Hills, 90210,* and female identity.[2] I listened to regular viewers of *90210* talk about the show, and in doing so I developed some theories about the relationship among television, talk, and identity. I talked with 36 girls and young women from sixth-graders (11 years old) through college age (age 22), basically following the ethnographic cultural studies model. I talked with some individually, most in small preexisting groups of friends; also, we watched the show together in real time as it aired, and I tape-recorded what they said while viewing.

One important key to our relationship with television shows and films is ways in which the shows intersect with our notions of who we are. Most of us have grown up with the notion that identity is something we have, almost like a possession; and whether it's an ego, an id, and a superego; or a set of traits and attributes; or abilities and talents, we generally speak of identity as something that is both part of us and relatively stable.

Students of identity and identity-construction such as Gergen,[3] Shotter,[4] Sampson,[5] and Edwards and Potter[6]; and poststructuralist feminists like Weedon[7] and Butler[8] suggest that identity is less a set of finite traits and attributes than an ongoing process. And this process is deeply linked to our interactions with others. Within every interaction, there emerges a certain implicit construction of who "we" are; who "they" are; who "I" am; who "you" are. And the meaning of these words is going to vary depending on the interaction. For these theorists, identity becomes a fluid set of possibilities to which we may or may not have access. For example, as I write here I'm presenting myself as a scholar. But with my mother I present myself differently; I construct still a different identity with a lover or with a child. A multitude of different selves, different identities, are available and accessible to me— even as they are modified and reconstructed every time they emerge in interaction. And rather than talking of identity as a set of consistent traits, we can refer to a repertoire of presentational frames.

A good deal of identity construction goes on in talk. Furthermore, different kinds of interactions open up different ways of attending to self and other. In particular, important identity work goes on during talk about television. One of the capacious ports through which television enters our lives is our talk about it; as we talk about television, we construct identities for ourselves and others. These identities, I would argue, have enormous implications in what they permit us to say, and what they don't permit us to say; what sorts of "selves" they make accessible, and what kinds of "selves" get closed down or marginalized.

Beverly Hills, 90210 is a prime-time soap opera chronicling the lives of a group of upscale students, who first attended two fictional schools, posh West Beverly Hills High School (the numbers in the title refer to its envied ZIP code), then alluring California University. Dedicated viewers with whom I talked reported arranging their weekly schedules—homework, shower time, night classes, etc.—to free themselves to watch *90210* and its spinoff in the following time-slot, *Melrose Place*. The show was a phenomenal success, and helped establish the surprisingly successful Fox network. It is going into its seventh year this fall, and it still retains a large audience share.

The Discursive Construction of Identity

Friends deals with a group of twentysomethings who live in a New York apartment building and basically do a lot of hanging out together. Owing to a combination of idealism and ineptness, they are not destined for any kind of success, material or otherwise, although they never stop trying to beat the odds.

90210 stars four women and four men; *Friends* stars three women and three men.

The two shows—and a whole group of clone and spinoff shows and films such as *Singles* (1992) and *Reality Bites* (1994)—are united by their at least superficial emphasis on community. Each deals with a group of friends; and what is constantly foregrounded is the nature and importance of relationships. The whole notion of community is a loaded one nowadays, of course, as we are bombarded with discursion about its dissolution and the ways in which technology isolates and restructures it. We can conduct love affairs on e-mail and flame over the Internet. And much of our politically correct emphasis on inclusiveness leaves us with a vague sense that it is wrong to want to belong to a group everybody else can't belong to, making the characters' exclusive communities seem all the more enviable. For example, Bellah et al.'s *Habits of the Heart*[9] offers an insightful discussion of the way North American culture, in particular, presents us with an almost insoluble dichotomy between our cultural admiration of the autonomous individual, the pioneer, the Horatio Alger, and our need for community. We can see echoes of this dichotomy in the feminist literature as well.

And the hunger for community plays an important role in the popularity of *90210* and *Friends*. One of the things I heard over and over from *90210* viewers was a longing for the stable community they saw portrayed on the show. It would be so wonderful, they said, to have people like that who would always "be there for you," as the theme song for *Friends* puts it. The opening montages of the two shows vividly depict, over and over, the joy of community and connectedness. For *90210*, the montage shows the ensemble posing and mugging for a group snapshot, while the *Friends* montage is drawn from scenes from episodes.

In both shows, many of the opening one-shots portray the characters as involved in conversational interaction, apparently with off-camera buddies. Like these interactive characters, my respondents expressed themselves with great excitement, intensity, passion, and involvement. Most of the conversations of *90210* viewers concerned hairstyles, makeup, eyebrows, clothing, and boyfriends. Here's a sample (with respondents' names invented):

> MADDY: I love her hair.
> SANDY: I like Kelly's eyes.
> E.G.M.: *(to Sandy)* Yeah?

MADDY: I like her hair.

E.G.M.: She has dark eyes, doesn't she?

SANDY: I thought they were green.

E.G.M.: Oh, are they green?

SANDY: I think.

MADDY: I like her hair, 'cause I love the color of her hair.

E.G.M.: Yeah?

MADDY: It's just so light.

E.G.M.: Yeah.

MADDY: Mmmm, it's, like, not even dark. Just all light.

This was a type of talk that I heard over and over.

I came to believe that this talk accomplished several things. One important function was to establish a community among the viewers, a community with shared experience and expectations—a shared expertise, if you will, in terms of how females look. I should add that the talk was as often critical of characters' appearance as praising. But the point is, they all knew to talk about appearance. That kind of talk provided an important base for the community. And as you can see, that talk often perpetuated a certain stereotype—blonde hair, green eyes; thin, expensively dressed.

Even more, the talk either implicitly or explicitly judged a female's worth on the basis of her appearance. Consider the following:

JANE: I like, like the most characters, my favorite one is like Kelly.
    I like how she dresses.

    . . .

E.G.M.: Do you have a favorite?

KATEY: Um—probably Kelly too. 'Cause like she's the prettiest out
    of all of them. But sometimes Donna, she can be pretty. Like it
    depends on what her hair looks like.

ALL: *Laughter.*

KATEY: Sometimes she can not look pretty.

E.G.M.: Yeah. And then you don't like her?

KATEY: Yeah.

I would suggest that repeatedly attending to females on this level not only perpetuates the notion that a woman must be concerned with her appearance, but also suggests that on some level she is defined by how well she lives up to certain specific

The Discursive Construction of Identity

standards of appearance. That's a proposition that feminists have been struggling against for a long time.

The same point can be made about dating. In the talk of *90210* fans, dating was foregrounded as the main business of the community. A huge amount of time was spent discussing who was dating whom, who might date whom, and who should date whom. Not only was dating foregrounded as crucial, it was also presented as something that was governed by a complex set of rules negotiated in endless discussion. For example, when Kelly (Jennie Garth) started dating Brenda's (Shannen Doherty) ex, Dylan (Luke Perry), there were interminable conversations about whether it was "right" to kiss your best friend's ex-boyfriend:

> CASEY: My friends and I, my [sic] and my best friend, talked about this just last night, and got in this huge big fight with these two guys that we were hanging out with, that we've never been with anyone that the other person has ever hooked up with.
> E.G.M.: Uh huh.
> CASEY: I just couldn't do that. I will never kiss the same guy that my best friend's ever kissed. Unless it's like my dad. *(laughter)* [garbled] kiss my dad. So I mean, it's like, I don't know. I could never do it.

This type of talk accomplishes the same sort of thing as talk about appearance: it perpetuates a stereotype that is ultimately self-defeating for the speaker. Talk about dating defines a female in terms of her relationship with a male and positions the locus of control as external to herself. A female's job, in this logic, is to reify the cultural rules and follow them. Her relationship with her boyfriend is not based on common interests, compatibility, or mutual support and love, but rather on conforming to externally imposed rules of behavior; and her identity is based on what rules she follows and how well she follows them. You just *don't* kiss someone your best friend has kissed. (And you just *do* put a price tag on your kiss.)

The point is not that *90210 makes* viewers think of themselves that way. Rather, as these girls and young women talked eagerly and intensely about *90210*, they constructed a certain kind of female identity. And their talk was the foundation for a community based on this way of attending to oneself—a community that perpetuates and reinforces that particular way of being. This type of talk also meant that other ways of being, other female identities, got marginalized. Consider an episode in which David (Brian Austin Green), one of the regulars, decides to take piano lessons. His teacher is Holly Marlow (guest star Sydney Brown).

In the first scene of this subplot, Holly is discovered playing the piano in a practice room. From David's point of view, we hear passionate, tempestuous music and see her from the back, with her long, flowing, light-brown hair. David quietly enters the practice room for his first lesson, ostentatiously holding the piece of music that he will play. When—turning his way—Holly asks if he brought the music, there is a long and pregnant pause, then he realizes she is blind. However, the piece of music David has prepared is one Holly knows and can play from memory (this fact is taken for granted in the text). The lesson proceeds well, with David making great progress.

Reproduced below are some of the teenagers' reactions during viewing.:

> *(Holly in practice room, playing.)*
> KAITLIN: Oh, no. The beautiful woman piano teacher.

When the viewers first encounter Holly, her character has certain possibilities—"the beautiful woman piano teacher." In a way that phrase says it all—locks her into a genre-specific identity, laden with tantalizing expectations, whose potential relates to appearance and to dating. However, as the scene proceeds, the viewers eagerly accept the text's clever invitation to find "something wrong" with Holly.

> *(David meets teacher. David's point of view shot as we see teacher's face for*
> *the first time and hear her talk. She speaks with exaggerated mouth ges-*
> *tures, quite slowly, with virtually no animation in her face or voice.)*
> MARY: There's something wrong with her.
> CHRYSE: She's weird already.
> KAITLIN: Her teeth.
> MARY: Maybe she's paralyzed.
> KAITLIN: She's got definitely something weird—SHE'S BLIND!
> MARY: Yeah. Good call, [Kaitlin]. *(Laughter)*
> HOLLY: *If you really want to have fun with me, you can move the furniture*
> *around.*

When the girl I've called Kaitlin guessed that Holly is blind, the guess was received as something she discovered, not something the text revealed ("Good call, Kaitlin") and it was also presented as the culmination of the suspicion that there is "something wrong." So now we've established the mistake in our initial impression—which, while it was limited, still had certain possibilities that are presently closed down. Once the girls established that Holly's most important trait is her blindness, they could instantly spin out a plot line:

KAITLIN: OK. I predict in future episodes, she like asks him out, he thinks about it, he kisses her, and then he decides he could never go out with a blind woman.

As it happens, I am a musician, and my first thoughts about Holly related to the difficulty of learning music when you are blind. Everything must be learned by ear (by listening to recordings) or by rote (having someone else teach you the notes), and of course you always have to play from memory. To me, she represented an admirable subject position, a triumph over a handicap. However, this position was not explored by either the text or my viewer-respondents. Instead, they focused on her (presumed) inability to relate to a man. Because of Holly's blindness, constructed as something "wrong," the girls were ready to pick apart Holly's identity, to focus on the negative. They immediately began to search the text for support for Holly's "weirdness":

> (David plays and Holly listens. At one point, she corrects his fingering, playing the passage to demonstrate her point. David plays on with growing success and confidence.)
> HOLLY: Let the music play you.
> ALL: Laughter.
> KAITLIN: OK, there's a cheesy line right there.

"Aha!", Kaitlin can be understood as having said, "I told you she was odd. And there's proof, right there."

The television text is complicit in this read, of course. On one hand, Holly is portrayed as competent (although she is blind, she can instantly and faultlessly play the piece David has brought in) and an inspirational instructor (by the end of the lesson, David's playing is miraculously transformed). On the other hand, however, and throughout, the "markers" of otherness are preserved in Holly's face, voice, and dialogue, inviting viewers to see her as "cheesy." As the pretentious and scripted-sounding line, "Let the music play you," suggests, Holly's primary emphasis is on imagining attractive images such as water-skiing in the spray rather than on improving David's technique. And the implication that when she performs she lets the music play her undermines her skill and accomplishment by placing her in a passive position.

The text is both open and closed: while presenting the possibility that a primary characteristic for Holly could be her musical skill, it invites the viewer to see this skill from a distance, always linked to her "otherness." And this position was adroitly and pleasurably read by the viewers, who continued to work to bolster that identity for Holly:

> *(Lesson continues)*
> MARY: She's a cheeseball. I don't like her.
> *(Holly tells David to imagine he is water-skiing as he plays.)*
> HOLLY: ... *feel the spray in your face ... the wind in your hair ...*
> KAITLIN: In your hair?
> *(David is playing much better.)*
> MARY: *(sarcastically)* It's a miracle!

In a few minutes, the girls reached a comfortable conclusion that Holly is "a cheeseball." The possibility that Holly's character, her subject position, her identity, could be accessed by the viewers is first opened—and then closed down in favor of the easy dismissal: there's something wrong, David could never date a blind woman, she's a cheeseball, I don't like her.

This was a process that occurred repeatedly in encounters with the *90210* text. One other brief example is provided by the character of Lucinda, a divorcee and feminist (Dina Meyer). Like Holly's, Lucinda's identity was constantly explored and then closed down—as a divorcee she was called "on the loose"; her feminism was easily dismissed as "politically correct." Instead of actually exploring alternate identities, the viewers created a sense of "us-them," of who is acceptable in our club and who isn't, based on a certain, restrictive way of constructing female identity.

As can be seen by these examples, in their talk about *90210,* the viewers also spoke of themselves as in a community with the characters. What I observed over and over again was that, when talking about the show the viewers would speak of the characters as they would speak of friends. "We" tended to become, not "myself and my friends" but "myself, maybe my friends, certainly myself and the characters":

> JOAN: Always seems like Brandon gets into—
> MEETRA: I wish we could just find one nice person.
> JOAN: One nice girl for him. That's why I kind of wanted Kelly.
> But, he always gets the bad end of deal, it seems, always. All these girls.

"I wish we could find one nice girl for him." These young women can't do anything for Brandon (Jason Priestley). Brandon is a fictional character. But they position themselves in their talk as in a community with Brandon, as his friend. And I would argue this has important identity implications in terms of who "we" are and who "they" are; who "I" am and might become. This discursive community sometimes took precedence over viewers' real-life communities.

We have seen already that viewers often reported arguing with their real-life friends over the fictional community. Sometimes, these arguments actually got quite painful. In one of the high school groups I interviewed, we finished watching the show and had begun discussing it when one of the girls was called out to the phone. In her absence the group negotiated a construction of what the best and worst parts of the episode were. When the girl returned from the phone call, I asked her what her favorite part was, and she gave the "wrong" answer—i.e., not what the group had concluded in her absence. The other girls made terrible fun of her and I think she felt uncomfortable.

This notion of the self-in-community-with-the-characters played out in an interesting way when it came to discussion of moral issues. 90210's producer, Charles Rosin, has been quoted as saying that an important part of the show's purpose is the presentation of teenage issues—teen pregnancy, drug abuse, etc.; and as hoping that the show would help young people to consider these issues thoughtfully.[10] I went into the interviews expecting to hear that level of discussion. But, in listening to the young viewers I found something different. Just as the scene with the piano teacher seemed, to a textual analysis, to present intriguing alternate subjectivities that were closed down in viewers' talk, other shows seemed to present important moral issues and were just not attended to in that way. During the time of my study, David got involved in drug use. When asked directly about this issue, viewers would parrot back politically correct answers—we know enough not to do drugs just because David did drugs. But when actually watching the show, what they did was work to exonerate David, to excuse him from responsibility, in an intense desire to have him escape the consequences. As one viewer said, "I didn't want him to still do drugs but I didn't want him to get caught." David is a member of our community, and we don't want anything to happen to him. Over and over, moral issues were simply reduced to an "us-them" configuration.

In another episode, David's drug dealer, who is about to be "busted," gives his "stash" to David. Here's how two eighth-graders reacted to that scene. They are twins, and their voices sound so alike on the tape that I was unable to distinguish between them, which is why they are identified only by an initial:

> M: He's gonna get busted.
> M: Idiot! Idiot! I would never do that.
> . . .
> M: That was stupid to take it. I'd be like, "Here, you get in trouble,
>   go away." I'd burn it. I would like just throw it down the toilet.

The concern was that David was going to get busted—and that that would be unfair. Never mind that David has been stealing money from friends, mistreating his girl-friend, slacking off at school—the point is, he is one of us, one of our community, and while we don't want him to do drugs, we also don't want him arrested. In fact, we put ourselves completely in his shoes, exploring ways in which we would escape punishment if we were in his situation. "I'd burn it. I would like just throw it down the toilet. I would never do that."

When analytical talk occurred, it was around the topics of dating and appearance. I was struck over and over by the fact that during the most dramatic scenes the comments would be, "I hate her hat," or "She has new hair. Cute." Around drug use, the type of intense and rule-bound discussion we saw around the issue of whether you should kiss your best friend's ex-boyfriend never surfaced. There, it was black and white: not don't do it, but don't get caught.

As has become clear by now, the text is complicit in all of these constructions. As Fiske has argued, the television text is polysemic, semiotically rich, offering a variety of meanings.[11] But the text also invited the viewers to see Holly as "other." There *is* something "weird" about the way she talks, though unusual speech patterns are a strange attribute to give a blind musician who is presumably an acute and discriminating listener. In the same way, the text does highlight appearance, and dating, though there are other issues available to be talked about and never brought up.

It is perhaps obvious from these excerpts how emotionally engaged viewers were when talking about their show. They laughed and screamed and carried on; they deeply sympathized and empathized with characters. Not only were they perpetuating rules that are ultimately disadvantaging—they were eagerly becoming experts on what it takes to be part of a community that foregrounds appearance and dating. And they were also taking enormous delight in doing so. That, I would argue, is hegemony at work in microprocess. These girls and young women were engrossed in cooperating in a perpetuation of a system that disadvantages them. As they talked about the television text, they were working to formulate rules of behavior that guaranteed inclusion in a community that defines women by (a) looks and (b) relationship with men, a community that may not ultimately be in their best interests. They were seldom resistant, even when resistant identities were available in the text.

Only once in all my interviews did I hear a reference to the ways in which the mainstream identities might be disadvantaging. That was by the three high school students with whom I watched the episode about the blind pianist:

CHRYSE: I mean the whole like skinny woman thing. It's like—
ALL: Really! [garbled]

The Discursive Construction of Identity

CHRYSE: —a big like issue in my life. Also just because, like, I feel like the whole like anorexia thing is so much bigger than anybody realizes. It's like, I don't know a single girl that I wouldn't consider like preoccupied with her weight—

MARY: They're totally obsessed with their weight. I don't—

CHRYSE: Yeah.

MARY: Except for [Kaitlin]. You're not obsessed. [Kaitlin's] the only person I know who's not obsessed with her weight. Everybody else I know is just like *(sound)*, like that, all the time.

CHRYSE: Yeah, I mean, I feel like if I like look less at like the magazines and TV shows like that, then I don't feel as bad about it.

MARY: Yeah [garbled].

CHRYSE: But, it's really easy to just sit there and be like, you know, "Oh, she's really pretty, she's really skinny, she has like this long pretty hair, and she has all these nice clothes, and her face is perfect, I wish I could be like that."

E.G.M.: Mm-hmm.

CHRYSE: You know like—

KAITLIN: Yeah, and I'm sure that happens—

CHRYSE: It's really easy to do that, even if you're like, "Don't do that, don't do that!" It still happens.

KAITLIN: Yeah, it's in the back of your head.

CHRYSE: It's impossible not to.

While I welcomed this discussion as a sign that resistance is possible, I can't help but point out the resignation, the acceptance that it's impossible not to be seduced by television's images of what a woman should be.

•

In my interviews with viewers of *Friends,* I found much the same thing. First of all, I saw that enormous pleasure—that seductive hegemonic pleasure. When I turned on the VCR and let the opening credits of *Friends* roll for a group of seventh-graders, there was a perceptible feeling of, "Ah!" It's like that feeling some of us get when we hear that pop of the beer-can top, or (as my brother, who is a smoker, told me) that first inhalation of the cigarette as you're shaking out the match.

For the seventh-graders I listened to, a key function of *Friends* was to provide grist for their community conversations.:

DAISY: People quote *Friends* a lot. A lot.

ALL: Uh huh. I quote *Friends*. Yeah, me too.

DAISY: I do it as a joke though. But when for example when people, I remem—I just remember this one episode when people are like, um, when someone says a really stupid joke, Monica went, "Look, it's funny's cousin, not funny." I just remember that one.

As with *90210,* I heard talk about *Friends* that concerned appearance, cool clothes, the "Rachel" haircut. Without delving too much into genre differences, the fact that *Friends* is a comedy means that it relies even more heavily on stereotypes, and among the group of seventh-graders I listened to, the dumb blonde character, Phoebe (Lisa Kudrow), received considerable acclamation as the favorite character. Phoebe is the ditzy blonde to the max—and that was what they liked about her. In fact, one girl said she liked it best when Phoebe pretends to be dumber than she even is. Below are some of their comments:

ZOE: I like Phoebe because she's so funny. She says like—she—even though she's really ditzy, sometimes she does stuff, like, pretends to be ditzy. Like the last show she was, like, pretending to be, like, stupid so that she could get people out of this, the, like, really boring party. So I thought that—I thought that—that she's really funny.

. . .

E.G.M.: Do you have a favorite?

JENNIFER: OK, well, I guess my favorite would have to be Phoebe because I just—she's really funny to just watch. And I like—all the characters are really good, really funny.

E.G.M.: Do you agree?

DAISY: Yeah, um, I agree with [Jennifer] about um, that, that, I like Phoebe because she's, um, funny.

Phoebe is dumb—in fact, sometimes she even uses that quality, pretending to be more airheaded than she is, and they like that image of the female.

Phoebe has aspirations to be a singer, despite the fact that her lack of musical ability is a running joke. In one episode these girls recalled with great relish, Phoebe gets asked to make a music video, unaware that another singer's voice will be used instead of her own. Here's how the girls relished this moment that reveals Phoebe in all her ditzy glory, completely without self-knowledge and so dumb she can't even

The Discursive Construction of Identity

recognize how she has been manipulated. It's interesting to note how accurate their memory is, even though the episode aired almost two months before the interview:

> ZOE: Just one part that I thought was pretty funny, was when, um, Phoebe was doing the, uh, the music video, when it was like "Smelly Cat."
>
> ALL: Oh, yeah!
>
> ZOE: We were singing that one day that we were like singing—
>
> ALL: Everyone was singing it, everyone—
>
> ZOE: And then she goes, she was sitting um on the couch in the cof—what was it—what is it, coffee shop—and um um and they were watching it, and she's like, "Oh my gosh, I know." And they're like, "You know?" And she's like, "I didn't believe it, but I have such a beautiful voice, and now I know what my voice sounds like too." And they're like, "Uh huh."

When Phoebe finds out that another singer's voice has been dubbed into the video—a discovery she presents as a brilliant deduction—she then transforms the defeat into an opportunity for the voice-over singer, who she says deserves it:

> ZOE: And she's like, "I realized, my first clue was when they wanted me to sign a contract that said that someone else could sing for me." And they're like, "Really?"
>
> DAISY: No, they figured it out, they're like, um the girl, like, she she um her voice, she needs to like, um, she should go, she deserves this because she has a beautiful voice or something, at the end she finally realizes it or something, and she's like—
>
> ALL: Yeah, yeah.
>
> DAISY: She was a little thick, she was a little—she was a little spacy because she was like, "Oh wow, she deserves this."

Now, you might say, this is just a comedy, it's entertainment. And actually, the actress is quite talented, a wonderful comedian. But I would argue that as these young viewers get together and laugh, and sing "Smelly Cat," and repeat lines from the show, they are creating a delighted community of viewers based on perpetuation of a stereotype we might have hoped we had left behind.

I think we have realized the complexities of arguing that television provides role models, even though to us as citizens, teachers, parents, it feels intuitively right to say that. But it's a postulate very hard to "prove" through research. Despite the example above, in which viewers admitted they quoted *Friends,* the viewers I interviewed were very much aware that they weren't supposed to imitate what they saw on TV, and many had absorbed the limited effects model—television can reinforce but seldom converts—and dutifully parroted it back. The young people I interviewed talked a lot about the fact that you don't let television affect you, that there must be something wrong with a person who would imitate a TV character, they must be sick or mental, that television doesn't really affect *me,* that "my mom thinks I'm going to have sex because I see it on TV but I'm not going to do that, that's stupid." This is what I heard them say, repeatedly.

Yet what I observed was instance after instance of the shows not only influencing *what* the viewers talked about, but *how* they talked about it—in short, construction of female identity. I want to emphasize that this isn't just talk about Kelly's hair, or whether to kiss your best friend's ex-boyfriend, or the funny ditzy blonde. It's identity construction—opening some ways of attending to oneself, closing down others. Consider some disturbing interviews I had with a number of *90210* fans attending an Ivy League institution and studying to go to medical school. One woman commented on the fact that what she was forced to think about was her studies, but what she wanted to do was focus on her personal life, like the characters in *90210.* In another interview, the young woman was more explicit about her longing to be part of a "normal" community like the one depicted on *90210* and its companion show, *Melrose Place.*

> COURTNEY: I wish—I wish I were called to do like executive business-type work. I really wish I could just have like a normal life.
> RUTH: And I kind of—I considered that, but then—
> COURTNEY: Just like, you know—
> RUTH: —something—
> COURTNEY: Get up in the morning, go work out, you know, live the life of the professional and get—go to work in spiffy outfits and hang out with our friends after work for drinks.
> RUTH: [Inaudible] I feel like I'm doing something worthwhile.
> COURTNEY: That's so true. And I was like, I really wish I were called to do that, I'm just not called to do that. You know, I have to do what I feel like I'm called to do.
> E.G.M.: Which is med school?
> COURTNEY: Which is med school.

These young women have every expectation of enormous success financially and professionally, and also, as Ruth points out, of doing "something worthwhile" in the world. In a way, they are what a generation of feminists has worked a lifetime to achieve. Yet listen to the resignation in their voices as they face a life that doesn't revolve around spiffy outfits and hanging out with friends.

It seems to me we as academics have spent a significant portion of our lives striving to achieve, to define ourselves in ways other than wearing spiffy outfits, hanging out with friends, dating. While many of our mothers, I imagine, grew up planning to define themselves in terms of the men they married, many of us have constructed our identities differently. And many of us have devoted our lives to encouraging young people to achieve similarly. In one way or another, many of us have resisted the hegemonic invitation to walk down traditional paths of female identity. However, many young people today are not doing that. And I think there is something very wrong when a group of college students can tell me about how they choose their evening class schedules to accommodate their viewing of *90210,* or how a group of well-educated girls can describe how they quote *Friends,* sing me a song they learned from the show, then turn around and say, "Television doesn't really affect me. It affects what I talk about, but it doesn't affect *me.*" We are locked into our notion of identity as something stable and deep-seated, and into our notion of talk as—just talk. I have come to believe that identity is constructed in great measure in talk, and that talk in that situation counts as action.[12]

I would suggest that we need a new way of conceptualizing television effects—a discourse that says, when we talk about television we are constructing identities for ourselves and for others, identities that are strongly influenced by the television text. I think we might want to ask, "Do we want our girls and young women attending to themselves and others in the context of these communities of television characters? Do we want them taking a deep and abiding pleasure in a discourse that reconstructs and perpetuates the funny dumb blonde, or the notion that you are what you wear, or the idea that you are defined by whether or not you *have* a cute boyfriend?" What about hard work, and generosity, and responsibility to others less fortunate than ourselves, and achieving our potential in ways that can make the world a better place for everyone? What about the real issues of hate and abuse and violence, of rampant commercialism, and corporate control of individual lives? As academics we have a very real responsibility to address popular television in light of these issues, rather than seeing these issues in the problematic light of popular television.

Notes

[1] John Fiske, *Television Culture* (London: Routledge, 1987).

[2] I do so in fact in *Beverly Hills, 90210: Television, Gender, and Construction of Identity* (Philadelphia: University of Pennsylvania Press, forthcoming).

[3] Kenneth J. Gergen, *The Saturated Self* (New York: HarperCollins, 1991).

[4] John Shotter, *Conversational Realities* (Thousand Oaks CA: Sage, 1993).

[5] Edward E. Sampson, "The Deconstruction of the Self," in John Shotter and Kenneth J. Gergen, eds., *Texts of Identity* (Newbury Park CA: Sage, 1992); and *Celebrating the Other* (Boulder: Westview, 1993).

[6] Derek Edwards and Jonathan Potter, *Discursive Psychology* (Newbury Park CA: Sage, 1992).

[7] Chris Weedon, *Feminist Practice and Poststructuralist Theory* (Cambridge: Blackwell, 1987).

[8] Judith Butler, *Gender Trouble* (London: Routledge, 1990).

[9] Robert N. Bellah, Richard Madsen, William M. Sullivan, Ann Swidler and Steven M. Tipton, *Habits of the Heart* (New York: Harper & Row, 1985).

[10] Quoted in Marie-Claire Simonetti, "Teenages Truths and Tribulations Across Cultures: *Degrassi Junior High* and *Beverly Hills, 90210*," *Journal of Popular Film and Television* 22: 1 (1994), 38-42.

[11] Fiske, *Culture*.

[12] See Erving Goffman, *Forms of Talk* (Philadelphia: University of Pennsylvania Press, 1981).

The Discursive Construction of Identity

MARK CRISPIN MILLER

North American Youth and the Entertainment State: A Talk

> Though we may protest that, alas, we still do not know how to manipulate or control
> the things we inherit, we have been taught at least how to want and waste them.
>
> Leslie A. Fiedler, "The Two Memories: Reflections on the Thirties"

I've just finished teaching a course at Hopkins called "Shakespeare on Film." I would lecture on a play one week, then on a film version of that play the following week, so as to marry together literary analysis with film study. After starting with *Henry V* and Olivier's adaptation (which enabled us to talk about the Globe Theatre), we moved on to *Romeo and Juliet*.

The students read the play, and I began by asking them what they thought of the two young lovers and their passion for each other. There was a long pause, and then one student raised her hand and said, "They're really adolescent." I asked her what she meant by that and she said, "They're immature. They're selfish, and they're immature." There was another long pause, and then I said, a bit pedantically perhaps—and it's a point I want to emphasize today—that the concept of "adolescence" simply did not obtain in Shakespeare's day. There was at that time no notion of the "adolescent" either as noun or adjective—and, indeed, there really was no distinctive, influential concept of the "adolescent" as such until the post-war years. Certainly "adolescence" was not a general cultural and social concern until that time.

But suddenly, after World War II, there seemed to be, in our own midst, an alien sub-population of malevolent young trouble-makers in sunglasses and black leather jackets—"adolescents" with their own peculiar traits. They were like another species. That hadn't been the case in Shakespeare's time. After all, if you made it to, say, 36 years old back then, you were already stooped and gray, life expectancy being what it was. For that reason and others, there was no conception of the "adolescent" as a type, or of "adolescent behavior" as peculiarly and necessarily "immature."

Now, that answer was, of course, insufficient. The student didn't simply make an historical mistake, but was making, or so it seemed to me, a very interesting ideological revelation. To write the lovers off as "immature" and "selfish" is to dismiss the entire critical dimension of the play—that is, the experience of passion, which experience figures as a critical reflection on the status quo depicted in the petty world of *Romeo and Juliet*. On one hand, the young lovers are obviously, dangerously rash. They're oblivious of the consequences of their swift surrender to that passion. But there is, on the other hand, also nothing worth respecting in the world of the adults (as we now call them). That is a world of constant *vendetta,* of clan violence and endless homicidal rivalry—an impulse that's entirely pleasureless and destructive, so that the eloquent suicidal passion of those lovers stands as an ambiguous kind of contradiction to that world. Permit me to wax Marcusean, and suggest that *Romeo and Juliet* has no poignancy whatever if we don't recognize the uncanny value of the lovers' catastrophic union.

In other words, for this student and for many of her peers, the play failed to resonate—and I'm not blaming them, or bemoaning their ignorance or their illiteracy or anything like that. I actually felt saddened by what I took to be an inability, and an unwillingness, to recognize the play's utopian dimension.

If we're going to talk about youth and youth culture in the media, we have to think historically. We have to understand what we mean by "youth" and "youth culture"—indeed, what we mean also by "the media," because such meanings are not static.

I know we always say things like this, and we all nod and agree, but it's one thing simply to acknowledge the primacy of history, while it's another to try actually to bring to bear on the discussion some sense of the crucial differences that have been effected in the culture over time.

Let me begin by mentioning some famous ads for *Rolling Stone* that ran in *Advertising Age.* In the 80's, the magazine mounted a new ad campaign intended to tell people that the magazine was no longer counter-cultural—that it was not a hippie magazine, and in no sense oppositional, but a publication for successful people: yuppies.

The campaign entailed a series of visual contrasts, with the left page presenting something antithetical to something that was on the right page. The left was titled "Perception" while the right bore the title "Reality." "Perception" would, for example, be superscribed over a Christ-like hippie-type with very long hair, a ludicrous billowing shirt, brightly colored beads, and so on. On the right, under "reality," there'd be a fresh young MBA-type: short-haired, cool-eyed, neatly (and expensively) dressed. Or on the left you'd have a heap of home-made hash brownies, and on the right—a container of Häagen-Dazs. Or on the left, some loose change—pennies, nickels, dimes—with an American Express card on the right. In every case, as in a conventional "before-and-after" ad, you'd have the primitive Sixties-era relic on the left, and then the cleaner, newer, better version on the right.

They were witty ads. I don't deny their wit, but there's also something more than chilling about that playful and ironic suggestion that all that was then, while this is now—i.e., that unrestrained capital is the whole point of *Rolling Stone*. On the left, you'd have George McGovern; on the right, Ronald Reagan. And so on.

Such ads make a joke not only out of the old-fashioned past, but also—and more troublingly—out of the very longing for alternatives to what is now. The representation of the prior moment is derisive, while the present seems to glow with total newness, total "nowness," a perfect product-aura that promises no need for an alternative of any kind—that promises, in fact, no need. This dream of a wholly saturated world is envisioned throughout advertising as a landscape that is nothing but an endless highway. In countless ads, the planet looks post-nuclear. There's nothing out there. The best thing—indeed, the only thing—you can enjoy is your own car, which lets you speed across the surface of this devastated planet. That's it. There's no difference anywhere, no distinction possible.

And that same totality, or uniformity, which is manifest in individual ads tends also to be imposed by all the ads *en masse*—by the whole spectacle, in fact, that all of us keep tuning in to. I'd say that the gravest and most disorienting consequence of living in a world entirely saturated by a certain kind of media may be this effect of differencelessness, this seeming disappearance of history—the elimination of any sense that something else was, before this came to be; the elimination of any sense that, outside of this, there *can be* something else.

Thus one must somehow step outside of this big bubble to a get a sense of what's really going on inside the bubble; and one must also try to understand what it was like, here in the bubble, before now. I'm simply talking about the necessity of retrieving the bases of a critical perspective, which of course requires some overall contrast.

So what I want to do now is talk, somewhat ramblingly, using different kinds of evidence of what I take to be important cultural changes that have set in since, say, the 60's and before. These are differences that we can't recognize unless we take that effort to step back and look for them. They are especially important to discussion of the young, or youth—assuming that that really is a separate category. It's important, first of all, because the younger ones are those, of course, less likely to be conscious of those differences, and also because we ourselves aren't really fit to insist that the young be treated better or understood more fully if we don't know what obtained in prior times.

The first point I want to make—and I've ordered these points arbitrarily—is that, with the rise of MTV and rock videos, the definitive experience of modern youth culture has been completely altered. I'm talking about the experience of dancing to rock and roll music. The music has been curiously disembodied, as rock has ceased to be a music for listening to—in a car, and at parties—and has come to be a music that you watch.

I'm certainly not arguing that rock has lost its beat entirely, but that its mainstream aspect has become primarily spectacular.

There was a time when people would have thought this inconceivable—and I'm not talking only about rock and roll. Let me read to you from an article in the *New York Times* of March 19, 1939: "Telecasts to Homes Begin on April 30, World's Fair Will Be the Stage." As students of media history know, the arrival and development of TV were delayed by the traumatic interruption of the war, but in 1939 people were already talking about it.

Now, this is what Oren Dunlop of the *New York Times* had to say about television. Today, it sounds so touchingly naive that it could make you cry: "The problem with television is that the people must sit and keep their eyes glued on a screen. The average American family hasn't time for it. Therefore, the showmen are convinced that, for this reason, if for no other, television will never be a serious competitor to [radio] broadcasting."

The fact is that the kind of audience we have today had to be created—something I'll discuss by and by; but first I'll expound a bit on the disembodiment of rock. With its translation from an aural into a spectacular form, rock'n'roll has itself been changed in an important way. There has been a subtle process of psychic externalization, as the erstwhile work of individual fantasy has been taken over by TV: its advertisers, its producers, its enormous owners. Whereas you once could listen to a song and have your own pictures running in your head, now—if you watch the likes of MTV and VH1—you cannot help but see again, with your mind's eye, the images that were so expertly and so expensively concocted for the video.

In 1986, Jon Pareles wrote a very interesting column about what had happened to big-time rock concerts. Pareles noticed that even Madonna, who does dance music—and even Bruce Springsteen!—had audiences just sitting quiet and glassy-eyed throughout their shows, inwardly re-screening those delicious images. The point is not that people never go to concerts and dance nowadays. I'm not denying the fact or value of the mosh-pit, or making any sweepingly nostalgic statement. I'm simply noting that there's been a change. Large audiences for mainstream shows have tended to become more sedentary, because the music has become more spectacular, and spectacle demands a seated audience. (Rock performers, like country singers, are also now required to be much prettier, for the same reason.)

Allow me a viewer's free-association. I was watching the news coverage of Woodstock II in 1994, and there were all those kids having so much fun cavorting in the mud, and doing all the other things that they'd seen happen in the movie *Woodstock.* Thinking back on the first event in 1969 (or rather, on the coverage of the show: I wasn't there), I was struck by the fact that the kids at this second Woodstock seemed each to weigh a good twenty-five pounds more than their predecessors. That's just a random observation that I make as a culture critic, although there are of course statistics on teen obesity that would bear me out. If you watch a lot of TV, you'll probably get fatter. This is something that social scientists know, something that pediatricians know and, of course, it's something that Frito-Lay, Anheuser-Busch, Coca-Cola, Mars, McDonald's, Burger King and all the rest of them know too, since they advertise at just those times when you'll be sitting there and getting hungry, so that you'll stuff your face with *Whoppers,* tacos, *Pepsis* and potato chips, etc., and that does tend to you make you chunkier as time slips by.

Odd that the music, which our bodies love, should be disembodied by the same force that makes our bodies thicker, heavier, less beautiful. In any case, if democracy does indeed require actual physical assembly—a very quaint notion in the age of cyberspace—then the disembodiment of an experience central to the "youth culture" is surely something we should think about, inasmuch as that fractious "culture" formerly seemed a highly democratic influence.

The music's disembodiment pertains, as I implied before, to the general ascendance of TV. People don't sit around watching it for hours because they're stupid or because they lack imagination. (There's certainly a causal sequence here, but it's the other way around.) The rise of TV as the sole focus of one's attention, as the very core of one's whole day and night, as the virtual hearth in one's home—the medium's centrality is both a cause and consequence of the general disappearance of other institutions and associations. It's only the rightists who talk about the decline of "family values," and others of us tend therefore to be leery of that discourse, because it so often functions as a code for bigotry and sexual repression; but the fact is that, primarily for economic reasons, the family has indeed become more incoherent. Today TV has, for many children, become a vast commercial substitute for other kinds of associations and neighborhood recreations that have vanished, because of the rise of interstate highways and suburbia, the breakdown of the cities and the victory of the mall, and so on. The medium is itself a glittering, insufficient compensation for the ravages that have been crucial to its rise.

Some of the best-loved anthems of the young attest to the now-pervasive sense of bitter loneliness that all those screens can't ever really mitigate. I suspect that the great popularity of *Nevermind*, for instance, has much to do with how Kurt Cobain's songs have really moved a lot of kids who've listened to the lyrics, because so many children in this country have grown up with that experience of feeling orphaned— that experience which Cobain wrote about obsessively. Coming home to a house with no one in it, because both Mom and Dad have had to go to work—it's not the influence of evil feminists that has made that desolate feeling so widespread, but the fact that a declining middle class has been forced out into a shrinking marketplace.

Thus the music's disembodiment is one component or subcurrent of a general disintegration of society—a process that affects the family first of all, but certainly not only that fundamental collectivity. And as the spectacle, or TV, or "the media," has tended to supplant the external associations of the young (and others), so has it displaced our internal powers; a point I've made already, but on which I'd now like to elaborate. I referred earlier to the externalization of fantasy. If we want a more inflammatory term, we might refer to the corporate colonization of the mind—of countless individual minds.

There's a certain major cultural shift that might help us grasp the scale of that great seizure. It has been going on since, roughly, the mid-Seventies, and has concerned a feature of the old youth culture as important as—and closely bound up with—rock music.

Let's recall that, in the Sixties, there were innumerable young who felt themselves quite smitten by LSD and marijuana. (Of course, I was not one of them.) Those who enjoyed those drugs thought they found something intensely gratifying and exciting about that seeming inner journey—as in the cult of Aldous Huxley, whose book, *The Doors of Perception*, was, as you know, the source for the name of Jim Morrison's band. And of course there was Timothy Leary, who, charlatan though he seemed to be, was a very influential figure.

Often, since the Sixties, I have asked myself what happened to psychedelic experience. Is it that the acid isn't as good as it once was? What became of "psychedelia"? Where did it all go? Surely that odd disappearance has something to do with the slow decline of the utopian impulse, which not only relates to a play like *Romeo and Juliet*, but is a crucial cultural phenomenon. It's a devastating fact that the utopian simply does not really figure for us any longer, and we must talk about that change at greater length, since it has had a profound influence on the young.

But the disappearance of the psychedelic also has to do, I would suggest, with how communications technology has superceded, and now provides an all-pervasive ersatz version of, the psychedelic rush of yesteryear. The intense, fantastic visual and aural experiences of the Sixties, which used to be primarily in people's heads (and out of certain people's heads into the music), are now all over TV and in every cineplex. In a way, one's own individual trip is just redundant—if you're "tripping," you're deluded, and it's also a waste of money, since you can just hit the remote. Watch any pod of prime-time advertising, or drop into any cineplex, and you'll have something like the same experience that kids were rhapsodizing over thirty years ago. Go watch *Twister*. You don't even have to drop acid to watch it—the way that some people once dropped acid to go see *2001*.

Now, let me take this notion out of the realm of the illicit. This is not just a matter of what happened to narcotic fantasy, but of the extent to which all individual capacity has been minimized and derogated by the culture of consumer technology. "Leave the driving to us," in other words—or, "We do it all for you." To return to those ads for *Rolling Stone:* making your own hash brownies is just, like, really yesterday. It's over. We don't do that anymore. It's not just that those brownies had hashish in them—it's also that you made those brownies yourself. Now why'd you ever do that? Why didn't you just go out and buy some Häagen-Dazs?

As you watch TV commercials and scan the ads on billboards and in magazines, notice the repeated denigration of individual capability. This tendency goes way back. It goes back to Progressive attempts to assimilate the immigrant populations in the United States, where certain foreign customs were cast as unclean and unhealthy, so as to expedite "Americanization"—which generally entailed reliance on experts and commodities. That effort was ongoing throughout the Progressive Era and well into the Twenties, establishing that it was simply better, say, to buy prepackaged food than to go into a general store and scoop it from a bin. It was just more civilized that way. Now you wouldn't smoke a pipe, or roll your own—you'd buy your cigarettes ready-made. You wouldn't dip a pen into an inkwell, but buy a fountain pen, and then a ballpoint. These are just a few trivial examples of a general appropriation, or obviation, of individual functions, but of course the examples soon cease to be so trivial, but come also to include the ability to play a musical instrument, to write a letter, to do math, to read for pleasure; to daydream; to remember; to think.

It is this process of appropriation on which corporate capitalism has depended from the start. It depends on our reliance upon their "goods and services."

Let me come back to the subject of youth and the media. This is from a research paper written by Carlene Bauer, a graduate student at Hopkins. She did a study of the histories of both *Seventeen* and *Sassy*, the magazines for teen-aged girls. There are poignant and instructive stories to be told about them both. It's enlightening to discover that *Seventeen*, at the outset, was, for a few years, intent on treating its young readers as capable, as accomplished, as having interests and intelligence—and even civic obligations.

It's astonishing to read the very first issue—this is in 1944—and find the editor, Helen Valentine, inquiring about the intellectual pursuits of her young readers: "Are you a music fiend? A bookworm? A movie fan? Do you like art, history, poetry or humor?" It's even more astonishing to read those early issues and find charts explaining inflation, and articles defending modern art. Valentine treated her readers like "adults"—or let's say "equals"—assuming that their tastes and capabilities were not appreciably different from their parents'. She also urged them to regard themselves as citizens: "Never for a moment think, 'I'm only a girl in my teens, what can I do?'" Valentine encouraged her readers. "You can do plenty." This involved not only helping with the war effort, but also fighting racism.

It's a bit surprising, is it not? And yet there was, of course, already a counter-movement underway within the magazine. At the same time that the readers were being courted so respectfully, the message being sent out by the magazine's ad people was completely different. Out of earshot of those readers, as it were, they were being cast as nothing more than a source of advertising revenues.

The advertising types invented an exemplary young girl named "Teena." Teena was the average *Seventeen* reader, devised to make clear to the advertisers what a gold mine they could have in this magazine. They assured the advertisers that this Teena was a responsible citizen, but also "a copycat. What a break for you! Our girl Teena wants to look, act and be just like the girl next door." The social worth that editor Valentine extolled in print meant absolutely nothing to the advertisers, who were asked, "When is a girl worth $11,690,499?" That was Teena's "purchasing power," you see. So there were two different messages at work at *Seventeen:* inevitably, through the Fifties, the articles with headings like "Your Mind" would gradually disappear, while there were more and more ads for hope chests and all the stuff you needed to get married and be a good homemaker. It was inevitable because the magazine was fundamentally commercial.

The grand deprecation of individual capabilities has required—as if somehow to replace them—a compulsive irony. A facile irony has been, indeed, the crucial rhetorical principle of the culture of the spectacle. In no premeditated way, irony offers the major corporate interests—the advertisers and the media trust—a perfect way to seem to make connection with the young (and everybody else). The young— let's now call them "adolescents"—have their inevitable problems with their parents, with their teachers, with all figures of authority; and so what illusion could be more seductive than to have those bright, hip, snappy ads and shows and movies seem to tip the kid a wink, as if to say, "We know what it's like to be who you are. We're on your side (against them)."

There is an immense, not to say enormous sort of populist pretense going on here, as advertisers assure the spectator that the spectator him/herself—cynically detached and apathetic—is really pretty cool, as long as he/she stays out of it (although commercially connected). This pose has had political implications, inasmuch as that apparent coolness must entail political quiescence, a sneering quietism.

Let me read you something that a 24-year-old woman told a writer for *New York* magazine in 1982. This is from an article entitled "Attitude," which dealt with the widespread post-Sixties backlash against the fervor of the counterculture. "Idealism has given way to cynicism," the reporter writes, and then illustrates the point with this memorable bite: "I think your generation was very sweet to be outraged by Vietnam and Watergate. Incredibly innocent, dumb, stupid and naive, but very, very sweet."

You can't really argue with that judgment. There's always something potentially laughable about earnestness of any kind. We tend to use the word "earnest" pejoratively, because the culture places so high a premium on the posture of coolness that "earnestness" must necessarily smack of Puritanical smugness and repression—the worst traits of the grown-ups as we are all endlessly encouraged to envision them. (It's basically a cultural inheritance from the Twenties, adapted to the needs of multinationals.) This permanent mobilization against "earnestness" may blind us to the facts of who's in charge—for the rise of irony has bolstered the illusion that those really in control are not "earnest," stuffy, tight-assed types. The authorities are not authoritarian (and woe to him who can be made to seem so). Those with real economic sway in this system are thus concealed behind a wall of images that are all disarmingly cool (and hot!), bright, "irreverent"—in a word, sassy.

Interestingly enough, *Sassy* was quite an unusual magazine—and here I return to Carlene Bauer's findings. The magazine was started in the Eighties by an Australian feminist named Liz Phair, and it aimed at girls who weren't inclined to flip through mainstream magazines like *Seventeen*. The magazine had bite, it dealt clearly with the actual world its readers lived in—and so the Christian Coalition mounted a big campaign against it, because they thought it was too dirty, and consequently several major advertisers, including Maybelline, quickly headed for the hills. Eventually the magazine was sold to Peterson Publishing, owner of *Teen*, which is a very different thing from *Sassy,* as those of you who've read them both have doubtless noticed.

At the time of the sale, the head of Dale Lang Publishing, the previous owner of the magazine, was quoted thus: "In the last year or so, *Sassy* became more of a fringe publication than a cutting-edge magazine. It missed a large part of the teen market and concentrated on a small number of teens that don't relate to the mainstream. There was a darker side to *Sassy* and I think they alienated a part of their market."

Now that utterance is entirely typical of a certain bottom-line mentality—so we should think about it. The magazine is actually called *Sassy*— and it was evidently too damned sassy to survive. To be "cutting-edge" no longer means to risk offending or disturbing anyone—not even "a part of [the] market—and so the magazine had now to be made much less sassy, because it wasn't reaching quite enough young readers to entice the advertisers.

The point here is that the mainstream irony is always fundamentally innocuous. It poses no threat to those in power, asks for no changes, affirms no values, but functions only to have us snickering in assent.

•

Thus far I've been talking about cultural developments that may or may not have occurred in any case. To sit and watch TV, for years, within a world that has been spatially and socially arranged, as ours has been, for nothing other than commercial purposes, is certainly to make ourselves subject to certain large, predictable developments. But there's also another side to the story—and this is where the possibility for corrective action comes in.

All the developments that I have talked about thus far have each been worsened—intensified, accelerated—by the unprecedented control over all the media by a very few enormous profit-making entities. In other words, the developments I've been discussing each suit perfectly the long-term purpose of those entities, which purpose is always and only to increase their profits.

For example, it is entirely in keeping with that general purpose that the commodity stand as the ultimate criterion for all that is worthwhile in the spectacle, and in life (and that the spectacle be seen as life). This is another development, and one that pertains directly to the disappearance of the utopian, which I mentioned earlier. By now, the vague old promise of an actual (albeit imprecise) utopia—a hazy paradise located, surely, just over the next rise—has been displaced by the commodity: the new car, the new refrigerator, the new jeans or just the mouthful of cheap chocolate or cold soda. You can perceive the absence of the utopian today by looking back, say, at the culture of the Thirties—mainstream pop culture, or the propaganda of the left, or the rhetoric of uplift used routinely (and often quite sincerely) by the *colossi* of Big Business. At movie's end, they were always heading off into the sunset, as in *Stagecoach*, or otherwise venturing beyond the confines of reality into a better world. We find a different version of the same blurry utopianism in the escapist glamor of the advertising then—and a very different version in the Marxist-Leninist rhetoric of Thirties *agitprop*. All such vague, happy visions have now given way to the harder, cleaner outline of the brand-new product—or products, which now sing to us, "We are the world!"

This is not just a North American development, of course, but global; and it's not merely spectacular, but ideological, which is to say that the change can be discerned in people's thinking. I recall being struck by a moment in a recent TV documentary about Tienanmen Square, when one of the young Chinese activists was asked what he had been protesting *for*. He seemed nonplussed for several seconds, then said, "The freedom to wear Nikes."

The displacement of utopia by the commodity has necessarily entailed a growing incapacity for outrage. Certain noble goals and high principles having all been superannuated, there are fewer grounds, or occasions, for moral indignation. The resultant fatalism, which is especially striking when we see it in the young (because the young should be uncompromising in their optimism), has had as well another cause or source—one that, like the all-pervasive celebration of commodities, has also derived in part from the corruptive influence of the media trust. I'm referring to the mass coarsening of sensibility induced by an ever-more-explosive spectacle of violence.

The young have been especially deprived in this regard. What formerly could move, thrill, outrage and offend the audience now tends to leave kids cold. All of us who are parents, and those of us who teach film courses, have had the experience of colliding with a certain youthful incredulity that we could ever have been troubled, scared, exhilarated by this or that movie. I remember my son's reaction when he finally saw *Psycho*, which I'd been talking up, and also prohibiting, for years: "You think that's scary?" This is an example of a mass sophistication that Hitchcock himself perceived, when he noticed that the famous chase scene in *North by Northwest* (with the crop-dusting plane chasing Cary Grant into the cornfield) had been ripped off by several lesser talents who used helicopters, speedboats, motorcycles, blimps— whatever might arouse, again, the ever-more-jaded audience. And now there are kids who'll yawn through *Halloween*, and millions chuckle through *Pulp Fiction*. It's bigger than all of us, this process of sophistication, whereby we become harder to excite the more deeply immersed we are in media. To use Godard's old terms, we are "well-done," whereas the people in those places (if any) not yet saturated by TV are all still "raw."

In fact, we in the developed world are over-cooked by now—burned to a crisp, I'd say. But it would be a big mistake to see this routinization of the outrageous as merely an objective consequence of our having watched so much TV. It's a consequence also of the domination of the media trust, whose managers are interested only in the squeals of a particular huge bloc of viewers. It isn't cost-effective, they believe, to vary the intensity, to turn out smaller, quieter films for other, smaller sectors of the audience, and so the atmosphere is almost wholly raucous, screechy and percussive; and so the audience, increasingly, must have a certain kind of stimulation, since we ultimately are what we keep breathing in. What once was bold and daring—bare breasts and genitals, everybody screaming "fuck!"—is, therefore, now downright obligatory.

This sort of thing has surely had an influence on the style and moral posture of the hero as represented on TV and in the ads and movies. The same detached, impassive, dangerous figure that was once widely demonized (and, by Norman Mailer, romanticized) as "psychopathic" has by now become a cultural icon—as a real cool guy, and even as a hero. The wandering loner, expressionless, in tight t-shirt and shades, haunted The Ike Age as a menacing antithesis to the mainstream values of that era: hard work, conformity, "togetherness." Since the Seventies, however, that cool drifter has ascended into ideal status as a figure of the absolute consumer. About ten years ago, there was a print ad for the Honda *Elite*—I remember it from *Rolling Stone*, in fact—showing Lou Reed at the waterfront, standing very cool beside the motorcycle. He's wearing sunglasses, tight jeans and t-shirt, a black leather jacket; he has his thumbs hooked in his pockets, he's quite impassive in his shades, and faces us, legs spread apart, as if confronting us, either as a mugger or a hustler. Beneath the ad, it simply says: *Don't settle for walking.*

Get it? As in, "Take a walk on the wild side"—only now the illicit and anonymous encounter of the past has been transformed into a different kind of coupling: between Lou Reed and his Honda. It's just as loveless, both players are just as hard as any erstwhile cruisers, or any hustler and his john; but it's also completely sexless, an inhuman coupling of an extremely cool celebrity with a sleek, bright new machine. This is in no sense forbidden. Indeed, it's practically compulsory within the culture of consumption.

Elsewhere we see much the same uncanny rehabilitation of the psychopath—his translation from the ultimate outsider to the ultimate insider. Notice, for example, how the renegade enforcer has become an admirable figure: Mel Gibson in the *Lethal Weapon* series, Rambo (after the troubling and ambivalent *First Blood* [1985]) Schwarzenegger's heroes, Chuck Norris' and many others. For all his maniac impetuosity, his eagerness to break the rules—or in fact because of it—this raging button-man is now represented as true-blue, the hardest, most reliable of troops within the military or constabulary bureaucracy. No longer do we see the maverick as a danger, as we did in cop movies like *Detective Story* (1951) or *The French Connection* (1971), or the Dirty Harry films (with Clint Eastwood playing a pretty frightening sort of scourge), or in westerns like *The Searchers* (1956). Now the psychopathic grunt is no longer demonized but prized for his excesses—just like his real-life counterparts, such as Oliver North, or the elite troops throughout the Western military.

Whether or not the hero is a hulking killer, the mainstream media generally—including advertising—is now forever selling us a vicarious experience of power. We therefore should be careful when we invoke "empowerment" as a *desideratum*, because the very concept has become rather dubious. A hostile fantasy of personal "empowerment" is now routinely sold not only to insecure white males, but to every population large enough to help turn a new release into a blockbuster. This fact has certain implications for those of us who tend to look for signs of a salutary subversiveness in the products of the corporate media. The same vicarious ass-kicking that some of us would readily deplore in, say, a Steven Seagal movie might not seem offensive to us when it's worked into a film like *Thelma and Louise* (1991); but the move is just as brutal and manipulative no matter which particular bloc of viewers is being invited thus to fantasize. The target audience might be female, or it might be black, or—to come back to the subject of this conference—it might be pre-adolescent, as with a hateful piece of trash like *Problem Child 2* (1991)— but whichever profitable bloc the system's trying to incite, the bogus offer of "empowerment" is the same, psychologically and morally, and no doubt socially.

In all these cases, we see the same pretense at work—the same loud presumption of enlightenment, permitting us, as viewers, to look back at what was, and laugh it off. This presumption is now all-pervasive. Of course it absolutely permeates the spectacle, and as critics of the media we can pretty easily take note of the presumption when it finds expression in an ad or movie or TV show. It's not so easy, however, to perceive the very same presumption in our own critical thinking.

Indeed, the very faculty of "critical thinking" can easily be displaced by this enlightenment automatism. Just to trash what was, to the advantage of what is: whether this reflex works to glamorize a car, extend your *vita* or betray the revolution, in itself it's not progressive. (It's the "recidivist element" in the onward thrust of Enlightened cogitation, to quote Adorno and Horkheimer.) And because that reflex rules throughout the culture of consumption, usurping thought in many minds, any opposition is impossible if those who seem to be the dissidents are only "thinking" in the same way that the culture "thinks." If we are thus basically united with it, we can't hope to contradict it, our little ironies can't possibly impede the huge cold irony that moves it forward. Between us and it, it must prevail, if there is no transcendence of its basic tendencies, because its managers will always come across as cooler, newer, hipper than ourselves—cooler, indeed, than any mere human effort, gesture, movement, institution.

This is not to argue that the system is a monolith, affecting everybody equally and uniformly; nor is it to deny that individuals, or outgroups, are able to appropriate this or that detail from the spectacle—a slogan or a jingle or a logo—for their own wayward uses.

Let us face the fact, however, that the spectacle can impose near-unanimity on all who watch it, and has done so lately, several times. Sophisticated mass propaganda works here and now, just as it has throughout this century. It worked during Desert Storm, it's worked during U.S. Presidential campaigns, it worked at the time of the Hill-Thomas hearings. It makes little difference that the truth (or some of it) eventually comes out, since those belated revelations always come too late to be of any help to those who are discredited, defeated, killed. When the spectacle is good to go, it's a lot bigger than we are, and at that point there's nothing we can do about it.

•

What we must do, then, is start getting down to business now—before the next big drive or crisis comes, with every mainstream outlet saying the same things. What we need to do, eventually, is to democratize the media, which means that we must study how to break the enormous power of those commercial entities that now control the media globally. As I have said, the various disabling cultural trends of the last thirty years, although to some extent inherent in the mere forms of the electronic media, have also been accelerated and intensified by the likes of Rupert Murdoch, Disney, Viacom, Time-Warner, General Electric, Conrad Black. We ought therefore to make common cause with the increasingly uneasy audience around the world, and break those powers down.

It's crucial that we keep teaching media literacy, which surely ought to be a curricular feature in every school. (After all, in our humanities courses we've been teaching those who end up going to work as p.r. flacks, admakers and political handlers—and who end up using what they've learned from us. It's only right that we should now teach people to defend themselves against such propaganda.) Thus far, however, "media literacy" has been conceived primarily as an *ex post facto* knack or skill: we teach kids to decode the images, but not to grasp the nature and the purpose of the mechanism that spits out those images. That mechanism, with its too few owners and all-powerful advertisers, is a given, like the sun—and so that modest "media literacy" functions as a sort of intellectual sun-block, leaving the whole system quite intact. To be truly media-literate, one must know not only what those images might mean and how they're made, but also who is making them, and why. One also must know something of the history of that mechanism, the psychological and social consequences of its sway—and one's own rights, as one stands in the path of that great engine.

With the passage, down in Washington, of the Telecommunications Act in 1996, the situation has become extremely serious. It's as if an iron door has closed. The powers that control the media are less answerable than ever. Of course, most of us know nothing on the subject, because the U.S. press has largely failed to clarify the implications of the new law—and that's true also of the alternative press.

So what to do? First of all, we need to know who owns the media. I tried to make a start in this direction in the June 3 issue of *The Nation*, which is devoted to the problem of the media monopoly. Included there, is a four-page centerfold that demonstrates the size and interests of the four huge corporations that control the TV news in the United States: General Electric (NBC), Time-Warner (CNN), Disney (ABC) and Westinghouse (CBS). It's a very striking demonstration—enough so that that issue sold out in unprecedented numbers, and got quite a lot of mainstream media coverage. I mention this because it proves that there is now much serious concern about the media trust among the general public. Thus far the only American politicians who've addressed that concern—that is, who've exploited it— have been those on the right, such as Bob Dole and Pat Buchanan. Those folks aren't serious about dismantling the monopoly—indeed, in many instances they've actually helped strengthen it, because they want not to do away with it, but to run the thing themselves. You'll notice that they never hint at anything like antitrust, but merely go on vaguely scapegoating "the media" for political advantage, by hinting that a sinister "elite" is in control. (The implication is, of course, that that "elite" is Jewish.)

Such demogogic propaganda must now give way to accurate and detailed information on the media trust. It is we who can provide the public with that sort of information; and in order to do that, we need to have some conversation with that public, which will require us to stop talking just to one another, in a language that only we can understand.

There's a group in Philadelphia called the Cultural Environment Movement, whose purpose is to organize a broad-based antitrust movement—one that will extend beyond Academia, and beyond the bailiwick of media activists, to include a lot of other people who might not tend to think politically, but who are fed up with the noise and grossness and monotony of the mainstream media. The group was started by George Gerbner. Its founding conference took place in St. Louis in mid-March, and it was exhilarating, because there were people there from all over the world, and everybody started feeling pretty confident about this movement, which will attempt to use legal and legislative measures of all kinds.

Then there's Unplug—who've just opened a Canadian office. Unplug's purpose is to decommercialize the classrooms of our public schools. Their main aim is to get rid of Channel One, a daily 22-minute newscast beamed directly into middle schools and high schools—a newscast that includes commercials for major advertisers like Nike, Pepsi, Mars, AT&T. The deal is that the schools must make the daily viewing of those newscasts—and those commercials—mandatory; and, in exchange, they get to use the video equipment that the company provides them, "free." Basically, it's just a VCR, video monitors (with pretty small screens) and a satellite dish (that picks up only Channel One). The VCR is centrally controlled in every school, so that the teachers can't use the broadcasts individually, or critically. (The company that now owns Channel One is K-III Communications, which is owned by Kravis Kohlberg Roberts, the investment bank that owns RJR/Nabisco. K-III also owns *The Weekly Reader*.)

Unplug has done an excellent job at getting students and their parents organized to get the broadcasts out of their respective schools. The school boards in Santa Clara, California, and in a small in town in Missouri, and one up in Alaska, have all voted to get rid of Channel One. It makes sense that they would. We're talking about millions of dollars in advertising revenues spent by corporations that use up classroom time, that exploit the students as a captive audience, and that take advantage of a forum that's sustained by tax dollars—a forum, moreover, that should never be a venue for any propaganda, commercial or otherwise. The work that Unplug does is therefore crucial to the ongoing fight to keep the young protected from the media.

I hope that I haven't disappointed you by straying from culture criticism into these mundane political particulars. My point is, however, that we should all be straying this way, or else our theorizing will amount to very little.

ANVER SALOOJEE

Hollywood and the Black Youth of South Africa: Culture, Rebellion and Revolution

To fully comprehend the magnitude of the contribution made to rebellion and culture by the youth of Soweto, the very image of whom is evocative of rebellion and revolution, it is important to link popular resistance, the emergence of counter-hegemonic cultures, to broader socio-economic and political crises in society at large; and then to understand how the popular media depict the struggle of the black youth. Recognizing the commercial worth of the black struggle in South Africa, the western film industry depicted it in a number of films, appropriating the images of black struggles against apartheid; dissociating these images from the reality that gave rise to them; offering western audiences understandings of rebellion and revolution in South Africa via protagonists they could relate to—white people who were adversely affected by apartheid; and, thus, effectively recreating the struggle in South Africa in an image that turned reality on its head. The view reproduced showed the black South African struggle requiring the intervention of whites to ensure its ultimate success.

As Berger has pointed out, it is not sufficient to understand the language of images; what also matters is who uses that language and for what purposes: "If the new language of images were used differently it would, through its use, confer a new kind of power."[1] The first major western film about the revolt by the black youth of South Africa—Richard Attenborough's *Cry Freedom* (1987)—can best be understood at two levels. The first situates the film in the broad socio-economic and political context that gave rise to the events it seeks to capture. The second level assesses the internal coherence of the film, and uses semiotics to understand how the construction of binary opposites is used to create a new language of images about the struggle of black people in South Africa. Both levels of analysis are important in order to fully comprehend how the western film industry appropriates non-western reality through images, deconstructs it, and then reconstructs it in a form that at once turns it on its head and guarantees greater commercial success. Thus, when analyzing any film, especially one that claims to capture a large slice of reality by being a "docu-drama" or a "biography," it is important to see it in two ways simultaneously—at the macro level where it is situated in a broader socio-economic and political context, and at the micro level where it can be interpreted in terms of how the narrative is internally structured and socially constructed.

Theoretical reflections on populism; on the rise of popular democratic movements; on the rise of an alternate revolutionary popular culture; and on Gramsci's notions of hegemony, crises and organic intellectuals; provide important insights and interpretations which can be profitably applied to understanding both the significant role the youth of Soweto played in the development of Cultural Liberation in the South Africa of the 1970s; and the western film industry's uses of the image of black struggles for its own commercial and ideological purposes.

In order for the dominant class in any society to assert its rule it has to constantly "neutralize" the people by inserting "popular demands" and "popular culture" into the ideology of the dominant class in such a way that it ensures that class's hegemony. A challenge to that hegemony by the dominated classes can provoke a crisis in society. This is where Gramsci's notion of hegemony is critical.

Gramsci uses the concept of hegemony in two interrelated senses. In the first instance, hegemony is viewed as consensus not domination. Central to the question of consensus is social control and the maintenance of the social order, which in turn means consensus around a particular kind of society; integration into and acceptance of given cultural norms, and social, political and economic structures. Here Gramsci is concerned with how a dominant discourse comes to gain credibility and establish itself as "the" discourse. Or, as Lukes puts it, what is at issue is the power that arises from "shaping perceptions, cognition and preferences in such a way that they [i.e. social agents] accept their role in the existing order of things, either because they see or imagine no alternative to it, or because they see it as natural and unchangeable, or because they value it as divinely ordained or beneficial."[2]

Secondly, consensus at the cultural level indicates how the culture of the dominant class is taken to represent the culture and "general interests" of the entire body politic.

Gramsci saw hegemonic rule as the predominant form of political/social control and as the normal form of government in most industrialized countries. And the forms hegemonic rule takes are varied. While all hegemonic states are in a very limited sense mass based (to the extent that they propagate a dominant culture and ideology throughout society), they differ in the pervasiveness of their hegemonic apparatuses, the degree of consensus they achieve and the extent to which they can rule unchallenged by the dominated groups. But when the hegemony of the ruling class is ruptured and an hegemonic crisis ensues, conditions emerge for the use of extreme force by the dominant class, to continue to assert its rule.

What role does the media play in depicting and reporting the crisis? The answer is not clear cut. In *Policing the Crisis,* Hall et al., describe the media as "a key terrain on which 'consent' is won or lost."[3] The media, precisely because they are relatively autonomous from the ruling class, through their own "constructions and inflections" reproduce "the interpretations of the crisis subscribed to by the ruling class." The role of the media in "manufacturing consent" derives from its capacity to portray itself as the neutral "conveyer/ transmitter" of news events. The media however, are not simply passive transmitters of news. Through their selection of news items, the incidents they seek to cover and give prominence to, the items they wish to highlight, the media are in fact active agents who shape the contours of the message. In so doing the media transmit information, provide the ideological lens through which to view the "event," and set the agenda according to which some events are deemed to be crucial. The media "define the situation" and they do so in concert with other "primary definers"—sources in government and other institutions.[4] The media therefore reproduce "primary definitions" whereby they bring to our attention a crisis that already exists in the economy and society and is defined as significant by other powerful forces in society. According to Hall et al., "By consenting to the view of the crisis which has won credibility in the echelons of power, popular consciousness is also won to support the measures of control and containment which this version of social reality entails."[5]

At the heart of the above is an understanding that, the entertainment media exert a considerable influence over audiences, and play a vital role in the "construction of social reality." While on one hand we can see that it is reductionism to suggest that concentrated ownership of the media industry translates into absolute control over the message, we must remember Miliband's injunction that the apparent divergence of views found in the media should not obscure the power that concentrated ownership confers nor should it hide the reality that the range of diverse views in the dominant media is rather narrow.[6]

Whether one is analyzing the role of the media in reporting on domestic or foreign crises, the cultural terrain is most hotly contested. It is here that the struggle for the hearts, minds and consciousness of the audience is fought. The dominant group attempts to project its hegemony in the name of all, while the counter-hegemonic bloc is beginning to posit a revolutionary culture that calls into question the status quo and exposes its self-serving nature. On the terrain of resistance, including cultural resistance, the dominated classes put forward a viable, albeit antagonistic, alternative to the prevailing culture of the dominating classes.

ANVER SALOOJEE

In the case of South Africa, the hegemonic rule of white society was challenged right from the onset of colonialism in 1652. While the forms or resistance changed over time, the challenge to white domination reached a very different level in 1976 when the dominated groups, led initially by the uprising of the Soweto youth, challenged the apartheid state and began to consciously consolidate a counter-hegemonic bloc. The counter-hegemonic alliance took the form of a multi-class, multi-racial, multi-organizational populist movement.

The crisis of apartheid that South Africa was facing by the mid 1970s was marked by a number of features including: divisions within the ruling bloc on whether to pursue a path of increased repression or to "liberalize" civil society; a stagnating economy, a rising national deficit, and increasing unemployment; a massive increase in defense expenditures which exacerbated the fiscal crisis of the state; increasing militancy from black workers; and the rise of "Black Consciousness" as an alternate to the cultural hegemony of white South Africa.

The Black Consciousness Movement (BCM) in South Africa developed in a partial political vacuum created when the African National Congress and the Pan Africanist Congress were banned and many of the resistance leaders were imprisoned, killed or driven into exile. It developed at a time when the broken backbone of resistance was beginning to mend and the black working class was once again asserting its collective muscle. The Black Consciousness Movement began as a student movement and had its most profound impact on the black youth of South Africa. It developed and matured during the late 1960s to mid 1970s, when the South African economy had experienced its greatest expansion and the lustre of the boom years was wearing off. Internally, by the mid 1970s, South Africa's economy was in crisis, while politically its rule was being challenged by black workers and by black youth.

On June 16, 1976, the world awoke to news of a youth-initiated and youth-led revolt against apartheid, which began as a challenge to the right of the apartheid state to continue to extend its hegemony over the black people of South Africa via the imposition of an Afrikaans "language policy." The world was stunned by the response of the South African government to the youth protests: mass murder. The picture of a young person carrying the body of the first youth to be shot dead, Hector Peterson, was flashed around the world, and became the first national and international symbol of the Soweto uprising.

The youth uprisings also precipitated a more generalized crisis of the South African social formation. The Soweto uprisings, the murder of Steve Biko—a leading member of the Black Consciousness Movement—the banning of eighteen anti-apartheid organizations, the increasing militancy by black workers making economic and political demands, and increasing international pressure to reform apartheid,

Hollywood and the Black Youth of South Africa

massive unemployment, and a deepening recession all came together to provoke an organic crisis of the apartheid state. The political revolt by the youth of Soweto also resonated at the cultural level. In organizing themselves and their communities, black youth resorted to the use of culture in the form of songs and poetry of resistance: liberation songs, songs of resistance, poems enshrining the heroes of the past, plays extolling the virtues of struggling against racial domination all made their appearance in the midst of the Soweto uprisings. A cultural revolution and a cultural liberation were beginning to take hold alongside, and in a complementary vein to, political struggle. The iconography of the cultural revolution and liberation included liberation poems and songs; the *toyi-toyi* (a dance of spectacular undulating rhythms done in unison by the participants); plays about the uprisings (*Sarafina!*, *Bopha!*, etc.); and literature about the struggle.

Cultural Liberation had a number of crucial defining characteristics. First it espoused "Black Consciousness," the uplifting of the Black people of South Africa. Secondly, it espoused "National Liberation," the liberation of the people of South Africa from racial oppression. Thirdly, it espoused a "Transformative Culture"—the use of culture in all its forms and manifestations as a weapon in "Black Consciousness" and the struggle for "National Liberation." Beside standing in marked contrast to the dominant culture of South Africa, Cultural Liberation also marked a major departure from a previous tradition which tended to focus on the evils of apartheid and its victimization of the black people. The focus of Cultural Liberation was on the youth taking the initiative to fight an oppressive regime even at the expense of losing their lives. Sensing the potentiality of counter-hegemonic culture young people pushed it to the point where it began to gain ascendancy over the dominant white culture.

Around the world people were riveted by images of youth who had only their hands and sticks and stones, taking on the might of the South African state. While the youth of Soweto were fighting for liberation and simultaneously transforming their very existence, the western cultural establishment itself began to take notice.

The western film industry's view of the South African rebellion has gone through three distinct phases. The first phase was marked by a total disinterest in the Soweto uprisings. In the second phase, beginning with the film *Cry Freedom*, there was a recognition of the existence of the rebellion, but it was narrated through protagonists predominantly white western audiences could easily and directly relate to—white people negatively affected by apartheid, such as Bram Fisher, Donald Woods, or Ruth First. The third phase was a significant departure, in that there was still a recognition of the rebellion but now it was being narrated through name box office stars who could make the cinematic venture broadly commercially viable. In each phase the western film industry was consciously or unconsciously mediating the South African rebellion through discourses the western film industry was familiar with. The revolutionary populism of the black youth, their political and cultural revolution, was all but subordinated to other paradigms in film. Thus, the western film industry was reconstructing South African social reality and structuring information about that part of the world for western audiences.

Let us examine Richard Attenborough's *Cry Freedom*. The film starred Denzel Washington as Steve Biko, a leader of the Black Consciousness Movement in South Africa and a significant force in the resurgence of black youth on the terrain of resistance against apartheid there. The Black Consciousness Movement had its greatest influence among the black youth and students of South Africa. The ideas that influenced the leaders of the movement including Steve Biko developed while they were in university themselves, rejecting the domination of youth and student politics by white university students.

For his part in organizing youth, students and black communities and for promoting the ideas of black consciousness, Steve Biko was labeled a security risk by the South African state. He was apprehended by the state security police, and tortured to death. When his death in detention was announced, the Minister of Justice remarked that the death of Steve Biko left him "cold." The ensuing investigation resulted in a cover-up that protected the perpetrators. Donald Woods, a liberal white newspaper editor, had befriended Steve Biko, and had became an outspoken critic of apartheid. For his editorial criticisms he was banned and eventually had to flee South Africa. The Attenborough film was supposed to be about the life of Steve Biko, but it ended up being a film about the escape of Donald Woods (Kevin Kline), a white man hunted by the forces of apartheid.

Cry Freedom was the first feature length film on the struggle of the Black Consciousness Movement in South Africa made by an influential western director. At one level the film successfully highlighted the struggle against apartheid in South Africa. The timing of the production was perfect—it came as the Soweto uprisings in South Africa had gained international prominence. Apartheid had become the subject of international attention as well as international scorn. South Africa was rapidly becoming a pariah nation that Western nations—including Canada, the United States and Great Britain—were being urged to isolate. And the film successfully captured the crisis plaguing South African society.

But it was also cashing in on the world's attention, which television had focused on Soweto. Some of the most riveting scenes depicted the first few days of the Soweto uprising, where black youth confronted a very repressive para-military force armed both militarily and with an "attitude" to quell the youth rebellion by any means necessary. Global consciousness was being fed a steady diet of news reports, television documentaries and film documentaries about the horrors of apartheid, racial injustices, the mass killings of black youth; and a host of other atrocities; committed by the racially exclusive state in South Africa as it sought to protect white power and privilege.

However, an analysis of the internal construction of the film reveals a very disturbing pattern. The Attenborough film does not view black people in South Africa as capable of their own liberation from white tyranny. The struggle gains legitimacy only when a white man and his family are hounded and temporarily terrorized by the system. While crisis theory and Hall's perspective on media reporting were useful in analyzing the macro context of *Cry Freedom*, it is to semiotics that one must turn to unravel the internal mechanisms through which it reproduced a view of black people in South Africa not as active agents—the primary force—in the struggle against apartheid; but as secondary agents whose struggle derives significance from whites who are also victims of apartheid. The title of the film is evocative of the murdered black leader and the first half of the film does center on Steve Biko. It is in the second half of the film that its primary discourse unfolds—in the telling of the tragic impact of apartheid on a white family. The film becomes less the tale of the struggle of black people against apartheid and more the report of the impact apartheid had on liberal whites. The binary opposition[7] is one between black oppression and white privilege; between black resistance and death, and white power. Most reviews and accounts of the film stress the heroic character of Steve Biko and, in the same breath, the sacrifices made by Donald Woods.

The real significance of *Cry Freedom* lies in our recognition that the hero for the director is not Steve Biko but Donald Woods—who sacrifices the safety of his family and abandons his life of privilege in white South Africa. The discourse of Steve Biko is subordinate to the discourse of Donald Woods. And if binary opposites in a film reflect wider social tensions, then in subordinating the Biko discourse to the Woods discourse the film leads the audience to two crucial conclusions. First, whites suffered just as much as blacks from apartheid. And secondly, black people in South Africa are not to be seen as active agents and the primary force in the struggle against apartheid, but as secondary agents whose struggle derives significance from whites who are also victims of apartheid. Black people in South Africa, it is suggested, were not fully capable of their own liberation from white tyranny.

If awareness of the injustices of apartheid is what characterizes Donald Woods and prompts him to political action and to the sacrifice of privilege, then it is precisely this discourse that makes the lasting impression on the audience; for it marks the narrative and the structure of the film. This is exactly where the film departs from reality, for it was the black people of South Africa who were their own liberators. In the film Attenborough, as a white man, was providing his own primary definition of the situation. The internal ordering of the film and its internal structure represented South African reality in a very partial and incomplete manner which ended up reflecting the interests of the dominant white group in apartheid South Africa.

Cry Freedom, however, brings with it the air of authenticity. It professes to portray reality "as it is." The cinematic device of biography is a supposedly neutral, impartial and unbiased way of allowing reality to unfold as it "really" did. This presumed neutrality secretes its own value framework, however, best unearthed by the use of semiotics which allows one to engage with the internal coherence of the text and its various meanings and levels of subordination and superordination. Semiological readings of *Cry Freedom* enable us to dig beneath the level of surface reality to the ideological secretion hidden as a subtext in the message of the film—the narrative of Biko is subordinate to that of Woods; the struggle of black people gains significance only through the interventions of whites hurt by the system; and, finally, the loss of privileges by whites opposed to apartheid is superordinate and paramount while the injustices against black people in South Africa and their struggle against apartheid are subordinate.

Attenborough was reflecting another disturbing reality in *Cry Freedom*—that the western film industry was still ambivalent about the commercial viability of the black struggle in South Africa. While the western film industry was sufficiently attuned to the commercial prospects of making movies about the South African struggle, it was at the same time determining the narrative through which the struggle would be allowed to unfold profitably. And that narrative had to have a hero western audiences could relate to—a white man. The western film industry was not prepared to take audiences along a radically different path where the black youth of Soweto would themselves be the heroes American audiences would identify with. As Berger said in *Ways of Seeing*, "The means of reproduction are used politically and commercially to disguise what their existence makes possible. But sometimes individuals use them differently."[8]

A second film about apartheid, *A World Apart* (1987) starring Barbara Hershey, also involves a white journalist—Diana Roth—who defies the white government and is the first white woman arrested under the 90-day Detention Act. The screenplay was written by Shawn Slovo and was based on the life of her mother Ruth First, who was killed in Maputo when a bomb-laden parcel sent by agents of the South African government exploded as she opened it. Once again the film follows the pattern established in *Cry Freedom*—that the real horror of apartheid can be comprehended only if the narrative involves the discourse of white heroes.

By 1990 the western film industry had finally taken notice, and many movies were made depicting life in South Africa, the Soweto uprisings, and relations between blacks and whites in a racially divided country: *A Dry White Season* (1989), *Bopha!* (1993), *Sarafina!* (1992). The Soweto uprisings and the youth of Soweto had arrived on the film sets of the west. While *Cry Freedom* typified one form of films made about the struggle in South Africa, there emerged another tradition which concentrated on the struggles of black people in South Africa unmediated by white experiences. Black actors in the United States clamored to play lead roles in films about the black youth of South Africa: Danny Glover in *Bopha!* and Whoopi Goldberg in *Sarafina!* are just two. Unlike *Cry Freedom*, the latter two films, both related to events in Soweto, focused entirely on the lives and struggles of black people. Both were based on plays which came out of South Africa as renditions and depictions of the Soweto uprisings; plays written by inhabitants of Soweto who had not experienced the rebellion vicariously, and were interested in depicting the struggle of black youth from their own vantage point.

Sarafina! was the story of a black Soweto school teacher Mary (Whoopi Goldberg) who defies authorities, teaches a forbidden curriculum, and inspires black students to take pride in their heritage and themselves. She teaches the students to stand up for their rights and to search for truth.

Bopha! involves the struggle of a black Soweto family torn between competing interests and political directions. The father (Danny Glover) is a black policeman in Soweto at a time when the police—viewed generally as collaborators with the white government—are used as a significant force to quell the Soweto uprisings. The son (Maynard Eziashi) is a youth who plays an important role in organizing the youth to rebel against the system. *Bopha!* depicts the struggles and resultant tensions the family faces, struggles and tensions that reflect the real impact apartheid had on the lives of black people in South Africa.

At one level the stars of Hollywood began to popularize the struggle in South Africa in film. The western film industry had moved along a continuum, and was now prepared to make films about the black struggle in South Africa without using white South Africa as a reference point for audiences. But "name" black stars had to play the lead roles. Western audience identification with box office stars was necessary in order for a second wave of films about Soweto to emerge. Nor were these black stars content to make films about South Africa. As they learned more about South Africa and came into contact with cultural workers and leaders of the African National Congress of South Africa (ANC), they gained a different appreciation of the struggle in South Africa, and began to carve out a more politically interventionist role for themselves. They took to protesting against apartheid in front of the South African embassy in Washington.

At another level, the popularity of the South African struggle was at such a fever pitch that key players in the cultural and entertainment industry were not only boy-cotting South Africa, but were in fact donating their time and energy to actively orga-nizing against apartheid. Concerts, cultural events and even birthday celebrations for the then imprisoned leader of the ANC, Nelson Mandela were organized and held around the world.

In return, South African cultural workers were invited to the west and South African plays like *Sarafina!* played to sold-out audiences throughout the western world.

The western entertainment and cultural industry, the most powerful in the world, had become the champion of the oppressed black people of South Africa. The power of that industry to shape images in its own fashion is legendary. In the case of South Africa the jury is still out on whether the contributions of Hollywood increased the awareness of the American population about the condition of the black people in South Africa, and further, on whether this increased awareness translated into the American public putting pressure on their elected officials to do something about the situation in South Africa. But the involvement of major players in the cul-tural and entertainment industry in the west generally, and in the United States par-ticularly, and their willingness to publicly demonstrate their abhorrence of apartheid South Africa, did significantly embarrass both the South African government and the governments of the United States and the rest of the western world.

Though the youth of Soweto became icons of revolution in an international arena, it is not clear to what extent they altered the western image of the South African struggle; or to what extent Hollywood popularized it, giving it access—through what only the western film industry can afford—to an audience a struggle for liberation would not otherwise have reached.

Notes

[1] John Berger, *Ways of Seeing* (Harmondsworth: Penguin, 1974), 33.

[2] Steven Lukes, *Power: A Radical View* (London: Macmillan, 1975), 24.

[3] Stuart Hall , et al., *Policing the Crisis: Mugging, the State and Law and Order* (London: Macmillan, 1978), 220.

[4] Janet Woollacott, "Messages and Meanings," in Michael Gurevitch, ed.,*Culture, Society and the Media* (London: Methuen, 1982), 91-112.

[5] Hall,et al., *Policing*, 220.

[6] Ralph Miliband, *The State in Capitalist Society* (London: Weidenfeld and Nicolson, 1969), 219; see as well, Mark Crispin Miller and Janine Jaquet Biden, "The National Entertainment State," *The Nation* 262:22 (June 3, 1996), 23.

[7] On binary opposition see Woollacott, "Message," 95.

[8] Berger, *Ways*, 30.

TIMOTHY SHARY

The only place to go is inside: Confusions About Sexuality and Class in *Clueless* and *Kids*

In 1995 two distinctly different films about teenagers were released to distinctly different audiences: Larry Clark's *Kids* was a low-budget *vérité*-style examination of a group of teens in Manhattan which contained such frank discussion of sexuality, particularly sexuality among minors, that it was initially given an NC-17 rating by the Motion Picture Association of America and was eventually released unrated only in limited distribution; Amy Heckerling's *Clueless*, with a larger budget and a star teen performer whose tale of high school struggle centered around social acceptance based on class and attitude as well as sex, became, with its PG-13 rating and wide release, the highest-grossing teen film in recent years. At first glance one may find the differences and similarities between these two films to be purely academic, but the release of *Kids* and *Clueless* represents what could be a crucial movement in the way cinema addresses teens on-screen and in the audience, that population David Considine has labeled "screenagers."[1] The ways in which *Clueless* and *Kids* examine sex and class for their young characters indicate the precise reasons why these films are such important teen texts.

Ultimately, what is radical about *Kids* is obvious: its graphic confrontation with the dangerous and detached lifestyles of a group of urban teens whose engagement in sex and drugs is killing them. The radical aspect of *Clueless* seems less apparent, if only because the film presents itself as a vapid exposé that treats teen issues casually if not condescendingly: we are tuned into the idiosyncracies of current youth in such a way that young people's confrontations with serious youth issues appear relatively unthreatening. However, these two films are significant especially because they enforce particular perspectives on the American cinema's broader presentation of youth, a topic which has been problematized, if not minimized, since the release of *Pump Up the Volume* in 1990, as we shall see.

In the early '80s such films as *Porky's* (1982), *Fast Times at Ridgemont High* (1982) and *Risky Business* (1983) inaugurated the modern teen sex comedy, a genre that was closely linked with the traditional teen drama in which young people struggled to come of age. Throughout the later '80s the popular teen film refined its take on sex as the era of AIDS took hold: previously carefree sexual adventures were gradually replaced by either melodramatic visions of "troubled" youth (e.g. *River's Edge* [1986], *Less Than Zero* [1987], *Heathers* [1988]) or sanitized fables that largely averted sex (e.g. *Can't Buy Me Love* [1987], *Some Kind of Wonderful* [1987], *Dead Poets Society* [1989]). By the release of *Pump Up the Volume,* a film that points to a multiplicity of complex youth problems while enjoying the entertainment value of teen angst, Hollywood seemed to have reached a limit in addressing young adults, as the number of teen films declined considerably between 1991 and 1994. The critical exception was the African American youth drama.

When *Boyz N the Hood* and *Straight Out of Brooklyn* premiered in 1991, their gritty realism and street-smart style granted the films an instant credibility. These films were far removed from the adolescent adventures of the '80s, revealing a population of young people confronted on a daily basis by murder, drugs, and poverty. Like their '80s predecessors, they still explored issues about sex and love, family problems, and the difficult quest for adulthood, but here that difficulty was more daunting—and the consequences more threatening—than in the vast majority of teen films made in the past 20 years. With the release of *Juice* (1992) and *Menace II Society* (1993) Hollywood tuned into the dramatic (and financial) potential of the black urban youth crisis, leaving television to address the white suburban milieu in shows like *Beverly Hills, 90210, Blossom,* and *Saved by the Bell.*

By the mid-'90s the brief wave of African American youth films had nonetheless subsided, leaving open many meaningful questions about the representation of current screenagers. Was the prevailing male perspective going to be maintained? (Of the many African American youth films in the early '90s, only one, *Just Another Girl on the I.R.T.* [1993], focused on the female experience.) Were attitudes about poorer youth shifting toward class awareness and away from sentimentality? Were serious problems like crime, drugs, and sexual disease going to be confronted as well; and if so, how authentically? Indeed, if Hollywood was going to present the youth experience at all, would it welcome a heightened realism or resort to a safer naiveté? But with *Kids* and *Clueless,* Hollywood did both.

The five years before *Clueless* and *Kids* may well have been a hibernation period during which the minimizing of teens on-screen reflected a Hollywood predisposi-

*Confusions About Sexuality and Class in **Clueless** and **Kids***

tion against dealing with youth. 1991 could have been a watershed year for teen films with the publication of Douglas Coupland's eponymous book *Generation X* and the release of Richard Linklater's equally eponymous film *Slacker*, but these texts shifted attention to the post-teen twentysomething population, as the wave of corresponding movies over the next few years (e.g. *Singles* [1992], *Reality Bites* [1994], *Threesome* [1994]) attested. With the emergence of the "Generation X" genre in the early '90s, Hollywood could have avoided addressing teens even longer, and may have, had the new genre been more successful. By 1995 the time was ripe for Hollywood to reconsider not only the teen box office potential but moreso the conditions of teen life that had been renegotiated in the past five years, especially in the wake of the African American youth films. What remained to be seen was the form that new teen films would take.

The teens and pre-teens that populate *Kids* not only exist in a world removed from structures such as high school and family (we are led to believe that the story takes place during summer vacation and only one parent is featured), but seem to be removed from any livelihood other than the conquest for sex, drugs, and alcohol. In films like *Clueless* and earlier teen dramas like those of the John Hughes variety (e.g. *Sixteen Candles* [1984], *The Breakfast Club* [1985], *Ferris Bueller's Day Off* [1986]), high school and family provide the system against which teens rebel and through which they develop their social roles. *Kids* posits that its characters' social roles have been firmly developed outside of school—to be sure, even though there are dozens of teen characters in the film who associate with one another, not once is a reference to school friends or activities made by any of them. Unlike the vaguely similar *Where the Day Takes You* (1992), in which the out-of-school teen characters are homeless runaways dealing with troubled pasts and seeking more promising futures, *Kids* presents its characters as familiar with, and at home in, their territory and otherwise content to just make it to the next party. Thus, they have little discernable identity other than hedonistic ignorance. In praising the film, Amy Taubin deduced that *Kids* "suggests that adolescent socialization is less determined by culture than biology."[2] These teens obviously didn't need school or parents to develop their streetwise instinct for sexual and chemical gratification.

The lack of institutionalized social structure allows for moral conditions in which youths are forced to make decisions usually reserved for adults, and this is especially problematic since these children lack the wisdom needed to comprehend the consequences of their actions. The minimal adult presence in *Kids* calls attention to the guile of a culture that necessarily but unrealistically excludes all but the young (as if these characters function in the same artificial environment of the *Peanuts* comics, only with excessive decadence) and further blurs the distinction between youthful innocence and adult accountability. In terms of sexuality, the teens' actions can be a matter of life (pregnancy) or death (disease), and yet *Kids* allows the gravity of its characters' circumstances to be spoken in an aloof visual and verbal irony. This tactic might be effective in appealing to the young viewers who were supposedly prevented from seeing the film, but it evacuates the kids in *Kids* of much literal understanding about the dangers (and certainly the joys) of sexuality. In comparing the directors of *Clueless* and *Kids*, Tom Doherty proposed that "if Heckerling is an indulgent mother having fun with her kids, Clark is the absent father, looking on detachedly, counting on the spectator to invest the narrative with moral meaning."[3] *Kids* is thereby oddly reactionary: we are ultimately shown that sex can be bad despite how much people claim to enjoy it, and the moral and philosophical complexities of this position are left largely unexplored.

Perhaps much of the conquest for pleasure that permeates *Kids* is based on its distinctly masculinist perspective; or, as bell hooks claimed in more aggressive terms, "What is being exploited [in *Kids*] is precisely and solely a spectacle of teenage sexuality that has been shaped and informed by patriarchal attitudes."[4] The film revolves around two teen boys, Telly (Leo Fitzpatrick) and Casper (Justin Pierce), the first of whom begins the film's day-in-the-life by deflowering an apparently pubescent girl while the other is drinking a 40-ounce beer and reading *Hate* comics. The few girls who are presented in the film are less developed characters but, as an early scene shows, they are just as sexually excitable as the boys who pursue them. The one conspicuous exception is Jennie (Chloe Sevigny), who first reveals that she only ever had sex one time, with Telly, and soon afterward discovers that he has infected her with HIV. The film's narrative thus becomes something of a picaresque journey for Jennie as she tries to find Telly before he infects another girl by the end of the day.

Despite Jennie's presence in the story and the one dialogue scene offered between girls, Harmony Korine's script never offers a balance or reprieve from its objectified positioning of young women. Perhaps Korine was making a statement on the difficulty girls face in dealing with urban boys today, for he appears himself as a friendly nerd who meets Jennie at a rave and, with empty consolations, forces her to take a drug that he insists will make her feel better. By the end of the film Jennie is so stoned that she cannot even protest when Casper rapes her, in a scene made all the more brutal by the fact that immediately before it she finds Telly but is too late to stop him from having sex with yet another virgin; and by Clark's sustained filming of it for two and a half minutes. Thus the film cheaply offers a false empowerment for its female characters, who initially appear confident in their knowledge and appropriation of sex, but who are ultimately victimized by it. The film is not mere-

Confusions About Sexuality and Class in **Clueless** *and* **Kids** ly sexist or patriarchal, it endorses an understanding of youthful sexuality that is degrading for both genders.

Clueless offers a more complex hypothesis on the nature of sexuality among teens, as its virginal main character, ironically named Cher (Alicia Silverstone), negotiates a wider range of social roles that are not all related to sexuality *per se*. Cher narrates her story in a voiceover that recalls and accentuates the style of the film's inspiration, Jane Austen's *Emma*. In describing her perspective on boys, Cher notes that high school boys are unacceptably immature for her tastes (making the extra-textual reference, "Searching for a boy in high school is as useless as searching for meaning in a Pauly Shore movie"), and for the first half of the film she remains uninterested in pursuing romantic or sexual involvements. Instead, she devotes her time first to the "project" of matchmaking two of her teachers, clearly for the purpose of improving her grades, and then to transforming a new student named Tai (Brittany Murphy) from a frumpy outcast to a costumed cutie so that she can become part of the small but popular crowd in which Cher travels. Only after she has achieved these romantic and sexual changes in others does she turn to herself.

Meanwhile, a dramatic tension is set up through a rather candid conversation between Cher, Tai, and Dionne (Stacey Dash) about Cher's virginity. After Tai expresses her preference that men have straight (as opposed to crooked) penises, Dionne points out that Cher is "hymenally challenged," to which Cher rejoins, "You see how picky I am about my shoes, and they only go on my feet." Cher's implication that she has been careful and patient, not to say discriminating, in waiting to have sex (at the age of 15) is thus equated to a fashion statement and, as Amanda Lipman points out, Cher's "strong sense of morality is purely pragmatic."[5] Sex for Cher must be rationalized and purposeful. Tai makes no such concessions to virginity and Dionne, who initially resists losing her virginity with her boyfriend, later gives in after the "emotional" experience of surviving a drive on the L.A. freeway. This leaves Cher with the tension of being inculcated into sexual practice for the rest of the film.

What happens in the second half of the film in terms of Cher's sexual development is most unusual considering the traditions of young romance. First she develops a crush on a new guy at school (Justin Walker), who is sophisticated and cool and who clearly shows an interest in her. Despite Cher's best efforts at attracting him, which include sending herself presents, she discovers that he is gay (an over-informed friend telling her he is "a disco-dancing, Oscar Wilde-reading, Streisand ticket-holding friend of Dorothy"). This revelation prevents Cher from further pursuing her awkward crush (at least her gay friend becomes a great shopping companion), but as if her romantic/sexual momentum can't be stopped, she next finds herself in the conflict of being attracted to her college-age stepbrother, Josh (Paul

Rudd). Heckerling sets up this relationship with scenes that do not alleviate its incestual implications: Josh gazes longingly at Cher when she dresses up for a party and then tells her father (his stepfather) that he's going to the party to look after her; two scenes later, Cher encourages Josh to stay around for spring break, reminding him that he's not really her brother. Then, in what turns out to be a serendipitous soul-searching shopping trip, Cher realizes that she's in love with Josh, and next finds herself trying to hide her tense feelings for him. Josh and Cher eventually break this tension when, after a session of mutual compliments, they share a passionate kiss. While such an attraction between step-siblings may be understandable, the potential problems that could arise from acting on it are diminished for the sake of preserving the romantic trajectory of the film. When Heckerling ends *Clueless* with Cher and Josh kissing again at the wedding of her teachers, after Cher has fought hard to catch the bouquet, we are left to infer that the world of sexuality has become so difficult for teens to navigate that Cher's choice of her step-brother for a boyfriend is completely rational despite its dilemmas. Literally "staying close to home" may ironically be the smartest sexual choice of all.

Kids does not make sexuality for youths appear effortless either, however, the film's one-dimensional perspective, i.e. that boys are dogs and girls are no better, denying the psychological intricacy of the issue. The main, if only, consequence of sexuality in *Kids* is the potential spread of HIV, a serious issue to be sure; but Telly's habitual practice of deflowering virgins is left on the moral surface. When Telly's friend Casper tells him, "How you gonna fuck two virgins in one day? It's gotta be against the law," Telly takes further pride in his pursuit. Unlike the morality lessons learned in other movies about youth, the dangerous lesson of *Kids*—that sex and drugs can be deadly—is never realized on-screen. The film concludes with Telly visibly infecting another girl with HIV and reciting in a voiceover, "When you're young, not much matters.. . . Sometimes when you're young, the only place to go is inside. That's just it—fucking is what I love. Take that away from me and I really got nothing." This ending may be meant as further ironic commentary on the fact that Telly is likely to die from his fucking practices, but he is never forced to confront them while we watch. As Owen Gliberman said in his review of the film, "We never get to see if the little son of a bitch has a soul after all."[6] I am not proposing that *Clueless* necessarily offers a more "realistic" perspective on teen sexuality, only that the perspective offered by *Kids* is incomplete and misogynistic when compared to *Clueless*, and that such a perspective, when presented in the "graphic" style that Clark works in, is dubious and deceptive.

Sexuality and gender are issues central to many films about young adults, but there is another potentially radical address that *Kids* and *Clueless* pose, which is their ways of handling class. There have been some youth movies over the past 20 years that played out the economic status of their characters for the sake of considering intragenerational differences of privilege (e.g. *Valley Girl* [1983], *The Breakfast Club, Say Anything* [1989]). These films usually highlighted the struggles of couples as they recognized their class differences or the class disparities within a group, and in every case the point was made that friendship or love could transcend financial status. That transcendence is not a goal of the narratives of *Kids* and *Clueless*, for these are films that plainly acknowledge the class of their characters and then proceed to reinforce the false "privilege" that their status represents: in the case of *Kids*, the characters' lack of disposable wealth can be seen to justify their lifestyles of crime and hedonism, while in *Clueless* the characters' excess of wealth rationalizes their consumption and their nonchalance.

Some mention should also be made of the differing commercial practices connected to the productions of *Kids* and *Clueless*. Clark's film is adamantly independent and low-budget, shot on location with high-speed film in predominantly natural light, and thus preserving on a technical level the meager moral conditions inhabited by its characters by metaphorizing their surrounding. Heckerling had the backing of a substantial budget from Paramount (allowing for an extensive wardrobe, expensive cars, and spectacular sets), and several companies' products are clearly displayed and used throughout the film, commenting further on the literal and figurative consumption that is intrinsic to the characters' lives and Hollywood filmmaking practice. In one particularly telling scene, we see from Cher's point of view as she walks through a room looking at teachers. Suddenly she is seized by the sight of a candy bar, naming it aloud as if its material presence and personality in the room cannot be avoided. Both films are thus produced within the class conditions that are depicted in their narratives.

Kids portrays an ambiguous group of youths in terms of their living situations—some only mention having parents while others seem to have no family at all. We become aware that Steven, whose parents own the rather swank high-rise apartment where the kids have their climactic party, is at least middle-class, while it remains unclear if most of the characters in the film are really from the poor backgrounds that they appear to be from. Telly's class status is the one most clearly articulated, and it becomes an index for his peers. When he briefly returns home in the afternoon, his family's modest apartment speaks of their working-class position: Telly's father is away at his job while his mother is home breast-feeding, and the apartment is decorated with a sparse mixture of family snapshots and newspaper photos or posters. Telly tells his mother that as he and Casper have been out looking for jobs but have been unsuccessful, he needs money; when his mother refuses, Telly sneaks into her room and steals some, which he soon afterward uses to buy drugs. Clark films this sequence in the same casual, familiar manner as the rest of the film, demonstrating that the stealing and lying these youths engage in is routine and systematic. For Telly, Casper, and the rest of the group, jobs and money are indeed irrelevant, as their lives revolve around the ongoing acquisition of drugs and alcohol, which they steal or share, and sex, which is only slightly more negotiated.

This condition of excessive consumption is nonetheless figured very differently from that which is engendered by conspicuous wealth. In *Kids,* consumption has become a means of celebrating squalor and aimlessness while preserving communal bonding. These young characters not only lack jobs, they don't have any discernable skills other than the ability to maintain consumption. In another revealing scene, after Telly and Casper buy marijuana with their stolen money, a friend demonstrates how to hollow out a blunt cigar to smoke the dope. Clark films this sequence in a how-to manner, as the character takes us through the process ("break it, scrape it, lick it, dump it, smoke it"), instructing us on a technique which demonstrates the humble sophistication of dope smoking. This yields an attitude which is again indicative of the film's ambivalence toward class: you don't need a lot of money to be a hip youngster, but you do need to know how to engage in the common customs relative to your peer group. A striking parallel is found in *Clueless,* although this film necessarily presents a considerably different class perspective since the main character comes from apparently unlimited wealth and is well-versed in the practices of conspicuous consumption. Richard Corliss succinctly claimed, indeed, that the film is simply about conspicuous consumption: "wanting, having and wearing in style. And in L.A."[7] Because that consumption is so conspicuous it is easy to perceive as being harmless, too: the shopping trips and fashion concerns of Cher and her friends are not as dangerous, we may think, as the more private sexual and drug experiences of the youths in *Kids.* Nonetheless, the characters in *Clueless* are still having sex and, in lesser quantities, indulging in drugs—potential crises which are in real life undiminished by the more visible practices of buying clothes, driving in fancy cars, and hanging out at cafés. If money seems to have the effect of diversifying teen hedonism, it really serves only as a distraction from potential problems common to all young people.

Cher, like the characters in *Kids,* is certainly not interested in employment, but this is because her father apparently provides all the money she asks for. What becomes the more crucial class question in *Clueless* is how the fortunate use their financial power to influence—or stifle—change, as Cher attempts to become altruistic in her efforts to help people around her, gaining popularity (and a boyfriend) for herself and molding Tai as an acceptable member of her clique. There is a distinct sense of irony behind Cher's attempts to "improve" the world through her good fortunes: she struggles to help others in a way that is not self-serving, and finds this most difficult. When she joins a cause like the Pismo Beach disaster relief, Heckerling further parodies her ability to actually help people by having her donate such impractical items as caviar and skis. There seems to be no escape from the vapid consumption that ensures Cher's upper-class status, and even though it makes her more popular and visible at school, her wealth is nonetheless a liability in her understanding of the world around her.

The level of teen acceptance that is sought by characters in *Kids* via sex and drugs is thus figured very differently in *Clueless*, which incorporates upper-class materialism as a means of de-emphasizing sex and drug problems and thereby shifts the notion of acceptance to a more idealized vision of self-improvement and social change. Perhaps in this sense *Kids* speaks more of the truth about the disempowerment and *ennui* of most youth, who do not enjoy upper-class lifestyles; yet where *Clueless* demonstrates Cher's strained efforts to understand and utilize her privilege, *Kids* encourages its characters to wallow in their under-privileged conditions. Again bell hooks' critique is to the point: "There is no resistance to domination in [*Kids*], merely a primitive embrace of ruling paradigms."[8] The characters in *Kids* never speak of an interest in future life goals because the film is too busy celebrating the pleasure-filled present. Even Jennie, who fears she is going to die, never has an opportunity to consider the tragedy of her life. In the end, both films demonstrate class conditions for their young characters, but both are unable to offer any meaningful alternatives to the problems class conditions pose: the rich and the poor are locked in different prisons of nescience.

Despite the wide appeal of a film like *Clueless* and the art-house interests of a film like *Kids*, both films indicate that the traditional representations of youth that were seen in American cinema over the previous 20 years may be changing considerably. The graphic aspects of *Kids* would be enough evidence of this, but I argue that there could be a deeper change, in that *Clueless* and *Kids* are the new paradigms for addressing youth issues today. On one hand, we have a seemingly innocuous comedy which highlights issues as being important to teens without exploring how paramount those issues actually are to teens themselves; and on the other we see teens engaged in a level of serious behavior that is so extreme in its representation the protagonists' lives are reduced to vulgar debauchery. *Clueless* presents the supposed "Hollywood" version of '90s youth, paying lip service to social change while remaining steadfastly concerned with self-fulfillment; *Kids* presents youth strictly in adult terms, inflaming adult viewers with its nihilistic vision of the kind of teen crisis they most fear. A split image of youth has been established.

TIMOTHY SHARY

One of the greatest dilemmas in studying youth films is the fact that teens themselves are very rarely involved with the production of films about them. (The fact that Harmony Korine was a teen when he wrote *Kids* has often been used to grant the film an exaggerated verisimilitude.) In fact, children and teens are one minority of the population who are, perhaps necessarily and understandably, blocked from controlling their representation in global media. Until young people are more widely incorporated into the media process they will have to endure the adult perspectives that are given to them. As of 1996, those perspectives make teens either harmless and self-indulgently unproductive or dangerous and destructive, and the youth movies of the past year—*Fear* (1996), *The Craft* (1996), *Mad Love* (1995), *Angus* (1995), *Empire Records* (1995)—continue that inadequate and unrealistic division. Perhaps I am being naive in thinking that less extreme representations might soon appear because, after all, cinema is about the extreme. But until or unless more inclusive and comprehensive films about youth are produced, we may remain clueless about who kids really are.

Notes

[1] David Considine, *The Cinema of Adolescence* (Jefferson NC: McFarland, 1985), 14.

[2] Amy Taubin, "Chilling and Very Hot," *Sight and Sound* (November, 1995), 17.

[3] Tom Doherty, "Clueless Kids," *Cineaste* 21:4 (1995), 16.

[4] bell hooks, "White Light," *Sight and Sound* (May, 1996), 10.

[5] Amanda Lipman, "*Clueless*," review, *Sight and Sound* (October, 1995), 46.

[6] Owen Gliberman, "Bold Before Their Time," *Entertainment Weekly* (July 21, 1995), 47.

[7] "To Live and Buy in L.A.," *Time* (July 31, 1995), 65.

[8] hooks, "Light," 11.

Confusions About Sexuality and Class in Clueless and Kids

SUSAN SHERR

Media Framing of Children-at-Risk

On April 19, 1995, the world watched in horror as rescuers removed crushed bodies of children from what remained of the bombed Alfred P. Murrah Federal building in Oklahoma City. Many adults lost their lives as a result of that crime, but it was the image of a baby carried in the arms of a rescue worker that resonated widely, and it was the children who were collectively mourned.

While the tragedy of the bombing in Oklahoma City is undeniable, there are children who suffer and die daily as a result of poor health care, mistreatment by adults and urban violence. If recent studies are any indication, up to 50% of children between the ages of 10 and 14 in the United States can be categorized as "at risk."[1] However, there is no national mobilization to solve a problem that has, and will continue to have, profound influence on society. It appears that something is working against the "natural" instinct to protect children that was in evidence during the aftermath of the Oklahoma City bombing. Part of the explanation for the disparate responses to endangered children may be located in the same media that produced moving images of the young bomb victims in Oklahoma. The framing of media stories concerning children who are at risk from social problems may be exerting influence over people's response to the plight of at-risk children.

If we conceive of children as all individuals under the age of 18, it is easy to think of many areas in which children are deemed culpable for problems in the United States. Pointing to the high incidence of teenage motherhood has become a panacea for those wanting to trim the welfare budget or mandate traditional value systems. It is argued that the moral breakdown of society is manifest in the large numbers of young people engaging in sexual activity and producing unwanted children. Feelings of injustice are rampant among employed Americans about providing tax money for these children and their still-juvenile parents. Furthermore, gang violence is repeatedly referred to in assessments of the danger in our streets. Learning through the media that children are shooting teachers and each other in the classroom or on the playground shakes the foundations of people's understanding of what is good and just. All of the above can lead individuals to view children as threatening the secure structure of American society. For a long time, the dominant ideological view of children has been that of innocent beings in need of protection,[2] but what social changes occur when people begin to believe that they need to be protected from children? What can motivate people to help those children who are at risk within society if the prevailing notion is that society is at risk from children?

First we must ask where these disparate views of children as either enemies or victims come from. There are two main alternatives for framing news stories about disadvantaged youth, (a) children as victims, and (b) children as enemies; and the degree to which one frame or the other predominates in news coverage may be influential in determining how American society is perceiving children. The former frame has the potential for fostering community involvement in the improvement of children's lives. The latter frame, however, is more likely to inspire a punitive response. Instead of promoting activation toward changing social structures that are detrimental to children's welfare, such children-as-enemy frames evoke a desire for punishing the offending parties.

Certainly, the question of why the media would focus on a framing of children as enemies must be addressed. It is hypothesized by Gitlin and others that the media serves to perpetuate the dominant ideologies formulated and enforced by society's elite institutions.[3] Gitlin's notion of framing involves the selection of certain details and events that will be reported on, to the exclusion of others. By ignoring or marginalizing certain voices, this selection serves to reinforce dominant ideologies. In order to use this construction of framing as a reference point for analyzing portrayals of children-at-risk, it is important to know what American society's dominant ideologies about children are. This enables an assessment of whether they are being represented in the media to the exclusion of other frames. What, then, is American society's hegemonic notion of the value of children, and is it now in a state of change?

Fuchs conducted an analysis using economic principles in order to establish whether Americans are underinvesting in their children, and found some indications of what he categorized as misallocated resources.[4] For example, the majority of educational expenditures in the United States go toward funding higher education, whereas in Europe, pre-school education receives a higher level of funding. With public subsidies for higher education being predominantly allocated to those with average and above average income, the greater part of funding for education is not being delivered to children who would be termed at risk.[5] Furthermore, approximately 25% of all children fail to complete high school. While Fuchs does not report whether these statistics have changed over time, they provide some indication of the priorities of American society.

The rise in the teenage suicide rate during the 1960s and 1970s is another indicator of the decrease in the well-being of children. In addition, Fuchs reports the probability of a tripling in the number of maltreatment cases reported per 10,000 children between 1976 and 1985. Although a national increase in real per-capita income occurred during the 1980s, there was also an increase in the number of children living in poverty. By the mid-1980s, twice as many children as adults were living in poverty, with the poverty rate among black children 2.5 times that of white children.[6]

Wolfe argues that the United States is neglecting children by directing the greater part of funding toward senior citizens.[7] While the poverty rate of the elderly has been steadily declining, the poverty rate for children has exceeded that of the elderly since 1974. Wolfe compares the various benefits available to poor elderly people with those for poor children and demonstrates that children receive less governmental assistance. She also denotes the disproportionate political power of the elderly, who constitute a larger segment of the population than do the parents of children; and, of course, children have no voting power, and, therefore, no political voice of their own. Conversely, the interests of the elderly are supported by the powerful lobbying organization, the AARP (American Association of Retired People).

Historically, adults were not always held responsible for their abuses of children, and particularly not for neglect that led to juvenile criminal behavior. One of the first social movements involving child welfare was the nineteenth-century "house of refuge movement."[8] Those who were part of this movement advocated removing children from abusive families and placing them in group homes. No legal action was taken against abusive parents, and Pfohl argues that the purpose of placing the children outside the home was not to aid the children themselves but to save society from future delinquents. Analogous to this is the recent proposal by United States House Speaker Newt Gingrich suggesting an increased use of orphanages. Regardless of how one views the potential efficacy of such a plan, it is reminiscent of the "house of refuge" movement. It is evidently possible to note a regression in society's treatment of abused children.

Political realities dictate that the needs of the elderly take precedence over the requirements of the young. It is also argued that people fear for their own safety from abused and neglected children, and the well-being of children is generally decreasing. In depicting certain children as dangers to the social order, the media are apparently conveying an embedded and potent social ideology.

SUSAN SHERR

Gamson et al. discuss the concept of framing as organizing principles that "hold together and [give] coherence and meaning to a diverse array of symbols."[9] Like the schema of social psychology, the frame is a way of structuring information. Essentially, sociologists conceive of framing as the selection or exclusion of certain aspects of reality to be prioritized or marginalized over others as well as the identification and labelling of certain elements of reality.[10] A news frame can function dually as both an element of the news construction and an instruction as to how the news should be cognitively processed. In order to analyze this two-sided nature of news frames, Pan and Kosicki formulated a model for frame analysis[11] that functions to "link news texts to both production and consumption processes."[12] This analysis outlines certain structural elements, used to construct a frame, that not only create the structure of the news story but provide clues to the audience as to how it should process the text.

According to Pan and Kosicki's analysis, the frame exists in both the news story and in the mind of the news consumer. Pan and Kosicki refer to Minsky's work, which uses the frame concept to explain computerized knowledge representation. In this context, the frame is "a template or data structure that both organizes various bits and pieces of information and is indicated by more concrete cognitive elements."[13] Defining the frame in this way aligns the concept closely with that of the cognitive "schema" or "script." If a schema is a cognitive system that determines how we make sense of the world and what we expect to find in it, then a news frame functions as a device for formulating our understanding of the news itself and what we expect the news to tell us.

When a news story is framed in a certain way, information is formulated so that certain specific elements of an issue are attended to more completely by the individual's cognitive resources. To serve as examples of criteria for this information, Pan and Kosicki enumerate four main framing device categories or structures. Under the heading of syntactical structure fall the headline and lead of the news story. The headline is defined as the most salient clue to how to interpret a news story, with the lead being the second most important. The news constructor uses the headline and lead to immediately convey the theme of the news story. These devices then serve as clues to news consumers to help them cognitively process the frame. In determining frames for televised news, I substituted for the headline and lead of the typical print story, the introduction and establishment of the news story by the news anchor. Generally, prior to the beginning of a story about a particular incident of juvenile crime or the broader issue of violent youth, a news anchor or host introduces the piece. The formulation of this lead can establish a frame for understanding the story.

In creating this preliminary analysis of television news frames of children-at-risk, I examined examples from ABC News (both nightly news broadcasts and news magazine shows) and CNN programming. These networks were chosen because of the availability of transcripts for them on the Lexis/Nexis database. I searched from March, 1995 through March, 1996. Some recent examples will be discussed as well.

Because there is often some effort made by journalists to examine a news story from more than one perspective, children can be depicted differently throughout a broadcast. The frame is determined by the way a story is established either by an anchor's leading comments; or by the direction the story takes with its initial audio and video text. In addition, if one framing of children clearly predominates over the other in a story, that determines the frame of the story regardless of periodic references that fit another frame. One example of the anchor's framing power can be found during a CNN news broadcast of November 12, 1995. In leading up to *Law and Disorder*, a special presentation about the emphasis on fighting juvenile crime, CNN featured several broadcasts about youth violence throughout the end of November, 1995. On November 12, Catherine Callaway conducted a discussion with law enforcement and justice department professionals about punishing juvenile criminals. Callaway began her segment by reporting that "as the overall crime rate is declining, the U.S. is reeling from a juvenile crime wave, especially violent felonies," and speculated that "maybe we've just raised a generation of kids that are just beyond help."[14] The first panelist, a superior court judge, then responded by agreeing that "we have probably done that . . . we have a generation now of kids that are so violent, so out of control, that something drastic has to happen." Regardless of what other guests thought about this issue, or what statistics would be brought up during the course of the broadcast, the story is framed by the perception of children too dangerous to exist in society and too evil to be redeemed. Immediately articulating the possibility that society is faced with a generation of children who are beyond rehabilitation, the anchor establishes the children-as-enemies frame as the one in which this dialogue will occur.

Another CNN broadcast of November 12 focused on the problems of juvenile delinquency as well as possible solutions. Once again a frame was created that demonized the offending children rather than enumerating the social conditions that produced them. Among the first guests featured was Assistant District Attorney Doris Williams-McNeely who, in a statement replete with veiled racial references, constructed a frame for understanding juvenile offenders. Williams-McNeely told CNN correspondent Brian Cabell that she "had cases where I've talked to witnesses where the juvenile bragged about what they've done. I had a case where this—when I was talking to a witness about a guy that was shot, basically had his head blown off, and the witness said this kid had made up a rap song about killing the—

blowing the man's head off."[15] In order to make her story more vivid, the Assistant District Attorney stopped in mid-sentence while reporting in a straightforward manner that the child in question sang about "killing" another person, and instead termed the act "blowing the man's head off." As in the previous example, the first voice heard in the broadcast was the one insisting that violent children are ruthless and not able to be helped or rehabilitated.

A member of the Atlanta Urban league, Ursula Haughabrok, rejoined by asserting that there is no such thing as a bad child at the age of 12 or 13 and that children require only understanding and time in order to correct their behaviors. Cabell, however, prevented any adjustment of the news frame that might have resulted from this statement by articulating the opinion of "some" that "too much understanding, too much leniency . . . is not fair to society at large." As an activist, Haughabrok attempted to reframe the issue in order to depict children as victims of neglect deserving of society's effort and time. Cabell, however, maintained the framing of the story that was established at the onset: violent children are society's enemies and deserve to be punished as such.

Both Sides With Jesse Jackson is a CNN program moderated by Jesse Jackson that features a combination of background reports and panel discussions. On December 10, 1995, Jackson hosted a program dealing with violent juvenile crime, the discussion of which was preceded by journalist Brian Todd's background report. The series of experts featured in this sequence demonstrates the imbalance in the presentation of opinion to be found in news stories of this kind, and that results in the predominance of the children-as-enemies frame. The viewer is first shown United States Attorney General Janet Reno addressing the "intolerable" rates of juvenile violence.[16] Reno is followed by a judge from Prince George's County Maryland asserting that young perpetrators of violent crime are acting out of "hedonism," with no regard for how their actions impact upon others. Following that claim, a crime victim tells the audience just how violent actions affect others by calling his experience a "life-long sentence of misery."

After the victim completes his statement, a teenager confesses to the viewer that he is aware of all the bad things he has done and wishes he could change them, but Brian Todd tells us that change is not easy in conditions that breed violence. This introduction allows the voice of victimization to be heard briefly. American University professor Jamie Raskin explains that "if you raise people in a situation without any hope, without jobs, without economic livelihood, you're going to find crime." However, the conversation is then turned to Prosecutor Kay Hanlin, and, consequently, back to the cruelty of juvenile offenders. According to Hanlin, "If someone is 11 or 12 and they're committing a murder, you know they've thought it through, they've planned it, they've intended it, it's cold-blooded, they're certainly old enough to accept the responsibility for it."

As in many of these types of reports, the dominant voices are those describing children as uncontrollable animals. In fact, one police officer on Jackson's panel refers to the children's criminal actions as "sub-human" behaviors. These types of statements are easy to comprehend, vivid, and require little background knowledge to create their desired effect. It is easier to invoke affective responses with terms such as "sub-human" and "cold-blooded" than with more victim-related terminology like "dysfunctional families" or "poor education." Similarly, sights of children being pushed into police cars or standing in court are more readily available for capturing on film, and more comprehensible once captured and aired than footage of children's victimization. Generally, it is only after a child is killed, abducted or very seriously abused that we are exposed to coherent images. So, the daily conditions of children's lives that put them at risk of becoming violent criminals do not easily lend themselves to portrayal on the nightly news.

The issue of whether children are depicted as victims or dangerous criminals in television news is complicated by the fact that children are often the ones victimized by the violent behavior of their peers. This includes not only shooting and drug selling, but sexual violence as well. ABC's news magazine *Prime Time Live* discussed the increased sexual vocabulary and sexual actions of very young children.[17] The show began with footage of children responding to filmed sexual images and their parents observing those reactions; and ultimately progressed into an analysis of children who force their peers to perform sexual acts. Most of these children are victims of abuse, but, according to journalist Diane Sawyer's report, not all are. One girl was allegedly forced to perform oral sex on a male classmate while the teacher sat at his desk reading. The boy was not punished for the crime, supposedly because the girl did not scream for help. Diane Sawyer asked the girl to show her hand to the camera to demonstrate how small she was. For the purpose of this analysis, this type of story is problematic. While the report was about a victimized child, the victimizer was himself a grade school student. Especially in a case such as this one that discusses sexual abuse, it is possible that the image of the victimizer is more powerful than that of the victim. News norms favoring novelty would support a story about a child who takes the role of sexual abuser, because while the perpetration by adults of acts of sexual abuse upon children is—unfortunately—a familiar story to viewers, the act of one child violating another in a sexual way is more likely to be considered an aberration and therefore more newsworthy.[18]

Similarly, the news features increasing numbers of very young violent offenders who hurt other children. Again, the potency of the violent image is greater than that of the victim because of its anomalous nature. Very small children are traditionally vulnerable figures, but it is shocking, and therefore more interesting, to see them as dangerous. As coverage of juvenile crime becomes more prevalent, the novelty of seeing young criminals decreases. Only by surprising the audience with younger and younger criminals can juvenile crime continue to be compelling news.

The need to convey more sensational news stories can also result in the articulation of a problem that may be far less pervasive than a news audience is led to believe. On February 2, 1996, *ABC World News Tonight* conducted an investigation of three 13-year-old boys who built a bomb in order to blow up their school. They learned how to create explosives through information acquired on the Internet. Without citing specific incidents, and in fact specifically informing viewers that there were "no national statistics" available, journalist Aaron Brown reported that teenagers were "building bombs in New York and in Vermont, in the East, in Mississippi, and in Texas, in the South; and across the West." While the news story is filled with frequent references to the culpability of the Internet in providing instructions for the creation of dangerous explosives, bomb-building teenage boys are a more tangible object of fear than an amorphous electronic network of information. Psychotherapist Steve Crimando also informs the viewers that children who build bombs are not cognizant of the destructive ramifications of their actions but instead are seeking "thrills." While this analysis is meant to suggest that children are not truly violent but are only looking for a good time, it conveys the frightening message that individuals are building bombs for fun without comprehending that they might hurt themselves and others. In fact, this conceptualization of the problem creates a colder image of children than one that understands young people to be responding angrily to some injustice they perceive in their lives.

A new term for violent children is gaining prominence in media discourse. The word "superpredators" is becoming the standard indicator of remorseless children who commit violent crimes with neither regret nor fear of retribution. According to the prepared testimony of Bobby Moody, Second Vice President of the International Association of Chiefs of Police, given before the House Economic and Educational Opportunities Committee's Early Childhood, Youth and Families Subcommittee, Princeton professor John DiIulio developed this term as part of his prediction that the United States will face a large increase in violence from the children who will become teenagers in the next ten years.[19] DiIulio is quoted as saying that these children are being raised with no supervision, love or moral guidance and probably with abuse. They have no future orientation and no goals. The children use gangs as substitutes for real family structures, and they come under pressure to use violence as a means of survival in a society which they believe offers no other opportunities.

The ABC news program *20/20* conducted an investigation into the issue of "superpredators" during their April 26, 1996 broadcast. Several excerpts from an interview with DiIulio were featured. Again, the story was presented with images of both violent children and victimized children. One scene showed correspondent Tom Jarriel wandering through a playground and projecting that the youngsters innocently playing today would be the perpetrators of an enormous crime wave of the future. The shadows of children hanging from rings resembling swollen handcuffs were shown, an image which was echoed shortly after with footage of a child being placed in actual handcuffs.

Later in the broadcast, Jarriel interviewed a boy scarred from wounds received two weeks earlier (according to the boy) from a sawed-off shotgun. The boy was asked to lift his shirt and show the camera the many injuries to his skin. Faced with the number of holes in the boy's back, the correspondent—and presumably the viewer—is surprised that he survived. What is more jarring, however, is the cavalier manner in which he discusses his ordeal. The boy appears neither traumatized nor angry about his victimization. These figures of children impervious to their violent surroundings and the ramifications of their actions are both prevalent in stories of children-at-risk and uniquely disturbing. The only reasonable response for a viewer to have toward a human being who appears to be disinterested in his or her own death, or in being made to suffer legal retribution, is fear.

The problem of juvenile crime is real, and a mobilization of society's resources will be necessary even to approach solving it. If television news coverage continues to portray the issue as sprung by a generation of ruthless predators feeding off society, fear will certainly increase. However, it is questionable whether inducement of fear will lead to formulation of solutions. As with news coverage of most issues, a broader, more contextual examination of the problem of children who are at risk—of becoming criminals and of being hurt—would do a greater service to children themselves and to the greater society in which they will grow into adults.

Notes

[1] Carnegie Council on Adolescent Development, *Great Transitions: Preparing Adolescents for a New Century* (New York: Carnegie Corporation, 1995).

[2] Joel Best, *Troubling Children* (Hawthorne, NY Walter de Gruyter, Inc., 1994).

[3] Todd Gitlin, *The Whole World is Watching* (Berkeley, CA: University of California Press, 1980).

[4] Victor R. Fuchs, "Are Americans Underinvesting in their Children?" *Society* 28:6 (1991),17-20.

[5] Fuchs, "Underinvesting," 17-18.

[6] Fuchs, "Underinvesting," 18-20.

[7] Barbara L. Wolfe, "Treating Children Fairly," *Society* 28 (1991), 23-28.

[8] S. Pfohl, "The Discovery of Child Abuse," *Social Problems* 24 (1977), 310-24.

[9] William A. Gamson, David Croteau, William Hoynes, and Theodore Sasson, "Media Images and the Social Construction of Reality," *Annual Review of Sociology* 18:385 (1992), 384.

[10] Zhongdang Pan and Gerald M. Kosicki, "Framing Analysis: An Approach to News Discourse," *Political Communication* 10 (1993), 51-64.

[11] Building on Erving Goffman, *Frame Analysis: An Essay on the Organization of Experience* (Cambridge MA: Harvard University Press, 1974).

[12] Pan and Kosicki, "Framing," 55.

[13] Pan and Kosicki, "Framing," 56.

[14] "At Issue—Juvenile Delinquency, I" CNN News, (November 12, 1995), 7:11 a.m.

[15] "At Issue—Juvenile Delinquency, III" CNN News, (November 12, 1995), 9:04 a.m.

[16] *Both Sides With Jesse Jackson*, Cable News Network (December 10, 1995).

[17] "Age of Innocents—What Children Know About Sex," *Prime Time Live*, ABC Television (May 10, 1995).

[18] Lance W. Bennet, *News: The Politics of Illusion* (New York: Longman, 1988).

[19] Bobby Moody, Prepared Testimony before the House Economic and Educational Opportunities Committee Early Childhood, Youth and Families Subcommittee (April 30, 1996).

SARAH E. TERES

Negative Gender Stereotypes in Disney Animation

A close examination of animated feature films will reveal a disturbing trend toward perpetuating negative gender stereotypes. These films provide gender definitions, gender regulations, and reflections of the gender rules of Western culture. As animated feature films are usually associated with the Walt Disney Company this study restricts itself to Disney features; but the examination of Disney films is also essential because their core audience is children. Children are mesmerized by the singing, dancing, and amusing aspects of these films, while actively internalizing underlying messages. Therefore, the effects of negative gender stereotypes will have long-term implications for society.

Jerry P. Houseman documents several experiments demonstrating the impact of underlying messages of films in his dissertation *A Study of Selected Walt Disney Screenplays and Films, and the Stereotyping of the Role of the Female*.[1] The first study examines 1500 subjects randomly sampled outside movie theaters via a nationally distributed survey. Subjects responded to surveys before and after viewing a film. The results were statistically significant with regard to subjects' attitudes being changed as a result of seeing a film: with regard to the treatment of Jewish people, Neo-Nazi groups, and women's place in society. This experiment lacked a control group, and there were no controls for intelligence, education, or socioeconomic status. However, the idea that one viewing of one film can change a person's attitude is astonishing.

A second study presented by Houseman examined 815 subjects, all college students at Pennsylvania State University. The subjects responded to a questionnaire to determine subjects' general attitudes. The subjects then watched several Disney films, afterward completing a second questionnaire to ascertain if an animated film would produce an attitudinal change. The results were statistically significant, demonstrating that an animated film could affect attitude. Animated films also have an effect on cognitive learning according to a third study, which was comprised of 3000 subjects between 8 and 16 years of age. These subjects were shown a film, and immediately tested for recall of events and characterizations presented within it. They recalled 90% of what they saw on film, and three months later their recall was still 90%. This last study does not mention repeated viewing, though it bears mentioning that children enjoy repetition, and will often view a favorite film 20 or more times consecutively.[2] Perhaps it is this constant viewing that results in substantial increments of "learning" of the material by viewers. If continual viewing ensures a recall of 90% for film subject matter, what effect does this have on additional cognitive learning processes? Does this type of "learning" lead to the internalization of stereotypes? How could behavior be affected, especially in children?

The media are problematic because children model what they see and are very influenced by vicarious rewards and punishments often experienced by animated characters.[3] Observational and cognitive learning theory, with regard to gender stereotypes, both suggest that children will develop behaviors and attitudes congruent with media stereotypes well beyond childhood. Gender stereotypes saturate the media, and though a single exposure to negative stereotypes may be ineffectual, a potential lifetime of exposures has an enormous impact.

This impact is negative for both men and women, though the effects are quite different. For men, the continual viewing of negative stereotypes influences their perception of women as helpless, mindless objects. However, the effects, both short-term and long-term, are more focused on women. Influential films may discourage women from developing positive self-esteem, from pursuing education and non-traditional careers, and from becoming self-sufficient. Such films may encourage women to be more submissive and more insecure about their abilities, thus remaining invisible. Margaret Matlin, in her book *The Psychology of Women*, discusses these long-term effects and describes how they are often reflected in society. Men are generally more "valued" than women and more visible; and their careers tend to be more prestigious.[4]

Assuming the possibility of powerful long-term effects for women's self-esteem of negative gender stereotypes in feature animation film in general, it seems reasonable to expect that a close study of the work of Walt Disney Studios would reveal: (a) a majority of male central characters; (b) a reiteration of marriage as a central thematic goal, especially for females; (c) the portrayal of female characters as submissive compared with males; (d) a central figuration of self-sacrifice, especially of female characters; (e) a tendency for female disobedience to be disastrous in its consequence, compared with the male version; and (f) a tendency for males, not females, to possess power.

With an eye for these patterns, I viewed thirty Disney films (in English): *Snow White* (1937), *Fantasia* (1940), *Pinocchio* (1940), *Dumbo* (1941), *Bambi* (1942), *Cinderella* (1950), *Alice in Wonderland* (1951), *Peter Pan* (1953), *Lady and the Tramp* (1955), *Sleeping Beauty* (1959), *101 Dalmatians* (1961), *The Sword and the Stone* (1963), *Mary Poppins* (1964), *The Aristocats* (1964), *The Jungle Book* (1967), *Robin Hood* (1973), *The Rescuers* (1977), *The Great Mouse Detective* (1986), *Who Framed Roger Rabbit?* (1988), *The Little Mermaid* (1989), *Ducktails The Movie: Treasure of the Lost Lamp* (1990), *The Rescuers Down Under* (1990), *Beauty and the Beast* (1991), *Aladdin* (1992), *The Return of Jafar* (1993), *The Nightmare Before Christmas* (1993), *The Lion King* (1994), *Toy Story* (1995), *Pocahontas* (1995), and *The Hunchback of Notre Dame* (1996).

I examined main characters (only), those with dialogue in more than five scenes of the film, on the basis of their interaction with other characters; the personality characteristics displayed by each character; the type of dialogue used by each character; the activities of each character; and the end result for each character in the plot.

Negative gender stereotypes are perpetuated by Disney films. This conclusion is disturbing because at a time when children are developing self-esteem, and formulating ideas about future goals, they are subjected to Disney films. As previously mentioned, children enjoy repetition, and watching these films on a continuous basis affects their ideas about gender roles. Disney films often have strong central characters, all of whom may be influencing the attitudes of children on a long-term basis as they grow into adulthood. More male characters are presented in these films than females, subjecting young children to the idea that women are invisible; that they are unimportant, secondary, and merely serve a decorative purpose. For males, this encourages treating females as inferior, but for females this exposure encourages disappearance as a response.

In other words, girls learn to shrink away from commanding attention. This may be why beginning as elementary students, boys garner more attention than girls, and are more outspoken, a trend that may develop as early as three years prior to attending school—depending on exposure to animated films—and continue throughout an individual's education. If young girls have internalized the idea of invisibility by three or four years of age, school may exacerbate their sense of insignificance. If the idea of invisibility is internalized at such a young age, does it reappear in adolescence as anorexics attempt to (literally) disappear? It would be interesting to conduct longitudinal research to discover how female invisibility in Disney films affects body image for women.

The body images presented for young female characters in Disney films, difficult, perhaps, to animate on celluloid, are impossible to achieve for human beings.

The use of the "Kewpie-Doll Syndrome"—Konrad Lorenz's theory that all infants possess large foreheads, large eyes, tiny noses, and soft roundish features—for (young) female main characters is extensive. "Kewpie-Doll" characteristics make infants appear more lovable and elicit increased positive attention from care givers.[5] The young, female Disney characters are drawn with "Kewpie-Doll" characteristics, while simultaneously possessing large breasts, small waists, straight hips, and tiny feet. The style in which these characters are drawn seems to suggest that only females who look like infants are attractive. However, in the films these characteristics elicit attention and care from male peers, not parents.

It appears that "Kewpie-Doll" characteristics are also a necessary aid to women for reaching the "ultimate" goal: marriage. Though 31% of the male characters also desired marriage, it was often not a primary goal but a necessary means to an end. For example, Beast must win the heart of Beauty by his twenty-first birthday to save his life, and to become human. Prince Erik must marry the Little Mermaid to inherit his kingdom, and to retain the love and trust of his country. The Prince must marry Cinderella to inherit his kingdom, and to appease his angry father who is anxious for another heir to the throne. For young female characters the goal of marriage is itself a driving force, often facilitating escape from a bad home environment. Whether because "Some day their prince will come," as in *Snow White*; or because, as for *Cinderella*, "A dream is a wish your heart makes," young maidens busy themselves throughout their day, dreaming of a man who will sweep them off their feet and marry them. Often these young maidens fall in love at first sight and, in the cases of Snow White and Sleeping Beauty, are literally saved from death by a kiss from a stranger they marry immediately after waking from a disempowering coma. This device encourages the idea that in order to be complete as a woman, one must be married. However, many characters must enlist the assistance of a Fairy Godmother, or some other magical creature, to become attractive enough to marry. For example, Cinderella requires the aid of her Fairy Godmother to make her into a marriageable maiden. Sleeping Beauty's life is saved by her Fairy Godmothers, Flora, Fauna, and Meriwhether, though her life is spared only so that she may eventually marry the prince she was betrothed to at birth. The Little Mermaid sells her voice to the Sea Witch, and uses her father's soul as collateral, so that she can take human form and attract the young Danish Prince Erik. And Pocahontas asks a magical tree to help her see her future love.

Thus no matter how beautiful you may be, no matter what your talents are, it is apparently still not enough. This message may be internalized by young girls to mean that they are never going to be good enough at anything they do, let alone find a husband, because even princesses must have preternatural help. Impoverished with invisibility, a young girl's self-esteem will invariably be weak. She has seen that

Negative Gender Stereotypes in Disney Animation

she must not only find a husband but also be invisible enough to be attractive, though at the same time she will need supernatural powers to be worthy of a man. She must marry the man she secretly wants to be. It is the only choice afforded to her if she is to maintain the gender stereotype presented through animated heroines. To become a full-fledged woman in the social world presented in Disney films, you must be a wife. Unmarried women invariably become villainesses/sorceresses/wicked witches. They are portrayed as power-hungry, self-centered career women who are ultimately destroyed by their own vanity.

Susan J. Douglas discusses these ideas in her book *Where the Girls Are: Growing Up Female with the Mass Media*, mentioning that Disney films send the message that to be a successful woman you must "be dumb, keep your mouth shut, and learn to make Spam and Velveeta croquettes. To have it all you must be a martyr."[6] Vanity is equated with evil, and the only solution for evil is death. For example, the Evil Queen in *Snow White*, Ursula the Sea Witch in *The Little Mermaid*, and Malevecent the Wicked Fairy in *Sleeping Beauty* all meet their demise by the film's end. For young females, the only behaviors rewarded in Disney films are submissiveness and self-sacrifice.

Though I found 17% of male characters submissive, and 27% self-sacrificing, the males coded as submissive were infants or preadolescent. In the case of Dumbo, Bambi, and Young King Arthur in *The Sword and the Stone*, their submissive behavior is generally seen as negative and transformed into power by the finale of the film. The males coded as self-sacrificing are generally attempting to rescue a female in distress, prove their true love for a female, or, as older males, trying to save a child. For example, Aladdin is self-sacrificing in order to rescue Jasmine, the Beast to prove his love to Beauty, and Mufasa the Lion King to rescue his cub Simba.

The females coded as neither self-sacrificing nor submissive are young or preadolescent, and are generally punished for their behavior, then later redeemed as they become submissive and/or self-sacrificing. For example, the Little Mermaid is a strong, independent young woman who must sacrifice herself to reverse the punishment of seeing her father lose his soul. Jasmine must become submissive and sacrifice herself to save her father and Aladdin from the evil Jafar she refused to marry in *Aladdin*. Nala, the young lioness in *The Lion King*, must become submissive to Scar in order to protect her mother and aunts, ;and Sally in *The Nightmare Before Christmas* must sacrifice herself to save the Pumpkin King and the Land of Halloween. Pocahontas must become submissive to save her family and friends after disobeying her father's orders to ignore John Smith. The idea that women must be submissive and self-sacrificing is continuously demonstrated in Disney films. Young girls learn vicariously that submissive and self-sacrificing behavior is rewarded and assertive, self-preserving behavior is punished. Often female characters who are not submissive and self-sacrificing lose their families and homes in Disney films, and are outcasts. What little girl would be assertive and self-preserving if that behavior resulted in never seeing family or friends again? The message is clear for young girls: behave and be loved.

The idea of *behave and be loved* is also an element within the hypothesis *disobedience leads to disaster*. For female characters, disobedience does lead to disaster, and the authority disobeyed is usually a father, or father-figure. The Little Mermaid, Jasmine, and Sally all suffer fierce punishment for their disobedience. For these females, the attempt at independence wreaks havoc for everyone around them, and the only way for them to right their wrongdoing is to acquiesce, or become submissive and self-sacrificing. For the male character, disobedience leads to adventure, and a disaster from which he emerges a powerful hero. For example, Mowgli in *The Jungle Book* disobeys and becomes a man; Aladdin is able to marry Jasmine, and becomes second in line to the Sultan; a young Simba disobeys the authority of his uncle Scar and becomes the Lion King. The message here is clear: males should be encouraged to disobey and assert their independence, for this is the only way they may fulfill their destinies as men and inherit the power rightfully owed them. For females, the signal is that any attempt to assert independence, achieve a non-matrimonial goal, or separate from a father or father-figure will lead to destruction. But if females are not taught to develop an independent voice, no one will ever hear them scream.

Female characters in Disney films are forced to remain powerless, too. Only 26% are powerful, and with the exception of two (Fairy Godmother and Mary Poppins) these female characters are villainesses. The messages presented to young girls through Disney films ultimately lead to the underlying theme that women are neither deserving of, nor entitled to, power. Women in power are presented as cruel, corrupted, incompetent, and destructive. Yet power is presented as the ultimate goal for males. Young girls are shown images of how wonderful power and strength can be, though they are told they may never possess them. They cannot be trusted with, are not worthy of, power.

There are many researchers who have examined this issue of women and power, generally focused on Myths of Matriarchy. *Women's Realities, Women's Choices* as well as Bram Dijkstra's book, *Idols of Perversity: Fantasies of Feminine Evil in Fin-de-siècle culture* highlight that all cultures have myths of matriarchy.[7] Many cultures have myths for a time when women had power greater than, or at least equal to, that of men. These myths are focused on explanations for why women no longer have power, highlighting the moments women were relieved of their power. Myths in western

Negative Gender Stereotypes in Disney Animation

culture such as "Adam and Eve"; and the creation myths of many non-western cultures such as the Yanomamo of Brazil, the Maya of Mexico, and the !Kung of South Africa; all describe women as having lost power because they were ruthless, or too easily tempted to maintain power; that, in short, women are weak leaders, and must be prevented from attaining power. Power has long been the domain of men, and in essence, all negative gender stereotypes presented in Disney films ultimately lead to preventing females from attaining power, and to discouraging females from wanting to attain it.

This perpetuation of negative gender stereotypes through Disney films has been shown to have long-term negative consequences for children. What is now more discouraging is that technological innovations have enabled new generations of children to view old but refurbished Disney films, as well as other animated films and cartoons, on demand and in unlimited quantities. A study by Aimee Dorr and Dale Kunkel provides figures for the percentages of families in the United States with access to new media technology. As of 1988, "over 90% of families own a VCR, 80% have cable television, and 3% have a satellite dish."[8] Many children will now have access to more negative gender stereotypes than any other generation. These facts simply highlight the idea that negative stereotypes will be perpetuated in the future unless parents and educators take the long-term implications seriously.

On an encouraging note, the most recent Disney films may be the beginning of a new era in animated film aimed at changing the perpetuation of negative gender stereotypes. It is difficult to ascertain whether the change is due to a greater percentage of women now employed at Disney than in the past, or an actual concerted effort on the part of Disney to gradually eliminate negative gender stereotypes from their films.

The 1995 film *Toy Story* did uphold the traditional preponderance of male characters over female ones, though two new elements in the depiction of females were added in this film. First, the authority figure in the world of the young boy Andy was his mother. Disney films have often been criticized for their lack of maternal figures, though in *Toy Story*, it is the father figure who is absent. The second element is the presence of Bo Peep. Though the only female toy, Bo Peep is not ineffectual, and is a trusted and important toy member of "Andy's Room." In fact, Bo Peep is instrumental in negotiating Woody's forgiveness after a debacle with Buzz Lightyear. The film's final credits also indicate that numerous women contributed to *Toy Story*, an influence which may have made *Toy Story*'s tale more equitable.

The 1996 release, *The Hunchback of Notre Dame* also maintains a higher percentage of male characters; however, it introduces Esmeralda, a character who shatters the mold of Disney female stereotypes. Although Esmeralda is depicted as beautiful, and does maintain a semblance of the unrelenting physical standards set by most Disney heroines, she is drawn with womanly proportions and womanly features quite different from the "Kewpies" seen in other films—unexaggerated forehead, eyes, and mouth; small nose. The character of Esmeralda remains independent and strong throughout the film.

Toy Story and *The Hunchback of Notre Dame* present positive images for males and females, as well as positive story lines to bolster young children's self-esteem. Perhaps they are the cornerstone for new images to be expected from Disney, ones which can eliminate negative gender stereotypes from animated films, and encourage children to recognize their own power and self-worth. Perhaps, children's recognition will begin in pre-school, and in the words of Buzz Lightyear, continue "to infinity and beyond!"

Notes

[1] Stockton CA: University of the Pacific, 1993.

[2] Houseman, *Study*.

[3] Teresa L. Thompson and Eugenia Zerbinos, "Gender Roles in Animated Cartoons: Has the Picture Changed in 20 Years?," *Sex Roles* 32: 9/10 (1995), 651-673.

[4] Margaret W. Matlin, *The Psychology of Women*, 2nd ed., (Fort Worth TX: Harcourt Brace Jovanovich College Publishers, 1993).

[5] David R. Shaffer, *Social and Personality Development* (Pacific Grove, CA: Brooks/Cole Publishing Company, 1994), 150.

[6] (New York: Random House, 1995), 27.

[7] Hunter College Women's Studies Collective, *Women's Realities, Women's Choices: An Introduction to Women's Studies*, 2nd ed. (New York: Oxford University Press, 1995); and Bram Dijkstra, *Idols of Perversity: Fantasies of Feminine Evil in Fin-de-siècle Culture* (New York: Oxford University Press, 1988).

[8] Aimee Dorr and Dale Kunkel, "Children and the Media Environment: Change and Constancy Amid Change," *Communication Research* 17:1 (1990), 21.

RAÚL TOVARES

Under Construction: The Mexican American Youth Gang Story and Local Television News

The image created by the news media of Mexican American[1] youth as members of criminal gangs is to a large extent false. Many local television news stories contribute to the maintenance of this stereotypical view of Mexican American teenagers and young adults by packaging information that depicts this group as pathologically violent, addicted to controlled substances and beyond the control of legitimate authorities.

In contrast to such images, several researchers report that most gang members are not prone to violence,[2] that recreational drug use in the Mexican American youth gang is as common as that among the young, urban poor in general,[3] and that gang members demonstrate a high degree of conformity to social rules and regulations.[4] These discrepancies between local television news stories about Mexican American youth gangs and the findings of several researchers call for a closer look at the process by which these stories are constructed.

Approaches to the study of news production can generally be assigned to three broad categories: political-economical, sociological, and cultural.[5] The political–economical perspective of newsmaking, based on the Marxist philosophy of production, posits that the owners of capital maintain a system of production that facilitates and promotes their ideas and values, in turn facilitating and promoting their rule.

Some writers dismiss the Mexican American gangs of East Los Angeles in the 1940s as power-oriented fabrications of the police and the press. McWilliams[6] notes how only days after the Japanese had been removed from Los Angeles, newspapers in that city began to give prominence to "Mexican" crime and "Mexican" juvenile delinquency. Relatively minor incidents involving Mexican teenagers and young adults were played up by the newspapers and the police in the spring of 1942, "to build up, within a short period of six months, sufficient anti-Mexican sentiment to prepare the community for a full–scale offensive against the Mexican minority."

Writing about the early part of 1942, when the Los Angeles Police Department and the Los Angeles press were focusing on and dramatizing delinquency in Mexican neighborhoods, Gonzales notes:

> This period can be seen as the time during which the 'gang' image was developed and 'marketed.' During this time the Los Angeles community was being informed as to the extent and nature of these 'gangs.' Thus, the 'gangs' were *created* and *defined*.[7]

The political economic critique of news production has been criticized primarily because it assumes a linear model of communication, in which "someone" does "something" to "someone else." Up until the 1950s the more simplistic models of this type proposed that a sender of messages could in fact change and control the receivers of messages. The model explained the effects of propaganda on the public. While it is true that more modern versions of this model acknowledge the influence of different persons, institutions and social organizations on the process of news production, at their core remains the belief that a small elite controls the creation of messages that are distributed to the masses.

The sociological approach privileges the organizational system that has been developed to manage the demands placed on newsworkers.[8] One of these demands is the production of news stories on a daily basis. According to this model of news production, the newsworker is said to suppress his or her values, beliefs, and standards in order to produce reports within the constraints imposed by the need to deliver stories day-in and day-out.

The "beat system" and other routines of production are designed to facilitate the processing of information into news stories in a timely manner. This system is tied to the need, in a capitalist system at least, for the news media to earn a profit. Routines of production lower the cost of gathering and processing information into news stories but also serve to socialize reporters to the values and beliefs of the sources they depend on for story material. One problem with the sociological perspective of news production is that it cannot account for a more aggressive stance that is sometimes assumed by newsworkers. Culver[9] cites the case of Madison, Wisconsin, where reporters were at odds with the police department over the issue of whether or not there was a gang problem in that city. The police were reluctant to admit that there was a gang problem while the news media accused the chief of police and his staff of covering it up.

Cultural models seek the explanation for news production in the symbols found in the culture in which news is produced. Cultural symbols are said to provide the ideology through which the material for news is filtered as it is developed as a story. In order to explain how news stories are constructed one must consider the culture that surrounds the newsmaking enterprise.[10] The assumption here is that news stories do not rest on facts that can be uncovered but instead exist only as part of the context in which they are reported. As Roeh states, stories related as news "are, to put it bluntly, no less narratives than are stories of the imagination of desire, which refer to the wishful or the fantastic."[11]

In her analysis of the gang phenomenon in Phoenix, Arizona, Zatz concluded that "it was the social imagery of Chicano youth gangs, rather than their actual behavior, that lay at the root of the gang problem in Phoenix."[12] Zatz points out that gangs and gang-related crimes were a reality. However, contrary to their vigorous and organized reaction to gang-related crime, the police did not organize special units to deal with regular street crime, corporate crime and other types of illegal activity. She notes in her study of court referrals in Tucson, Arizona, that those Chicanos believed to be members of gangs were mostly guilty of having been involved in "minor squabbles." Only one referral out of 518 "gang boys" was for a non–fighting violent crime. Zatz explains that the imagery of gangs as "violent" converged with the imagery of Mexicans as "different" to facilitate the police and media promotion of a "moral panic" about gangs. Identifying Mexican American youths as responsible for community disorder paved the way for an increase in the number of social control agents in the *barrio*.[13]

Not clear in Zatz' study is the exact role ethnicity played in the creation of the moral panic about Mexican American youth gangs in Phoenix and Tucson. Moral panics related to youth gangs have been created in societies much more homogeneous than many of the communities in the U.S. that are currently said to be experiencing gang problems. In many cases social class differences, rather than ethnic differences, seem to serve as a basis for the creation of a moral panic about youth gangs.[14] This should not be interpreted as a denial that ethnicity plays a role in the youth gang discourse, but rather as recognition that the role of ethnicity in this social phenomenon, and how it interacts with other factors—such as social class, proportion of the ethnic population, immigration patterns, and quality and quantity of media coverage—are far from universal.

After interviewing and observing newsworkers at three television news departments in Austin, Texas and discussing the Mexican American youth gang phenomenon with police officers, social service providers and community leaders, I found that the police do have significant influence on the construction of the youth gang story. However, newsworkers and community leaders can also exert some influence.

RAÚL TOVARES

Overall, a cultural model of news production best explains the complexities of production of the Mexican American youth gang story.

First, the police can influence the production of youth gang stories by making information available to reporters. A reporter assigned specifically to the "police beat" begins each day with a trip to the police or sheriff's office of public information and the courts. At these locations a reporter can look through records of all the arrests that have taken place in the last twenty-four hours or the trials that are currently being held. Finding gang stories often takes a bit more work, however, because the word "gang" will often not appear in official police reports. Reporting a story as a gang story requires that the arresting officer or public information officer tell the reporter explicitly that the person arrested is a known gang member or is believed to be a member of a gang.

Another way that the police can contribute to the construction of the gang story is through organized events sponsored by the police department. In the late 1980s, after consulting with the Los Angeles Police Department, the Austin Police Department began to offer the youths in East Austin—believed to be a haven for gangs—an opportunity to play organized baseball. Youths who admitted they were members of a gang were accepted into the program, in a move described by Ken Williams, Deputy Chief of the Austin Police Department:

> We provided an incentive for those kids to join a gang, because if they joined a gang they could play baseball all summer – we supplied uniforms, balls, bats, a place to play, coaches, and we did it, and so we legitimized the gangs.[15]

One of the consequences of these baseball games was that politicians, community leaders and police officers saw opportunities to further their personal careers and programs. Politicians would show up at the games to have their pictures taken with the kids they claimed they were helping stay out of gangs. Many police officers and community leaders joined the "cause," granting interviews, supplying sound bites and setting up photo opportunities.

> Every time we had one [a baseball game] all the radio, TV, local media . . . was there.. . . And about the time we realized what happened we were also getting word from L.A., "Hey guys you got to quit this. This is creating a monster."[16]

Newsworkers also got caught up in the gang hysteria that swept the country after the release of the film *Colors* (1988):

All of a sudden they [adolescents] see this movie [*Colors*] and this whole thing of gangs and banding together and doing all these great, crazy things and they started doing it. Well the media started picking it up, because about that time you had this wave of information coming out of California saying that we had a huge gang problem. Well the media here locally says, "How big of a gang problem do we have in Austin?" see? Gee's not much. "Well, how much is not much?" And so they kept pushing. And then we found that, inadvertently, and certainly being well intentioned, the media legitimized the gangs in Austin by naming them.[17]

Here is an example where the police initially did not want to acknowledge a gang problem. This is similar to the case reported by Culver.[18] The news media, according to Deputy Chief Williams, took the initiative and decided to "expose" the gang problem in Austin.[19] It should also be noted that several police officers referred to *Colors* and *The Warriors* (1979) as sources of information about gangs that had greatly influenced local youths.

Most significant for the production of the Mexican American youth gang story is how reporters and their sources work together. One reporter produced a three-part series on a gang prevention program known as PURGE (Parents United to Repress Gang Evolvement). The series explored the positive impact that a gang suppression program was having on youths in the community. This reporter explained that, while making his usual rounds, he had received a tip about the program from an employee at the police department. He then went to the Juvenile Justice probation officer who was in charge of the program. The reporter was told that because he had given the probation office fair treatment in the past he could be "trusted" to produce a three–part series on the PURGE program. The officer agreed to give the reporter access to the training camp where PURGE participants engaged in outdoor activities—similar to basic army training—designed to build their self-confidence and self-esteem. Of utmost importance is how a reporter's relationship with a police employee led to a tip about the PURGE program. Also, the probation officer in charge of the program first had to feel that the reporter *could be trusted* before allowing him access to information about PURGE. This is an example of how a reporter is socialized into the process of cultivating sources who can supply information for stories.

Still another influence on the construction of the youth gang story is the community leader. Opinions varied among Mexican American leaders in Austin about how to conceive and approach the gang problem. But the evidence suggests that reporters gave preference to community leaders who accepted the assumption of a growing gang problem. Some community leaders soon learned how to use the *threat of gang expansion* theme to gain access to the news media and promote community projects.

One example of the strategy of attracting media attention by playing up the gang expansion theme was provided by Victor Aquino, president of the Southeast Corner Alliance of Neighborhoods (SCAN). He stated that in 1993 there was a shooting near his home in the Dove Springs neighborhood of Austin. The shooting was the result of an argument between an adult Mexican national and three African-American teenagers.

> The media portrayed it as a gang-related shooting but it never was. But we said fine, let's leave it alone, because we knew there was . . . a lot more problems, and gang-related problems, that we needed to address . . . we didn't know if these three kids were involved in a gang or not.[20]

The reason for not challenging the media's interpretation of that shooting as "gang-related" was that the neighborhood had been trying to get the attention of city leaders in order to secure funding for a host of services that it lacked, including a community swimming pool for the children.

> We said . . . let's use this to go to the city, to go to the police department, to say, "Look, these are the things that are happening out here." . . . We were trying to bring a community back that had . . . no services, no clinics, no recreation facilities, nothing, you know? . . . We used it as a tool to get some of the things that we've been getting in our community . . . the media made it seem like a gang-related shooting. We said, OK.[21]

A few years later the neighborhood had its pool and Aquino received an award for his efforts to rid the neighborhood of gangs and drugs. SCAN was held up as a model of how citizens can work together to bring a neighborhood back from near ruin by youth gangs.

However, there was another faction in East Austin that appears to have been ignored by the media. This faction resisted the notion that their neighborhoods were on the verge of being taken over by gangs. Gavino Fernandez, a community leader from East Austin associated with *El Concilio*, was highly critical of those members of the Mexican American community who were willing to play up the fear of gangs.

It's a falsification of reality . . . It's political. If the media is buying into it, hey, they'll [some community leaders] play to it. Here you have the media show up and they'll exploit the kids. They'll say, "All these teens these are wannabe's.. . . Had they not been in this program they'd probably be gang members right now." So the media goes out and they highlight the program.[22]

Fernandez went on to note how the actions of individuals were often associated with their "gang":

I don't see Latin Kings [doing a drive-by shooting], it may be some person that went and happened to know that this person was there at a party, an individual, but it's tied in to Latin Kings. For example, I might go . . . and rob a bank as an individual. "Oh, he's with the Concilio. It's the Concilio that went and robbed the bank." The Concilio had nothing to do with it. I was acting on my own as an individual. But see we don't get that kind of a possibility, it's got to be "gang-related."[23]

Although comments such as these would certainly add depth to the portrayal of Mexican American youths who are said to be involved in gangs, they were rarely, if ever, given air-time. One Mexican American reporter referred to the members of *El Concilio*, the organization that Fernandez heads, as persons who "bitch about things." The reporter went on to say that they resort to name calling ("racist, racial bias, bigots") instead of dealing with the issue of negative portrayals "in an educated way, like the Chamber (Hispanic Chamber of Commerce) wanted to do."

The data presented above demonstrate how the construction of the youth gang story for local television news is the result of the interaction of several players. Three of these, newsworkers, the police, and community leaders, regularly interrelate and at times promote the youth gang theme. At other times they may attempt to play it down. But they do not operate in a vacuum. Demographic, economic, political and historical variables can also influence the production of the Mexican American youth gang story. Much research in this area still needs to be done.

That the police exercise great influence over the construction of the Mexican American youth gang story should not be interpreted to mean that they can "create" gangs. Political-economic models of news production cannot adequately explain the construction of the Mexican American youth gang story. Groups of teenagers and young adults do congregate for camaraderie and support—the same reasons most people come together. Some of these individuals do engage in illegal, even violent, behaviors. Associating the behaviors of some individuals with the group, however, is an unfair process because it assigns guilt to those who were merely present near, or acquainted with, the individual or individuals involved in illegal behaviors. Such guilt-by-association leads to a distortion of the public image of minority teenagers.

The role of newsworkers is also influenced by several factors. The dependence on reliable sources for information, that reduces the cost of producing news stories, demands a relationship that has been built up over a period of time; and such a relationship involves benefits not only for the reporter who must deliver stories but for the source, who is seeking publicity. Many times the routines of production lead to exaggeration and reinforcement of stereotypical views of Mexican American youths as members of gangs. And reporters often search more aggressively for information about gangs than some sociological models of news production would lead us to expect.

Important also is how some community leaders are willing to promote a gang problem in exchange for access to city political leaders and bureaucrats. The gang theme can serve as a bargaining chip when negotiating with city leaders for goods and services. Again, a fear that can be best explained by cultural factors seems to motivate municipal leaders to provide some services in order to apparently stem the tide of a growing gang problem. These cultural factors are related to the fear of strangers, especially people of color. Recreational activities, education and social services have a long association with a belief that they will serve to assimilate participants to a White, middle-class lifestyle and accompanying values.

Closely tied to these fears is the mention of films like *Colors* and *The Warriors*. Popular forms of entertainment can be an excellent source for studying the attitudes and fears of the generation that produced and supported them.[24] The concern about lower-class youths, especially minority lower-class youths, controlling streets and neighborhoods, distributing or using drugs and engaging in violent behavior, is expressed in the two films mentioned. But the youth gang phenomenon was not created by Hollywood films, although they may have provided a focus for concerns people had about youth gangs. That focus makes a different impact on newsworkers, police officers, community leaders, and young Mexican Americans. The result is news stories—and consequently a perception of reality—built from hopes, dreams, fears and apprehensions.

It seems that local television news is incapable of presenting the Mexican American youth gang accurately. At best we can understand how these stories come to have the form and content that they do. By examining the underlying structure that supports such distorted views of Mexican American youths, the community may be able to organize and challenge its stereotypes. At the same time community members and students of media alike can learn that only through the long and tedious task of changing other aspects of culture can we change the news stories that culture produces.

Notes

[1] In this paper the terms "Mexican American," and "Chicano" are used interchangeably.

[2] Elizabeth T. Buhmann, *The 1992 Texas Attorney General's Gang Report* (Austin: Office of the Attorney General, Research and Policy Management Division, 1992), 3.

[3] Joan W. Moore and James Diego Vigil, "Chicano Gangs: Group Norms and Individual Factors Related to Adult Criminality," *Aztlan* 18 (1989), 27–44.

[4] James Diego Vigil, *Barrio Gangs* (Austin: University of Texas Press, 1988).

[5] Michael Schudson, "The sociology of news production," *Media, Culture and Society* 11(1989), 236–282.

[6] Carey McWilliams, *North From Mexico* (New York: Greenwood Press, 1990), 206.

[7] Alfredo Guerra Gonzales, *Mexican/Chicano Gangs in Los Angeles: A Sociohistorical Case Study*, unpublished dissertation, University of California at Berkeley, School of Social Welfare (1981), 136.

[8] Gaye Tuchman, *Making News: A Study in the Construction of Reality* (New York: The Free Press, 1978); Edward Jay Epstein, *News From Nowhere* (New York: Random House, 1973); Herbert J. Gans, *Deciding What's News* (New York: Vintage Books, 1980); Mark Fishman, *Manufacturing the News* (Austin: University of Texas Press, 1980).

[9] Kathleen B. Culver, "Feeding the Frenzy: Reporting on Gangs in a Midsize Midwestern City," Paper presented at the Association for Education in Journalism and Mass Communication Conference (1994), 32.

[10] Itzhak Roeh, "Journalism as Storytelling, Coverage as Narrative," *American Behavioral Scientist*, 33:2 (November/December 1989), 162–168.

[11] Roeh, "Journalism," 164–165.

[12] Marjorie S. Zatz, "Chicano Youth Gangs and Crime: The Creation of a Moral Panic." *Contemporary Crises* 11(1987), 129–159.

[13] As it is used here this word can be translated as "neighborhood."

[14] See Geoffrey Pearson, *Hooligan: A History of Respectable Fears* (London: Macmillan Press, 1983) for a study of "hooliganism" in Great Britain; and, as well, Stanley Cohen, *Folk Devils and Moral Panics: The Creation of the Mods and Rockers* (London: MacGibbon and Kee, 1972) and Dick Hebdige, *Subculture: The Meaning of Style* (New York: Routledge, 1991).

[15] Ken Williams, Deputy Chief of Austin Police Department, personal interview (July 25, 1994).

[16] Williams, interview.

[17] Williams, interview.

[18] Culver, "Feeding."

[19] Williams, interview.

[20] Victor Aquino, President of the Southeast Corner Alliance of Neighborhoods (SCAN), personal interview (June 7, 1994).

[21] Aquino interview.

[22] Gavino Fernandez, Coordinator, El Concilio, personal interview (November 1, 1994).

[23] Fernandez interview.

[24] John E. O'Connor and Martin A. Jackson, eds., *American History/American Film: Interpreting the Hollywood Image* (New York: Frederick Ungar, 1980), xviii–xix.

LAUREN R. TUCKER

Calvin Klein Jeans Advertising: Kiddie Porn or Media Ado About Nothing?

Since 1980, Calvin Klein's advertising for jeans, fragrances and underwear has pointedly challenged American attitudes[1] toward youthful sexuality.[2] Following the landmark *Nothing comes between me and my Calvins* campaign, advertisements for Klein's fragrance Obsession resonated with images of the sexual decadence and financial greed reflective of the lifestyles of the 1980s. During the early 1990s, supermodel Kate Moss and rapper Marky Mark, both featured with a minimum of a clothing and a maximum of suggestion, imbued Klein's advertising with the youthful sexuality that has become his trademark. The introduction of *cK one*, one of the largest fragrance debuts in history, included an advertising campaign featuring a multicultural mix of young, urban men and women who appeared to be as comfortable exploring same-sex as heterosexual relations. However, in August 1995, Klein launched a $6 million television and print campaign for *CK* jeans that so challenged the Puritan roots of American beliefs about youthful sexuality and self-determination that critics within advertising and the mainstream press alike accused Klein of promoting "kiddie porn" along with his jeans. This study offers a political critique of the kiddie porn frame, a media frame that obscures the problematic status of youthful sexuality and economic influence in the United States.

Klein's August 1995 jeans campaign (hereafter referred to as the August campaign) rejected the stylized mix of wealth, power and sexual seduction that characterizes his earlier efforts and the current campaigns of his contemporaries. Instead, the August campaign's low-key, low-budget look underscored the sexual vulnerability that was, ironically, quite determinedly asserted by the pouts and poses of the models. Directed toward a primary target of older teens and young adults, print advertisements were placed in upscale, adult-oriented magazines like *Variety* and trendy youth magazines such as *YM*. The television campaign was limited to large metropolitan markets, including New York and Chicago, and Music Television (MTV). The campaign featured young models, male and female, who were ostensibly auditioning for a photographer/director in what some called a "cheap wood-panelled" room. The models, who Klein and his advertising agency executives insisted were all over the age of 18, were scantily clad in a variety of denim fashions—vests, skirts and jeans. The television campaign featured a gravelly, male, off-camera voice asking models intensely personal, provocative questions concerning how they felt about their bodies and what would they like to do with their bodies in front of the camera.

Due to limited media acceptance and placement of the August campaign, most Americans did not see the ads until they were contextualized by the news media discourse as child pornography. While early criticism of the campaign was limited to the industry press and the activities of the American Family Association (AFA), a conservative political action group headed by long-time family values watchdog Donald Wildmon, mainstream media coverage of the nascent controversy brought the campaign into the national spotlight. The *New York Times, Newsweek, Time* and NBC's *Dateline* are just a few of the sites that offered audiences their first glimpse of Klein's campaign. In an apparent response to the pressure exerted through the maelstrom of media criticism and the threat of a government investigation, Klein prematurely withdrew the campaign and, for another first, offered a public apology that was published as an advertisement in the *New York Times*. Underlying the "kiddie-porn" frame are politicized discourses that mobilized the surprisingly visceral media coverage of Klein's jeans campaign and encouraged his dramatic and uncharacteristic retreat.

The kiddie-porn frame emerged within a dynamic political climate in which age became a hotly contested site of struggle over the distribution of cultural and economic resources in our society. In the United States throughout 1995, Republicans, Democrats, conservatives and liberals vied for the hearts and minds of the American voter as potential candidates prepared for the 1996 Presidential election. As national debates concerning media content, family values, and budget deficit reduction figured prominently in campaign rhetoric, age became a nexus connecting these disparate issues. Politicians accused Hollywood, Madison Avenue and the Internet of promoting sexual promiscuity and deviance among the young.[3] This anti-media discourse complemented the political focus on the financial and social cost to the American taxpayers of teenage mothers and illegitimate children, as conservatives argued for dramatic cuts in social welfare programs primarily affecting young people and women.[4] In addition, broader judicial interpretations of child pornography[5] combined with government reports that babies born to teenage mothers are more likely to be fathered by adult men suggested that misguided, oversexed children were complicit in their victimization by a deviant core of the adult population.

This political environment empowers the kiddie-porn frame's construction of youth as a victimized class that lacks the moral, cultural and economic will to resist Klein's seductive appeal. At issue are politically inspired, normative beliefs about the uncontainable aspects of American youth culture and its potential threat to the cultural and economic stability of U.S. society. The frame of kiddie-porn articulates a metadiscourse primarily structured by the discourse of Generational Equity. Initiated by aging Baby Boomers concerned about funding their current lifestyles and their impending retirement years, Generational Equity specifies that the elimination of the U.S. budget deficit requires deep cuts in social welfare programs, primarily those benefiting post-boomers and senior citizens.[6] While Social Security and other programs primarily benefitting seniors have been vigorously defended by organizations like American Association of Retired Persons, post-boomers, until recently,[7] lacked the political and economic resources of their elders in the struggle over the nation's wealth.

This struggle is manifest on the cultural front as well. Traditionally focused on fighting the senior citizens' lobby, the Boomer-dominated media and political establishments have depicted seniors as a class of Scrooges, hoarding the nation's wealth at the expense of a younger, more productive citizenry.[8] While little or no research has been conducted regarding the effects of the Generational Equity movement on the fortunes of post-boom generations, I propose that this discourse of age works with the established discourses of middle-class morality and patriarchy to define post-boomers as potential threats to the social and financial stability of society. The Generational Equity discourse specifies the need to cut social and educational programs that primarily benefit young adults, teens and children to provide middle-class tax "relief."[9] This discourse was bolstered by the negative images of post-boomers constructed by the media during the early 1990s.[10] Along with the discourses of middle-class morality and patriarchy, the discourse of Generational Equity defined Generation X and younger generations as socially deviant slackers who, unless contained by the more stable Boomer generation, threatened the American way of life. The frame of kiddie-porn supports these interests by articulating a metadiscourse symbolically denying the young any political, economic or social efficacy that Klein's marketing appeal may acknowledge.

This study empirically tracks these politicized discourses that structure the kiddie-porn frame by analyzing the patterns of key words, stock phrases, sources and themes within the coverage that describe, interpret and evaluate reality for society in some popular culture and journalistic presentations. Framing, originally conceptualized as individuals' use of mental structures to make sense of their physical and social experience, is a powerful discursive strategy when applied to the production and consumption of media content. It allows us to see how the media, employing "active agents with specific purposes,"[11] promote elite social discourses as the common sense of society.[12] The analysis of media frames offers a means of identifying the social origins of elite discourses and revealing the political and economic interests that underlie them.

This body of discourse consists of 31 mainstream and industry articles published during the period starting July 1, 1995 and ending September 30, 1995. This period covers the month before, the month during, and the month after the announcement of the withdrawal of Klein's campaign on August 29, 1995 and represents the *crescendo* of media coverage regarding the controversy surrounding the campaign. The following mainstream publications, those considered by professionals and academics to be reflective of national policy and broad audience interests, were searched, and the figures occurring after each title indicate the number of articles reviewed in each. They include: *New York Times* (5), *Washington Post* (1), *Los Angeles Times* (2), *Wall Street Journal* (5), *USA Today* (1), *Time* (1), *Newsweek* (1), *U.S. News and World Report* (1), and *TV Guide* (1). In addition, the following marketing and advertising industry magazines were searched: *Advertising Age* (10), *Adweek* (2), and *Marketing News* (1). While not exhaustive, this body of coverage resembles in breadth and depth the national media discourse generated during the three months specified for analysis.

The media coverage of the Klein controversy characterizes the fashion designer as a modern-day Fagin, the character who seduces children into a life of crime and social deviance in Dickens' classic *Oliver Twist*. Like Fagin, Klein is at once a "cynical businessman" in pursuit of a fortune, an overgrown child in search of attention, and a "dirty old man" in search of a thrill. Accusing Klein of having "created an . . . empire through risqué advertising,"[13] the media discourse admits Klein's tactics have generally brought the designer tremendous financial success. Yet, the coverage defines this success as ill-gotten gain at the expense of the cultural and social fabric. While other marketers may toe the line between good taste and bad, Klein epitomizes a journey into bad taste that is repeatedly referred to as having "gone too far." The discourse isolates Klein as a marketing pervert whose "castigation" by the marketing community and "the public" is well-deserved and long overdue. Ultimately, Klein's actions and his advertising are deemed to be the product of his individual greed, self-absorption and deviant character rather than an extension of the routine marketing tactics common to the industry.

As a cynical businessman, Klein stands accused of consistently overstepping the boundaries of good taste for profit. In this fashion, the media discourse about the

Calvin Klein Jeans Advertising

designer casts him as an opportunist whose history of exploiting young people leads to dangerous social consequences. Several reports link this history of exploitation—including the promotion of sexual promiscuity, teenage sex and anorexia—to the child pornography theme they associate with the August campaign:

> Calvin Klein is no stranger to provocative ads .. . . Ads featuring waif-like model Kate Moss have outraged some groups, which have accused Calvin Klein of promoting anorexia.[14]

Throughout the media discourse, Klein is said to be "at it again." Portrayed as the overgrown child who repeatedly "challenges" the public's sensibilities, Klein uses tactics no longer acceptable to the media community. Supporting the image of Klein as a self-willed, narcissistic child, the discourse condemns his marketing tactics as promoting "the classic infantile wish for an infinite self, free of all restraint."[15] Stock phrases such as "pushing the envelope," "went too far" and "crossed the line" characterize Klein as the wild child of the marketing community whose well-deserved drubbing came not a moment too soon. Similarly, Klein's public apology and defense of his campaign is viewed with the suspicion, impatience and scorn adults often reserve for unruly children who continue to pursue the wayward path: "Like the ads themselves—such limp apologia are not to be believed."[16]

To complete the Fagin myth, the media discourse also defines Klein as a "dirty old man,"[17] asserting the classic archetype of the adult who recruits the young for deviant activities. This image is further enhanced by references to the North American Man/Boy Love Association or NAMBLA. By comparing Klein's objectives to the infamy of an organization that promotes adult-child sexual relations, the discourse likens Klein's character to that of a child pornographer:

> The guy in the white panties (OK, briefs) is another case. His face, with its ring of curls, is so angelic, his blue socks and sneakers so poignantly boyish, that it seems the photographer picked him up in the park by offering him free ice cream and a ride in his car. Very NAMBLA.[18]

The media's description of the ads consists of patterns of stock phrases and key words that work in meaningful associations to define the August campaign as a perversion of legitimate fashion marketing and a threat to society's moral fabric. The media discourse surrounding the campaign homogenizes the variety of images and portrayals contained within the advertising into a unified archetype of child pornography. This process of homogenization reclassifies the specific characteristics of the ads—the age and attitude of the models, the styling, the set, the production values—and makes them meaningful as general indicators of child pornography. As a result, the coverage denies Klein's jeans campaign cultural and moral legitimacy as a marketing communication strategy.

The age—or, more to the point, the apparent age—of the models is a central criterion on which the campaign is judged. While only two of the models are identified by the coverage as under the age of 18, the discourse repeatedly refers to the models as "girls," "boys" and "teenagers," reinforcing the assumption that all of the models are underage and that Klein's campaign constitutes child exploitation. Yet, the media's descriptions of the ads are also rife with contradictory language regarding the age categories of the models: the terms "teen-age," "young men," and "boy" are applied without any qualification or reference to the actual ages of the models. But, as the following description of Klein's campaign illustrates, the models are considered "men" only when they are not doing anything defined by the discourse as abnormal:

> In some versions, the teen-age models are clad in denim shorts that reveal their underwear. In others, the young men are shirtless. In a magazine ad, one boy, legs splayed, wears a denim jacket, briefs, black nail polish, a tattoo, sneakers with cheap tan dress socks and an enigmatic smile.[19]

The media discourse discounts the models as working professionals in the fashion industry and instead (re)constructs them as the naive and helpless victims of the industry's most notorious renegade. The discourse interprets and evaluates the earthiness and languid physicality of the models in Klein's August campaign as "creepy," a distinction underscored by constant comparisons to the youthful exuberance and idealized physiques endemic to Klein's earlier advertising and the advertising of fashion's mainstream. Throughout the coverage, the models in the August campaign are defined in opposition to the aggressive sexuality of Marky Mark and the high-status stylization and sensuality of the ads featuring Brooke Shields and Kate Moss. The contrast establishes a binary opposition that portrays the models in the August campaign as immature, sexually deviant and of low social status. Within this context, the characteristics of the models are transformed by the discourse into indicators of "chickenhawk" porn:

> Sex is rather blankly offered here as a commodity by and for the bombed out and the hopelessly numb . . . like they're wearily going through the motions for a customer.[20]

Yet, the power of this transformation process relies on the moral evaluation of the images as a function of gender and class. The emotional effect of the kiddie-porn frame is enhanced by an emphasis on the way that the male models are portrayed in the campaign:

> One of the most offensive segments poses a young man alone, his face in that numb, deadened look associated with films that can be bought only in an adult bookstore.[21]

The discourse creates an association between the sexual vulnerability exuded by the male models and the homoeroticism and pedophilia suggested by references to the National Man/Boy Love Association. By repeatedly highlighting the fact that one of the male models wears black nail polish, the discourse makes what might have been an irrelevant feature meaningful as an indicator of deviant masculine behavior. It is the nature of the images of the male—and not the female—models that explains how Klein "crossed the line":

> Although in the culture, sadly, Lolitas are OK (super model Bridget Hall is now all of about 15), we cannot accept what look like pictures from a NAMBLA catalog as a fashion ad spread across the side of a bus.[22]

While the discourse barely acknowledges this double standard, the coverage makes it clear that the campaign's treatment of women as sex objects merely nudges the transitory boundaries of taste. In contrast, it is the image of the male models similarly portrayed that constitutes a truly serious challenge to society's morality:

> The pictures of the young girls in white panties (much as they did get many male viewers' endocrine systems going) were there as mere window dressing. It was the boys in short shorts who were the real story, the poignant boys who seemed like real prey.[23]

Defining the down-scale stylization and grainy photography of the campaign as "cheap" and "tawdry," the media discourse criticizes Klein's dramatic departure from the haute couture grandeur of fashion's mainstream advertising. The discourse evaluates the anti-design stylization of the campaign as a rejection of the mainstream cultural values of the fashion world, a world in which advertising traditionally seduces the middle class with idealized images equating good taste with high society. The wood-panelled room serving as a background for the ads is constructed within the discourse as a betrayal of good taste and, more importantly, a sign of immoral intent. The *New York Times* suggests that the "cheesily furnished rumpus room"[24] is reminiscent of adult magazines of the 1970s. The discourse transforms the campaign's low production values into a key indicator of low morals.

The media discourse employs an elite core of sources to substantiate the (re)construction of the campaign as kiddie porn. Direct quotes from advertising critics, marketing experts, and fashion industry spokespeople voice the criteria and standards by which Klein and his campaign are to be judged. Editorials and opinion pieces notwithstanding, the primary undertaking of news is to supply descriptive—albeit evaluative—material; to establish the kiddie-porn frame, reporters must therefore rely on sources to voice the moral evaluation and judgment prohibited by journalistic protocol but essential to their undertaking. The discursive power of the sources, described as a group by the term "critics," is often established in the lead:

> The designer Calvin Klein's abrupt about-face in withdrawing advertising that angry critics likened to child pornography . . . is generating fierce debate over whether there are limits in advertising . . .[25]

The lead is then substantiated by an elite source who uses the terms "child pornography" or "kiddie porn." The *New York Times* follows the above lead, for example, with the voice of advertising agency head Richard Kirschenbaum who warns advertisers to "think twice if they do something that smacks of child pornography."[26]

Despite references to "public outrage," the public is rarely given voice within the field of discourse. Only two articles reviewed cite teens or young adults; yet these voices are significant in their rejection of the kiddie-porn frame. One young viewer

> thought they were funny. That guy behind the camera was asking some stupid questions. I didn't get why he was asking those questions. It's definitely a sexual thing, but to say child pornography is stupid.[27]

This brief exposure of the opinions of the target audience is eclipsed by the dominant viewpoint, however, and the voice of youth is dismissed to the margins of "public" opinion.

The voices of the FBI and the American Family Association serve to endorse the kiddie-porn frame as the legitimate means of making sense of the campaign. Yet, the media discourse constructs both organizations as self-serving political nemeses. While media, marketing and advertising organizations support their critique of Klein's campaign with the fact of the intervention of the FBI and the AFA, the dis-

Calvin Klein Jeans Advertising

course dismisses the FBI's response as a political move "to show right-wingers that Democrats are not soft on kiddie porn"[28] while the AFA's Reverend Wildmon is defined as a political extremist:

> Among those objecting to this campaign are the Rev. Donald Wildmon, the sanctimonious, self-appointed arbiter of American moral values. But one need scarcely be a zealot or a prig to find these commercials—and the indefensible decision by MTV and others to air them—irredeemably repugnant.[29]

As a metadiscourse, the coverage of the August campaign employs the discourses of Generational Equity, middle-class morality and patriarchy to construct a frame in which the actions of youth can seem erratic, random and amoral. Hence, the kiddie-porn frame advances specific power relations that reify youth as a class lacking a rational framework in which their choices, be they sexual or economic, make sense. By denying the rationality of youthful decision-making, the elite group of middle-class adults can reject systematic approaches to understanding and addressing the motivations underlying the social actions of young adults, teenagers and children.

The kiddie-porn frame works by constructing a morality tale warning adults against addressing young people's independence from adult society. In his public apology, Klein avows to the integrity of his intent to address what he calls "the most media savvy generation yet" on its own terms. In effect, Klein's appeal to the self-determination of the young works to legitimize the promise and the problems articulated by the actions and symbols of the post-boom generations. In denying Klein's campaign and his subsequent apology legitimacy, the media discourse illustrates that the cost of opposing the dominant view of youth in our society is severe.

Ultimately, the kiddie-porn frame diminishes the significance of child pornography as a social problem as it works to shift political heat from the media industry onto Calvin Klein. It is significant to remember that the majority of the "public" would not have seen the August campaign if it hadn't been for the media coverage of the controversy. In response to the politically inspired accusations that the media industry has contributed to the erosion of middle-class values, the media elite cynically uses its privilege to compel society to see Klein and his associates as the "real problem." Hence, Klein is symbolically sacrificed while the frame of kiddie porn masks the interests of the media culture that created his success.

Notes

[1] This analysis is founded on the idea that the construction of youth—or any social group—in the media is the product of the dynamics of a specific social system, here the United States. Undoubtedly some of the particulars of this case, and of the media coverage of the Calvin Klein controversy, are applicable as well in Canada and other countries; and some are not. But regardless, the connection between political culture and media discourse offers a rich foundation for thinking about the structure and cultural politics of the generational conflict this case in many ways reflects.

[2] "Calvin's World," *Newsweek* (September 11, 1995), 60-66.

[3] Bob Herbert, "Mr. Dole's call to arms," *New York Times* (June 3, 1995), 19; n.a., "The Feds in cyberspace," *Newsweek* (September 25, 1995), 62; Vic Sussman, "Policing cyberspace," *U.S. News & World Report* (1995), 54-60; Stephen Labaton, "Computer stings gain favor as arrests for smut increase," *New York Times* (September 16, 1995), 1; Doreen Carvajal, "Pornography meets paranoia," *New York Times* (February 19, 1995), 4:4.

[4] Sue Woodman, "How teen pregnancy has become a political football," *Ms.* (January/February 1995), 90-92; Joseph P. Shapiro, "Sins of the fathers," *U.S. News & World Report* (August 14, 1995), 51-52.

[5] Linda Greenhouse, "Court rejects appeal of man convicted in child smut case with political overtones," *New York Times* (January 18, 1995), D20.

[6] Jill Quadagno, "Generational Equity and the Politics of the Welfare State," *Politics and Society* 17 (September, 1989), 353-76; Meredith Minkler, "The Politics of Generational Equity," *Social Policy* 17 (Winter, 1987), 48-52.

[7] Jeff Giles, "Generalizations X," *Newsweek* (June 6, 1994), 62-70; Joseph P. Shapiro, "Just fix it!," *U.S. News & World Report* (February 23, 1993), 50-56.

[8] Quadagno, "Equity," 353-76; and Minkler, "Politics," 48-52.

[9] Quadagno, "Equity" and Minkler, "Politics."

[10] Giles, "Generalizations."

[11] William A. Gamson, *Talking Politics* (New York: Cambridge University Press, 1992).

[12] Gaye Tuchman, *Making News: A Study in the Construction of Reality* (New York: Free Press, 1978); Michael Pertschuk and Wendy Schaetzel, *The People Rising: The Campaign Against the Bork Nomination* (New York: Thunder's Mouth Press, 1989); Robert M. Entman and Andrew Rojecki, "Freezing out the Public: Elite and Media Framing of the U.S. Anti-Nuclear Movement," *Political Communication* 10 (1993), 155-173.

[13] Kevin Goldman, "Calvin Klein halts jeans ad campaign," *Wall Street Journal* (August 29, 1995), B14.

[14] Bruce Horovitiz, "Calvin Klein ads draw criticism," *USA Today* (August 21, 1995), B1.

[15] J. Leo, "Decadence, the corporate way," *U.S. News & World Report* (August 28-September 4, 1995), 31.

[16] Rance Crain, "Rationale for CK ads feeble & hypocritical," *Advertising Age* (September 4, 1995), 18.

[17] James Brady, "Fueling, feeling the heat," *Advertising Age* (September 4, 1995), 1,34.

[18] Barbara Lippert, "Calvinist youth," *Adweek* (July 31, 1995), 34.

[19] Stuart Elliot, "Calvin Klein to withdraw child jean ads," *New York Times* (August 31, 1995), D1, D9.

[20] Leo, "Decadence," 31.

[21] Margaret Carlson, "Where Calvin crossed the line," *Time* (September 11, 1995), 64.

[22] Barbara Lippert, "The naked untruth," *Adweek* (September 18, 1995), 26, 28.

[23] Lippert, "Untruth," 26, 28.

[24] Elliot, "Withdraw," D1, D9.

[25] Stuart Elliot, "Will Calvin Klein's retreat redraw the lines of taste?," *New York Times* (August 29, 1995), D1, D9.

[26] Quoted in Elliot, "Retreat," D1, D9.

[27] "Teenagers wonder 'What's the fuss?'" *Advertising Age* (September 4, 1995), 35.

[28] Rance Crain, "FBI's move against Klein excessive, scary," *Advertising Age* (September 18, 1995), 24.

[29] Crain, "Rationale," 18.

ELIZABETH D. WAITERS

90210 in Black & White and Color: Inter-Ethnic Friendship on Prime Time Television

Beverly Hills, 90210 is the longest-running teen-oriented prime-time dramatic series to date. The program revolves around a middle-class Anglo-American family from Minneapolis, Minnesota adjusting to life amongst the rich and shallow in Beverly Hills, California. The father, Jim Walsh (James Eckhouse), is a successful accountant who has transferred to a large corporate firm. The mother, Cindy Walsh (Carol Potter), has no visible occupation outside the home. The series begins (in 1990) with the Walshes, all-American do-gooder Brandon, and his sister, popularity-seeking Brenda (Jason Priestley and Shannen Doherty), 15-year-old high school sophomores leaving their familiar surroundings and friends in Minnesota to transfer into West Beverly High School. The trials and triumphs of adolescent life are explored through the social, academic, romantic, and familial experiences of the Walsh family and the twins' attractive, Anglo-American and relatively well-heeled circle of friends: beautiful, snobbish Kelly Taylor (Jennie Garth); spoiled rich-kid Steve Sanders (Ian Ziering); sensitive, misunderstood Dylan McKay (Luke Perry); misfit peacemaker Donna Martin (Tori Spelling); intellectual, insecure Andrea Zuckerman (Gabrielle Carteris); and sycophantic wannabe rapper David Silver (Brian Austin Green).

By Fall 1995, as *Beverly Hills, 90210*'s sixth season is ushered in, the Walsh parents have left the show (relocated to Hong Kong for the father's job) as have Brenda (who is studying acting in London), Andrea (who transferred to Yale University), and Dylan (who left Beverly Hills to tour the country on motorcycle). The surviving main characters have graduated from high school and will begin their seventh season (Fall 1996) as college seniors. The transition from a racially exclusive high school to an ethnically diverse public university (California University, the fictional equivalent of the University of California at Los Angeles) affords the main characters of *Beverly Hills, 90210* an opportunity to interact with an increasing range of diverse people.

Three of the four inter-ethnic plotlines during the two seasons that chronicle the main characters' transition from high school to college involve interactions between African American men and the main male characters. Steve and his high school freshman "buddy," Herbert Little (Cory Tyler), stage an unsuccessful computer-tampering endeavor. Brandon and Jordan Bonner (Michael Anthony Rawlins), a newspaper editor from a predominantly African American high school, campaign to host a dance involving students from both high schools. And Brandon becomes an academic tutor for star basketball player D'Shawn Hardell (Cress Williams) during the main characters' first year of college.

Character behavior in these inter-ethnic plotlines follows a pattern in which one or both of the interactants tries to dominate the initial interaction, neither interactant sustains dominance throughout subsequent interactions, and finally, both characters reach a stage of cooperative interaction and mutual respect. But it is important to note that this last stage is achieved only after a climactic moment in which the African American character asserts dominance over the main—white—character. Consequently, at least between males, behaviors of mutual respect emerge sooner in relationships where the African American man begins the initial inter-ethnic interaction with a strong display of dominant behavior.[1]

African American male characters display stronger behaviors of dominance as the main characters move from high school to college. As a result, relationships with African American men become more complex as the main characters mature. Further character development and friendships with several main characters reward initial behaviors of dominance in African American male characters. The potential for an inter-ethnic relationship outside of the initial plot is therefore established within the first interaction.

The plot of the rival high schools' dance story is resolved within a single episode and illustrates the pattern of dominance, non-compliance and mutual respect that characterizes inter-ethnic relationships between main male characters and African American men on the series. It begins—typically enough, at a remove from the social activity that will turn out to be its apparent main concern—with the fatal shooting of two spectators at a high school football game on the campus of a predominantly African American school. The school board responds by cancelling the game scheduled between West Beverly and Shaw High that was to be played on Shaw's campus. Brandon becomes involved with a Shaw journalist in a campaign to host a dance between Shaw and West Beverly as a show of support between students of the two schools.

Brandon's first meeting with Jordan Bonner ends tensely, with Jordan storming off in disgust, but begins amicably enough. Jordan has followed Brandon out of the school board building, where the board members are still discussing the fate of the game:

(1) JORDAN: Excuse me. Who was that guy?

(2) BRANDON: He's the coach from my school.

(3) JORDAN: West Beverly, I presume.

(4) BRANDON: Yeah. I'm Brandon Walsh. *(Extends hand in hand-shake.)*

(5) JORDAN: Jordan Bonner from Shaw. *(Returns the handshake.)* So, ah, what did the coach have to say?

(6) BRANDON: Well, there won't be any formal decision made 'til Monday at the earliest.

(7) JORDAN: Anything else?

(8) BRANDON: Well, the prime concern is to make sure it's safe to play the game next week.

(9) JORDAN: No kidding. This is so unnecessary.

(10) BRANDON: Well, two people were killed.

(11) JORDAN: By a rival set from another school. It has nothing to do with you people.

(12) BRANDON: Well, considering we're supposed to sit in the same bleachers as the two people who were killed, I'd say yes it does have something to do with us. *(Touches Jordan's arm, briefly.)* Not to mention the fact that we're going to have twenty-five players down on the field.

(13) JORDAN: It was an isolated incident. You don't have anything to worry about, man. Unless some of your West Beverly homeys are planning something.

(14) BRANDON: Fortunately, we don't have much street violence in Beverly Hills.

(15) JORDAN: That doesn't stop you from being an expert on the subject now, does it?

(16) BRANDON: It's been really nice talking to you Jordan. *(Starts to walk away.)*

(17) JORDAN: They're going to cancel the game. You know that, don't you?

ELIZABETH D. WAITERS

(18) BRANDON: *(Comes back.)* No. What I know is that Coach
Chapman, Mrs. Teasley and the whole damn school board is in
there on a Saturday afternoon, trying to figure out any way they
can to make sure this thing happens.

(19) JORDAN: You know, Brandon, Brandon of Beverly Hills, you
don't know squat. *(Walks away.)*

The relationship between Brandon and Jordan gets off to a very tenuous start in
this conversation, with both interactants attempting to establish dominance in this,
their initial meeting. Although Jordan is at first in the deferential position of
requesting information from Brandon [1], [5], [7], Brandon approaches the interaction from a position of respect through confirming Jordan's presumption about
Brandon's school affiliation and initiating the handshake [4]. The conversation heats
up as Jordan provides critical commentary to Brandon's information about the killing
[9]. Brandon's attempts to establish dominance (by disconfirming Jordan's commentary [10], [12]) are matched by Jordan's counterdisplay of dominance (disconfirming Brandon's previous disconfirmation, then tendentiously offering sarcastic
feedback [13] and providing sniping commentary about Brandon's knowledge of
street violence [15]).

Brandon responds to Jordan's counterattempts at dominance by a further display
of dominant behavior when he attempts to end the interaction (politely, but firmly)
by summarily dismissing Jordan [16]. Jordan challenges Brandon to continue the
interaction by throwing putatively new information at Brandon's retreating figure
[17]. Brandon rises to the challenge by disconfirming Jordan's information and sup-
planting it with some putatively newer information of his own [18]. Jordan wins the
upper hand in this clash of dominant wills by disavowing Brandon's information;
though the disavowal is hollow, he has the last words and manages an exit that leaves
Brandon conversationally footless [19].

The second interaction between the two journalists begins with a resurgence of
dominant behavior from Jordan and ends with displays of respect from both interactants. The interaction begins *in media res* and takes place in the journalism room at
Shaw High School, where Brandon has taken it upon himself to visit Jordan to propose a joint editorial about the cancelled game:

(1) JORDAN: I'm sorry, Walsh, I didn't mean to insult your intelligence here, but either you are totally ignorant or naive in the
extreme.

(2) BRANDON: What is so naive about going to the school board

with a united front, telling them to move the game to a neutral field away from the violence?

(3) JORDAN: Switzerland! That's a neutral country, we can play the game there.

(4) BRANDON: Got an answer for everything, don't you Jordan?

(5) JORDAN: About this stuff? Yeah, I do.

(6) BRANDON: You know, I came here in good faith, man, and you just keep dissin' me. What's with that?

(7) JORDAN: *(Yells)* What do you want me to say? That it was very noble of you to trek down here? Man, you need to understand what's real. If we play this game anywhere but here, we might as well hand the community over to the gangs. The truth is, until we can afford to have everybody in this world live happily ever after, we need to take a stand right here. Where the people can see us, hear us, and understand that we are not afraid to be.

The conversation continues into the hall.

(8) JORDAN: This was Bose Hinton's locker. One of the kids that died? He was my friend.

(9) BRANDON: Was he a, uh, gang member?

(10) JORDAN: Does it matter?

(11) BRANDON: No, I guess not.

(12) JORDAN: See, what pissed me off was that both those dudes who died were my friends. And all I kept hearing from you was about a football game?

(13) BRANDON: Hey, man, it was never just the game. I don't know. The whole thing really got to me, you know?

(14) JORDAN: You should write a eulogy.

(15) BRANDON: I didn't know your friends.

(16) JORDAN: A eulogy for the game, man.

The greater part of this second interaction is filled with evidence of the co-interactant's mutual respect. They both self-disclose [6], [8], [12], [14] and listen attentively; Brandon communicates collaboratively by stating his intentions and requesting similar information from Jordan [6]; and Jordan affirms Brandon's view about being a know-it-all [5]. Jordan, however, produces a display of dominance when he assumes the role of Brandon's educator [7] and gives him the platform from which to later issue a directive (suggesting that Brandon write a eulogy [12], [14]). Brandon defers to Jordan's suggestion and they engage in the collaborative effort of simultaneously publishing side-by-side eulogies (Brandon's for the game, Jordan's for his dead friends) in their respective school newspapers.

Jordan's sarcastic [3], condescending [1] and patronizing [7] demeanor tests the sincerity of Brandon's display of friendship. Brandon maintains his position of respect throughout the interaction. He neither challenges nor defers to Jordan's display of dominance; he does not become antagonistic and he does not rescind his stance of friendship. Brandon's friendship is accepted and returned in the second half of the interaction as Jordan opens up to Brandon with personal information [8] and feelings [12].

The next interaction takes place at West Beverly, where Jordan returns Brandon's visit.

(1) BRANDON: Jordan.

(2) JORDAN: Brandon. How are you doing?

(3) BRANDON: Good. How are you doing?

(4) JORDAN: Okay. Got something for you, man.

(5) BRANDON: What's this?

(6) JORDAN: My editorial.

(7) BRANDON: Oh, I already programmed it into the computer, man. Didn't change a word.

(8) JORDAN: You were going to print that?

(9) BRANDON: Yeah, we made a deal.

(10) JORDAN: You really are naive.

(11) BRANDON: What do you mean?

(12) JORDAN: That was me getting through my anger. This is me getting through.

(13) BRANDON: *(Opens the envelope)* It's only two paragraphs!

(14) JORDAN: Yeah. Short, sweet, lean and clean. *(Snaps finger)*

(15) BRANDON: *(Reads aloud)* "Anything quieter than a gunshot people don't hear, and even then they don't listen for long." It's good.

(16) JORDAN: Thanks. A lot of people are going to get to read that thanks to you.

(17) BRANDON: And thanks to you I gotta redo the layout. *(They both laugh.)*

(18) JORDAN: So, what do you got for the readers of the *Shaw Courier?*

(19) BRANDON: *(Hands paper to Jordan.)* Hot off the presses.

(20) JORDAN: This looks very professional.

(21) BRANDON: Yeah, we try.

(22) JORDAN: Whoa, whoa, whoa, whoa, whoa, whoa.

(23) BRANDON: What?

(24) JORDAN: I appreciate the invite, Bro', but I think we're doing a huge thing here just by publishing these two pieces together.

(25) BRANDON: Yeah, but if we really want to shake things up, we gotta do something everybody's gonna remember for the rest of their lives.

(26) JORDAN: I think they will, man.

(27) BRANDON: Yeah, me too.

This interaction is composed of the give and take of opinions, feelings and camaraderie that characterize an established friendship. Self-disclosure [7], [12], active feedback to increase understanding and solicit further engagement [5], [8], [11], [23], confirmation of the partner's views [9], [14], [21], [25], [26] and undisguised compliments [15], [20] dominate this interaction. The only displays of dominant behavior in this scene [10] [22] [24] are quickly countered by the same interactant's behaviors of respect [12] [24], [26]. Brandon and Jordan's relationship has reached a stage of collaborative communication where they cooperate as friends and equal partners in a joint endeavor. Brandon, in fact, has been bold enough to invite Jordan and the rest of the population of his school to the West Beverly High School dance.

In the final interaction, Jordan attends the West Beverly dance and is introduced to Brandon's sister and friends. Some troublesome students from Shaw attend the dance and strike threatening poses (which they later discard as they relax and enjoy themselves on the dance floor). Brandon and Jordan's position of mutual respect is evident in the following exchange with Brenda:

(1) JORDAN: I just didn't see this [potential trouble] coming.

(2) BRANDON: No one could have, man.

(3) BRENDA: Are you out of your mind, Brandon? Anybody could have.

Here, Jordan's self-disclosure [1] is supported by Brandon's confirmation and agreement [2].

This last scene ends as Brandon places his arm across Jordan's shoulders and they walk off together in the direction of an integrated group of football players.

(4) JORDAN: Bose Hinton and Paul Browning, my two friends who got shot? They would have liked to have been here tonight. They would have liked you, Brandon Walsh. You would have pissed them off.

(5) MR. MEYERS: *(In passing)* Walsh pisses everybody off.

(6) NIKKI: *(Joins Brandon and Jordan)* So, who are those guys anyway?

(7) JORDAN: They're football players.

(8) BRANDON: Those are them, huh?

(9) JORDAN: Hmm hmm. Undefeated, untied, the masters of the universe.

(10) BRANDON: Really? 'Cause you see, I have this theory that if you get a couple of guys from one team, couple of guys from another team, together at, oh, I don't know, say a high school dance, that sometime, somewhere, like maybe 10 a.m. tomorrow, a football game will be played. Bet you they're looking for referees right now.

(11) JORDAN: There's no off on your switch, is there Walsh?

(12) BRANDON: It'll be a great game.

(13) JORDAN: Nobody could have predicted this.

(14) BRANDON: *(Puts arm around Jordan's shoulders.)* Jordan, my man, anybody could have predicted this.

This final interaction between the two editors ends on a much friendlier basis than their first interaction though the subject of their conversation at its point of greatest mutuality and warmth is a projected physical contest between their schools. The behaviors of dominance in this scene operate as displays of mutual respect. The interaction begins in mutual respect, with Jordan paying Brandon a backhanded compliment [4] and putting his own growing liking for Brandon in the mouths of his dead friends; and with Brandon providing active feedback as he brings the athletes into the field of the discussion [8]. Jordan assists in the centralization of the football players, confirming Brandon and leading the conversation forward a little aggressively as he touts his team's undefeated position and strength [9]. Brandon raises the ante on Jordan by positing, in abstract and theoretical terms that clearly spring from local and practical concerns, a possible formalization of conflict in a game structure [10]. Jordan's critical response [11] is framed teasingly in a manner of collaborative communication that invites a response from Brandon. Brandon ignores the critical edge to Jordan's comment, plunging forward with more information [12] that is subsequently ignored in Jordan's response [13].

Brandon's final comment [14] echoes Brenda's earlier remark [3]. Brandon's self-deprecating change of mind in the latter exchange, is phrased as a show of dominance (disaffirming both Jordan's current opinion [13] and his previous agreement with Jordan's opinion [2]). The comment is offered within a context of friendship, however, and resolves the antagonism that began their initial interaction. Brandon seems to say, "We have moved beyond the primitive point where I must try to dominate you, and you to dominate me. Now we are friends, and our teams can battle for dominance as we watch in unity."

Jordan's introduction to Brandon's friends leads to the subsequent reintroduction of his character in later episodes. He and Andrea meet again at a social event for students who have been accepted to Yale University. They begin dating and, through this association, Jordan becomes involved in a number of social occasions with the core characters. His involvement in future episodes is limited to that of a minor character, however, and little information (other than his plans to attend Yale) is revealed about him within the context of his friendships with Andrea and Brandon.

The pattern of interaction between main male characters and African American men in *Beverly Hills, 90210* suggests that African American male characters must assert stronger initial displays of dominance in order to achieve relationships of mutual respect and friendship with the main male characters. Mutual respect and genuine friendship must be fought for and won by the ethnic minority character, who is rewarded for successfully dominating the main male character. Between males, successful domination breeds intimacy.

The development of inter-ethnic alliances hinges upon the existence of mutual respect between inter-ethnic interactants. Behaviors of dominance, deference and mutual respect in initial interactions can either promote or inhibit cooperation, close friendship and/or romantic involvement between interactants. Approaching inter-ethnic interactions with respect for, and expectations of respect from, a co-interactant is therefore crucial to the formation of future meaningful relationships between diverse interactants.

The portrayal of inter-ethnic interaction on *Beverly Hills, 90210* brings peer role models within reach of diverse audiences every week. Pre-teens and teens from a variety of ethnic backgrounds have access to the actions of attractive peers involved in activities that often include a degree of social risk; and to the consequences of such actions. Inter-ethnic interaction in dramatic teen-oriented television series provides models of social behavior to young viewers who may have limited exposure to different ethnic groups. Behaviors of dominance, deference and mutual respect within these interactions supply vital social cues about the consequences of such actions for the development of inter-ethnic amity. In short, dominance and deference must be carefully staged and managed between high school and college students, in order for interactional participants to turn them from aggressive postures to engines which can drive balanced friendships effective for prime time television.

Notes

[1] The concepts of dominance, deference and mutual respect are relational terms that describe the degree of power and control that exists between two or more people involved in an interaction. Broadly, dominance implies an attempt by one or more interactants to maintain control of an interaction. Deference indicates one or more interactants' attempt to give control of the interaction to the other interactant/s. Mutual respect is evidenced by an interactant's willingness to share control of an interaction with the other interactant/s.

Behavior that indicates an interactant's desire to establish dominance over another interactant includes judgmental feedback (such as criticism or critical commentary) disconfirming the other interactant's views, ignoring the other interactant, lack of self-disclosure, rejecting or moving against (e.g., attacking) the other interactant, unwillingness to collaborate, and the giving of advice, directives, information, or physical or emotional support. Physical support can be task-oriented (e.g., sharpening pencils or fixing a car) or body-oriented (e.g., lifting someone over a wall). See Gale Auletta and John Hammerback, "A Relational Model for Interracial Interactions on Television," *Western Journal of Speech Communication* 49 (Fall, 1985), 301-321.

Deferential behavior is denoted by an interactant not expressing opinions (especially opinions that differ from the other interactant's), communicating a high level of agreement (even if this is not in the interactant's self-interest), not exerting influence over the discussion topics or interaction, allowing others to select the topic of conversation or direct the discussion, and requesting or receiving advice, directives, information, or physical or emotional support. See Auletta & Hammerback, "Model," 304; and also L. Henderson, B. Stanley Greenberg, and C. K. Atkin, "Sex Differences in Giving Orders, Making Plans, and Needing Support on Television," in B. Greenberg, ed., *Life on Television: Content Analyses of U.S. TV Drama* (Norwood NJ: Ablex, 1980), 49-63.

Indicators of mutual respect involve active feedback for understanding, confirming the other participant's views, self-disclosing, collaborative communication (e.g., requesting the other interactant's views and feelings and stating one's own), and empathic or attentive listening. See Auletta and Hammerback, "Model," 304.

RINALDO WALCOTT

Reading the Queer Narrative of Clement Virgo's *Rude:* The Politics of Third Cinema in Canada

While debates in cultural studies rage around black cultural productions, attention to black bodies has been minimal in the dialogues and conversations. I want to shift our gaze to the black body and the way in which Canadian Clement Virgo's film *Rude* (1995) maps it as a site for the writing of a contradictory socio-religious narrative of pain, threat and desire. Indeed black bodies in Western discourse are marked bodies, marked with the history of enslavement—or, to draw on an Elisonian metaphor, black bodies are both invisible and hyper-visible. Simultaneously, black bodies are unruly, resistant and the sites of various renewals. As well, black bodies are engaged in a performative struggle to produce their own markings.

My use of the body follows Michel Foucault's delineations of the term for understanding how discourses of medicine have intervened in the historical production of particular and specific ways for thinking and talking about the body and sex.[1] Foucault's micro-histories of how the discourses of medicine put into place an operational schema of discipline and regulation of the body, and how we think and act on questions of sex, clearly have implications for the reading of black bodies that follows.

Bodies as machines, bodies as docile, bodies as controlled by others are just a sample of the ways in which slavery operationalized and marked black bodies as a blank slate to be written on and inscribed with the desires of the master. As David Theo Goldberg put it,

> The new philosophical assumption that bodies are but machines, opened the way to some extreme novel development in technologies of physical power and bodily discipline. These technologies of discipline and power were superimposed upon human subjects; they

encouraged docility by reducing even *social subjectivities*, or at least some forms of *social subjectivity*, to physical dimensions and correlates.[2]

(emphasis his)

Slavery has had enormous impact on how we might think about bodies in the West. The operationalization of power on bodies to mark, discipline and control can be understood through the study of enslaved bodies. Such designations as breeder and stud stand out as examples of forms of domination, regulation, and discipline of the body-as-machine in slavery.

Ideas of black bodies as tied to nature, labor and savagery pervade our imagistic landscapes.[3] How do these images and representations relate to the enslavement of black bodies? How have black bodies resisted, reversed and undermined attempts to mark them? How have black people produced discourses of their bodies? What are the ways in which black people use their bodies as sites for the expression of joy, pleasure, pain, lack and desire? The varied cultural productions of black peoples have offered meditations on these questions as crucial for moving beyond the moment Stuart Hall has called "the end of the innocent notion of an essential black subject."[4]

Third cinema has been one of the sources where explorations into the end of the innocent black subject have taken place. Third cinema, characterized by its politically savvy insights, its poetics of critical left theory and aesthetics, and its ability to challenge political and cultural orthodoxies of all kinds unsentimentally, has really had no counterpart on the Canadian cinematic scene.[5] Thus the third cinema that I am referring to has mainly emanated out of Britain (in particular black Britain), various parts of the formerly colonized world—for example the Caribbean and Africa—and independent film making in the United States. Third cinema is characterized by the cinematic works of film makers from England: the Sankofa Collective, the Black Audio and Film Collective, Isaac Julien, John Akomfrah, Reece Auguiste, and Avril Johnson; and elsewhere: Ousmane Sembéne (Zaire), Felix de Rooy (Martinique), Haile Germina (United States), Charles Burnett (United States), Zienbu Davis (United States), Julie Dash (United States) and Euzhan Palcy (Martinique), to name a few. The output by these film makers in the late 1970s and early to mid-1980s challenged the ways in which we have come to understand and imagistically represent black communities.

Recently two feature films directed and written by black Canadians signalled the possibility of a late blooming of third cinema in Canada. But despite some ten to fifteen years of third cinema, these two black Canadian entries have failed to be as politically savvy, in terms of content, narrative and aesthetics, as their black British

The Politics of Third Cinema in Canada

and "third world" counterparts have been. The celebrations that have followed the release of Clement Virgo's *Rude* and Stephen Williams' *Soul Survivor* (1995) have failed to adequately address the truncated politics of the narratives and aesthetics in both films.[6] Though the films may be set in Canada, one wonders what makes them black Canadian films. One of the central tenets of third cinema has been the ability for film makers (like Isaac Julien, John Akomfrah and Julie Dash) to recast debates concerning place, space, history and belonging into their films; and to disrupt normative notions of nation and belonging; while producing in their work interesting aesthetic features which speak to complex manifestations of communities in the making. Thus third cinema did not announce itself on the scene by claiming to be representative. Rather, it questioned and brought a criticality to the very practice of naming and representing, as an incitement to critical dialogue and conversation.

The place of home, usually complicated by the hybrid practices of third cinema, is not at all in question in *Rude*. The film is set in one of Toronto's urban ghettos, and while stylized shots of the cityline are etched into the filmic text, place is not an issue. The voice-over of the pirate DJ Rude (Sharon Lewis), "The land of the Zulu Nation and the Mohawk nation meet . . . while the rest of Babylon gets to ponder its immigration policy," suggests not only that place might be important to the unfolding of the narrative, but also that the narrative will presumably relate Native issues to Black ones. These promises are never taken up in any sustained way. Instead, the dominating discourse of Jamaican heritage in the film creates an inability to address the multiple, archipelagic realities of blackness in Canada.

Virgo's *Rude* is aesthetically playful, populated with a host of features meant to signal the "blackness of blackness." Music is probably the most obvious sign of the attempt to bring a black aesthetic pitch to *Rude*. Reggae and gospel stand out as framing devices which play "speaking" roles in the film, punctuating speechless characters' actions. The instances of reggae and gospel, and sometimes rock, might be read (with some generosity) as the film's creolizing or hybrid moments, and it is true that the three musics in the film (reggae, gospel and rock) act as a ground for writing various kinds of distress onto characters. Yet the very specific use of these musicalities in particular scenes unravels any attempt at reading them as creolizing forces. For example, gospel is often the background music in the scenes in which Maxcine (Rachael Crawford), who had an abortion, appears. Thus, the socio-religio-narrative use of music tends often to act as a moralizing force in the film.

To merely signal *Rude* as the typical 'hood film would not do justice to the director's pyrotechnical talents. Virgo skillfully plays with a nonlinear narrative, varied camera angles and double takes of various sorts—whether of Jordan (Richard Chevolleau) repeatedly falling down or running but not advancing across the screen—demonstrating a significant talent for aestheticizing work. The aesthetic employed is mainly repetition, which is a fundamental element of black diasporic cultures and can be seen in any number of black cultural representational strategies. Yet despite these strategies by Virgo to distinguish *Rude* from the usual 'hood film fare, *Rude* cannot evade its influences. The film's narrative and the central tale are organized through the "usual suspects" of the 'hood film genre. Manthia Diawara, outlining some of the elements of the 'hood film—or what he has called "the new black realism"— identifies rites of passage, moments of crisis, black male responsibility for community, the existent violent realities of black urban living, characters who change with the unfolding story line and characters who move to a "higher understanding" of the world, all as elements of the genre.[7] These elements, all of which we find in *Rude,* are in some broad sense concerned with the black body, but do not and cannot account for critically assessing various forms of black resistance where black people, particularly men, refuse in constructing masculinities to mark their bodies as only victims.

Issues of crime and family breakdown pervade the imagined world of *Rude* with the central issue becoming the (re)gaining of black manhood for General (Dean Witt). The narrative of *Rude* consists of three tales which are kept together by the lubricating vocal twists of the title character. Here Virgo's choice echoes Isaac Julien's *Young Soul Rebels* (1991) which makes important use of a pirate radio station. The fundamental difference between Julien's use of pirate radio and Virgo's is the fluidity in which Julien's pirate DJ moves across place, space and time. Virgo's Rude is stationary, she moves neither metaphorically nor literally, this limitation being in itself an example of the ways in which Virgo's film creates a stasis in its conception of blackness. The tales of *Rude* unfold over an Easter weekend, consciously gesturing to issues of life, death and resurrection as central to the narrative. It is these three issues which propel the three tales of the film.

However I would point out that the socio-religio-narrative structure of the film fails to produce a politically transfigurative moment. We see in the three tales of *Rude* an overlapping narrative concern with a homogenized black male subject obsessed with the activities of producing and explicating a "right" black masculinity. Such a view fails to acknowledge the different ways in which black men live out their masculinities, in Canada and in the western world at least. Let us examine the tales.

Tale 1

A drug dealer named General returns home from prison to a wife (Melanie Nicholas-King) who has become a police officer; unemployed and penniless, he must put up with increasing demands from a growing son who desires various commodities (running shoes, ice cream, etc). General's dilemma is the choice of either returning to the drug trade so that he can be a father and "real" man to his son, through the ability to financially provide for him, or "failing" to represent manhood to his son. General's dilemma is solved when he refuses participation in the drug trade, which leads to a confrontation between him and the white drug lord Yankee (Stephen Shellen); the policewoman-wife shoots Yankee to protect her husband and son.

Tale 2

A window-dresser, Maxcine, is in distress, dumped by her boyfriend Andre (Andrew Moodie) who disapproved of her earlier decision to end an unwanted pregnancy. Maxcine is a kind of foil for Clement Virgo's filmmaking virtuosity. For example, she hardly speaks in the film. The camera pans to shots of her aborted love child, returned as a six- or seven-year-old ghost, dancing, while she tries to come to terms with her new, single life. And her experience is communicated to viewers via messages on her answering machine—a continuing fight with Andre, or that a gift of weed from her sister has been left in her mailbox—and by her emotional outbursts that result in her smashing the manikins which are the tools of her trade. By the end of the film Maxcine seems to have seen her love child walk away, suggesting that she has come to terms with her decision not to bear it and with her failed relationship with Andre.

Tale 3

Jordan is a boxer who is caught up in an emotional torment after participating in a gay bashing (or "lynching," as it is termed in *Rude*). Jordan must come to terms with his own homoerotic tendencies and as the film unfolds he begins the process of coming to terms and coming out. Jordan is finally emancipated when the man he helped bash retaliates by repeatedly slapping Jordan in the face. This incident happens while Jordan sits on the same bench the "lynched" man once cruised from. Jordan must endure this "beating"as his repentance and resurrection.

These are the three narrative tales of *Rude*. At stake in all three tales are bodies, we might even say bodies in trouble. Yet the narrative, cast in a religious mode, is unable to adequately demonstrate the political trouble these bodies are in. Instead they are used, together, as a canvas on which to paint a moral allegory of love and loss.

The Queer Body of Rude?

The three tales are tied together not only by Rude's verbal commands, which direct viewers to particular actions, but also by the theme of masculinity. In that light I want to focus here mainly on the last tale. Virgo has pinpointed it as the tale to teach the audience about homophobia. He is quoted as saying:

> What I saw and heard in black music: a lot of homophobia in the music and a lot of homophobia in the culture. I wanted to talk about this; I wanted to write a character that had this duality. When we think of young black men, we think that they are the ultimate symbols of machismo, of masculinity. I wanted to explore the idea of a young black man who is strong and a boxer, but the duality is that he is also gay.[8]

Any attempt to unravel the numerous assumptions behind Virgo's effort to bring a critical discussion of sexuality to black Canadian cinematic representations is mangled in these comments because the black/queer body is asked to stand in as the object upon which the inscription of violent heteronormative desires is played out. But films dealing with black/queer bodies—or with queer bodies in general—teach about homosexuality and homophobia as real, lived experiences, as well as providing entertainment. The film maker here is unable to be pedagogic about the ethical relations of race, sexuality and community without producing a victim. This particular writing of the body sits in opposition to the ways in which third cinema's best work has inscribed the body in cinematic texts.

In Julien's *Young Soul Rebels* the centrality of queer bodies to the ethicality of community is marked not only by the imaged and real violence of gay bashing but also, and in a politically radical way, by an extended love scene that questions heteronormative positions concerning sexuality and poses questions of racial border-crossing in sexual activity (a black man and white man make love).[9] To say that Julien practises a cinematic politics is to mean that the difficult, and messy, issue of representation is tackled in his work. His work, then, is the "unleashing of unpopular things"[10] as a way to engage in dialogue and conversation concerning important matters. It is this unleashing of unpopular things, of difficult knowledge, that the representation of the queer bodies in *Rude* significantly does not accomplish.

Hayden White offers a reading of histories of writing bodies in his essay, "Bodies and Their Plots."[11] White demonstrates how certain bodies are asked to inhabit specific histories. *Rude's* narrative asks the queer body to inhabit only the place of victimization. One can say that such a tale is well known and easy to tap into.

Consider, for example, William Friedkin's *Cruising* (1980) or Paul Verhoeven's *Basic Instinct* (1992). Why not ask the queer body to inhabit the site of pleasure, of joy, or the site that constitutes the only "normal," neutral, position in the film? Having Jordan engage in a gay bashing incident before he begins to come to terms with his homoerotic desires inscribes upon the queer body the very hatred that the writer/director might have hoped to dismantle with his film. White puts it this way:

> A drive may be disengaged from its original object of gratification and turned back onto its subject, so that what started out as, say, hatred of another ends up being expressed as hatred of oneself. This produces the masochistic body, the body that consist of little more than the sum-total of pain it has inflicted upon itself.[12]

What is at stake in *Rude* is bodies and their histories, or bodies in history. In many cases those histories are confounded through a socio-religious narrative which gestures toward a moralizing politic. What this postmodern moment of lost innocence can show is the various ways in which heteronormative positions can be—indeed are—postulated. The "story" or "plot" does not, in and of itself, guarantee a transfigurative moment.

Both *Young Soul Rebels* and *Rude* have as central to their narratives music and musical cultures and, by extension, practices of black youth culture. Specifically, hip hop stands out as the most evident cultural form in which we can begin to articulate a discussion of black bodies. The counter-poetics of hip hop cuts across a number of ideological positions ranging from progressively radical to nationalist. Black youths' cultural practices are representative of a moment characterized by the withering of post-emancipation/post-civil rights narratives of liberation. The importance of black postmodernity rests in the complex terrain of recognizing the contradictory moments of black youth cultures. Virgo's assertion that the motive for a tale about homophobia in his film was conditioned by homophobia in the music and culture is in fact based on an examination of only a very small number of musical styles and is thus a trap for our broader understanding of musical—and thus cultural—differences.[13] He fails to acknowledge black differences and to name in specific terms where, when and how black homophobia is uttered. Engagement in the politics of representation means that writers and directors take responsibility for their work and words. To critique a generalized black culture as homophobic is no longer sufficiently precise or useful.

Black youth cultures are concerned with the performance of bodies, and their use of bodies signals the various ways in which historical and contemporary social relations have been signified, inscribed and rewritten corporeally. Thus, bodies are not used as biological mechanisms only; but as sites for the contestation of social relations as those relations relate to actions of power on and through bodies. In Kingston, Jamaica, gay men refer to themselves as "sports" in the context of a culture that can sometimes be hyper-masculine and punishingly heteronormative. The use of the term "sport" unwrites the hyper-masculine, heteronormative implications of sporting bodies. The sporting body of the boxer in *Rude* could be read through a gaze that fixed that body in relation to the popularized heteronormative and hyper-masculine narratives of black male youth. But the use of boxing, and male assertions of self through violence, as ways of critiquing heteronormativity, constitute a refusal to see the extreme variation of queer sensibilities. This might be the fundamental difference between *Rude* and the work of Isaac Julien.

Because bodies, actual and imagined, are at stake, representations matter beyond merely the discourse of seeing ourselves. Representations have to account for something; they cannot be read through an apolitical innocence. Thus, across the three tales of *Rude* a number of images come together which can be seen to speak to the troubling politics of the film. In one scene Yankee injects blood that is potentially HIV-infected into a drug addict. Reading that scene alongside the tale of distress that Maxcine undergoes after her abortion and the bashing that Jordan participates in but is also a victim of, we find a moralizing tone that betrays any appearance of a radical politics. The writer/director seems not to see how these images and narrative representations leak into one another.

If bodies can be sites for pedagogy about anything today, then the reality of HIV/AIDS and the various ways in which it cross-cuts communities have to be taken into account in our commentary. That *Rude* is not conscious about the rhizomatic nature of how bodies relate, collide and connect in space is saddening. The various ways in which unprotected sex results in unwanted pregnancy and abortion; and the traces that such practices have in the context of drug use and sexual practices; combined with the ways in which queer communities have been politically active in terms of HIV/AIDS and the consequences for bodies, need to be taken into account. Because the film's structure does not allow for the possibility of its tales cross-cutting each other, we must conclude that Clement Virgo did not imagine an audience whose reading practices might assemble them.

But, as the film partially demonstrates through the sinister exchange of blood from one nameless character to another, bodies leak into each other and narratives and tales do, too. Bodies are not merely separate entities, discrete and infinitely individual, but they connect and come together—through sex, through talk, through glances, through intravenous sharing, and even through viewers' permeable reading practices—at various moments; and the resultant leaks can have important consequences, narratively and otherwise. Even if Virgo imagines his audience to be homophobic, and he has said as much—

> I assume the audience is homophobic and I have to take them along to the point where they discover that I love this character who's gay and they have to say to themselves 'hmmm, wait a minute, I've got to think about this.'[14]

—he must also know, but fails to acknowledge, that they do not have to read or experience each tale as a separate entity. In the war of representation that surrounds the politics of HIV/AIDS, even when intravenous drugs are a part of the story the underlying subtext remains one of a queer culpability. Thus Virgo's mission (impossible?) to "rescue" a gay subject is unwritten by the leaks in our readings of his tales, our tendencies to import traces of one tale into another. There must be another way to teach about love.

Postmodern blackness has its lineage in the discourses and movements of civil rights, black nationalism, feminism and gay liberation unsettling any easy assumptions about black community and sameness. The relations between histories and bodies remain clear. It is in black urban areas that bodies are consumed with drugs, high rates of infant mortality, AIDS and early death from firearms. It is the bodies which inhabit those places which provide the basis for the "authenticity" of much black cultural production. It is those bodies that are at stake in what we do, as folks engaged in the project of cultural work—whether as film makers or critics. If in the final analysis art speaks for some kind of politics, *Rude,* locked within a socio-religious narrative steeped in the politics of conversion, fails to register the kind of transfiguration that allows for thinking what might not have been thought before viewers encountered the cinematic representation.

Notes

[1] Michel Foucault, *The History of Sexuality: An Introduction,* Vol.1. Trans. R. Hurley (New York: Vintage), 1980.

[2] David Theo Goldberg, *Racist Culture: Philosophy and the Politics of Meaning* (Oxford: Blackwell, 1993), 53.

[3] James Snead, *White Screens, Black Images: Hollywood from the Dark Side* (New York: Routledge, 1994).

[4] Stuart Hall, "What is this 'Black' in Black Popular Culture?" in Michele Wallace, *Black Popular Culture* (Seattle: Bay Press, 1992), 32

[5] Teshome Gabriel, "Towards a Critical Theory of Third World Films," in Jim Pines and Paul Willemen, eds., *Questions of Third Cinema* (London: British Film Institute, 1989); in particular for a broad discussion of third cinema see as well

Mbye B. Cham and C. Andrade-Watkins, eds., *Blackframes: Critical Perspectives on Black Independent Cinema* (Cambridge MA: MIT Press, 1988); and Mbye B. Cham, ed., *Ex-Iles: Essays on Caribbean Cinema* (Trenton NJ: Africa World Press, Inc., 1992).

6 Rinaldo Walcott, "After the Celebration: The Discourse of Heritage in Stephen Williams' *Soul Survivor*," *CineAction,* No.39, 1996.

7 Manthia Diawara, "Black American Cinema: The New Realism," in Manthia Diawara, ed., *Black American Cinema* (New York: Routledge, 1993).

8 Marc Glassman, "Were Zulus Meet Mohawks: Clement Virgo's *Rude,*" *Take One,* Fall 1995, 20.

9 "Filling the lack in everyone is quite hard work, really..." A roundtable discussion with Joy Chamberlain, Isaac Julien, Stuart Marshall, and Pratibha Parmar; and Ruby B. Rich, "When Difference Is (More Than) Skin Deep"; in Martha Gever, Pratibha Parmar and John Greyson, eds., *Queer Looks: Perspectives on Lesbian and Gay Film and Video.* Toronto: Between the Lines, 1993.

10 Deborah Britzman, "Decentering Discourses in Teacher Education: Or, the Unleashing of Unpopular Things," *Journal of Education,* Vol.173, No.3, 1991.

11 Hayden White, "Bodies and Their Plots" in Susan Leigh Foster, ed., *Choreographing History* (Bloomington: Indiana University Press, 1995).

12 White, "Bodies," 230.

13 Progressive rap artists, like The Disposable Heroes of Hiphoprisy and Me'shell NdegeOcello are always overlooked when people talk about sexism and homophobia in black popular music.

14 Glassman, "Where Zulus Meet," 20.

STEVEN WOODWARD

Sudden in a shaft of sunlight: Krzysztof Kieslowski Looking at Youth

For Krzysztof Kieslowski Generation X, a generation whose lives are on hold, did not exist. He was not interested in creating pictures that place the individual neatly and simply within an identifiable class, an historical or sociological movement, a film genre that controls and determines action. He followed, in his films, much the same principle that Milan Kundera, along with other existentialist storytellers, employs for his novels: "Of the historical circumstances [in which my stories occur], I keep only those that create a revelatory existential situation for my characters."[1] Kieslowski's films, like the individuals within them, lie outside the generic conventions that power (and frequently overpower) the film medium. Danusia Stok wrote, in 1993: "To this day, Kieslowski claims to make features according to documentary principles as his films evolve through ideas and not through action."[2] His films, even those based on the Ten Commandments, are not moral tales, but instead have a superabundance of significance. As complex texts, they do not digest or simplify, but maintain the ambiguities and difficulties of the situations which they examine. Kundera characterizes the mission of the novel in similar terms, as complicating our picture of the world rather than reducing if for navigational purposes as do ethical and religious systems: "Man desires a world where good and evil can be clearly distinguished, for he has an innate and irrepressible desire to judge before he understands. Religions and ideologies are founded on this desire. They can cope with the novel only by translating its language of relativity and ambiguity into their own apodictic and dogmatic discourse."[3]

Kieslowski's resistance to such categories as inform the narratives of various media and propel marketing schemes and strategies may be a result of the fact that he lived for much of his life outside of the influence that consumer capitalism exerts on culture. He may have suspected that the idea of Generation X is a question of identifying a specific market niche rather than a provocative cultural phenomenon; further, that the idea of Generation X is provocative only insofar as it represents a problem for marketing—a glitch in the smooth circuit of desire and consumption. Of course, one could argue that the monolithic narrative of Communism was even more reductive than the perfidious schemata of consumer culture. But Kieslowski did not think so: "I've got the impression, which isn't well regarded, that public censorship is even more restricting than the political censorship which we were subjected to in Poland during Communism."[4] After all, while many individuals actively resisted the dogma of Communism, consumer capitalism is built on the idea of the endless interrogation, construction and seduction of the individual.

Having said all this, what then is the picture of youth that Krzysztof Kieslowski offered in the many films, both documentaries and features, that he made before his recent retirement and sudden death? Youth surely has its own "revelatory existential situation," and that situation is quite paradoxical. Setting out on life's course without any means of navigating, the young are the most vulnerable, but also the most likely to assume some extreme position—personal or political—that will free them from the continual anxiety of not knowing. As one critic wrote in relation to Larry Clark's *Kids* (1995) the youth of 15- to 24-years-old "embodies a moral authority very hard to beat."[5] If that moral authority is valorized in a film, then the youth becomes a rebel hero whose actions are a just comment on and condemnation of the system. Certainly, Kieslowski's *A Short Film about Killing* (1988) includes such a comment. One critic, Paul Coates, reflects that we never discover the exact motive for Jacek's murder of the taxi driver, though we might suspect that it involves "the country boy's need to assert himself in the city; youth's revenge on age."[6] But whether the circumstances that lead Jacek to murder are so extraordinary and specific to our own time, whether he is part of a Generation X, is another matter. Jacek might represent the shiftlessness of today's youth and the murder might be a form of protest against an enforced condition of suspension and *ennui*. On the other hand, Jacek's crime seems like the latest embodiment of the perennial Oedipal conflict. And Kieslowski doesn't valorize the criminal or the system that condemns him. Unlike *Kids*, Kieslowski's films always picture the youth, whether troubled or not, in relation to other generations, other ways of being. So Jacek's story is only one of three stories in the film.[7]

One of the central tenets of all Kieslowski narratives is surely that moral anxiety cannot and should not be evaded. While the youth is the emblematic figure of this moral anxiety, the difficulty and necessity of moral choice persists throughout life. One can free oneself from such anxiety through a commitment to some extreme form of action. *From a Night Porter's Point of View* (1977), in particular, gives us a view of the repulsive appearance of the world when all is reduced to the following and enforcing of regulations. "Rules are more important than people," pronounces the factory porter in this documentary. Of course, resistance to totalitarianism can also become a principle for the individual.[8] But by the time Kieslowski came to make *Decalogue* (1988), neither totalitarianism nor resistance to it was a viable course of action in Poland: in the ten films of the series, individuals must puzzle their way through the obscuring stuff that life presents, while the ten commandments echo faintly in the background, not as incontrovertible guiding principles but as intimations that humanity has been here before, that the issue of individual moral choice, not the social or political scheme, is the perennial problem facing humanity. And as Kieslowski himself remarked of the ten stories: "There are films about men and films about women. There are films about boys and films about girls. There are films about old men."[9] Not knowing is the universal human condition. Still, there is the constant temptation to erect false gods: the computer in *Decalogue One* that miscalculates the safety of the ice on the pond and thus, precipitates the boy's death; or the system of justice that the lawyer cannot dissuade from executing the murderer in *Decalogue Five/A Short Film about Killing*. Kieslowski's films of the 1990s are fascinating because they take this same theme of moral anxiety but modulate it to engage with democratic ideals and freedoms.

As Kieslowski moved from Polish-based and -funded films to the co-productions of the 1990s, it was inevitable that he would shift focus to adapt his films to the requirements of international distribution. But while he did so, diplomatically giving *The Double Life of Véronique* (1991) both French and Polish locations and protagonists (both played by Irène Jacob), his central concern never really changed. Kieslowski turned the circumstances of the film's financing to his own advantage: "All my films," he stated, "from the first to the most recent ones, are about individuals who can't quite find their bearings, who don't quite know how to live, who don't really know what's right or wrong and are desperately looking"[10] Weronika asks her father: "What do I really want, Papa?" Certainly, the answer cannot be found in politics. The fervent political events we see in the background of Weronika's life have no effect on her or on the decisions she makes. A statue of Lenin travelling through the town on the back of a truck may provide an ominous image, but it does not figure in the passage of Weronika's life. The greatest impact that politics have on her is that, while walking through a square where some kind of political protest is taking place, she is knocked down by a man who may be running toward or may be fleeing the scene, and her music scores are scattered. Politics may be noisy, but they are essentially inert. Weronika and her French counterpart, Véronique, rely on a totally different source for guidance.

STEVEN WOODWARD

What Kieslowski has always insisted on is accurate observation and description. As Witold Stok, one of Kieslowski's cinematographers, reminisces: "I remember talking to Krzysztof many times and he would insist that the world which is not properly described doesn't really exist. That was his main premise—just to see that little world we were living in and to quite honestly describe it."[11] This idea of accurate representation, difficult and equivocal, as the only real basis on which we can make our decisions is complemented, in *The Double Life of Véronique*, by the idea of the need for sensitive intuition, intuition involving a kind of self-observation. In this film, intuition is coded as a second self.

Kieslowski noted that observation and intuition are usually regarded as gendered concepts, when he said of the film, "*Véronique* is a typical example of a film about a woman because women feel things more acutely, have more presentiments, greater sensitivity, greater intuition and attribute more importance to all these things."[12] So Véronique does not notice the image of Weronika on the contact sheet in her bag, but feels an ineffable connection to her. On the same day as Weronika's funeral, Véronique is overcome by a post-coital sadness but attributes another, non-sexual significance to it. "It's as if I were grieving," she says. She drives to see her singing teacher, announces that she is quitting, and when asked why, replies unwaveringly, "I don't know. But I know I have to stop . . . now."

The Polish Weronika has had a few presentiments of her own fate, but they are not powerful enough to prevent her demise. Her aunt has warned her that the women of the family typically die while in apparently good health. And after her audition, as she sprawls on a park bench clutching at her heart, a sinister figure approaches her and the camera twists sideways. But rather than an angel of death, this figure turns out to be a flasher who mutely exposes himself (his penis-worm), then walks on. In comparison with these signs, the grief that Véronique feels after Weronika's death is a different order of warning, and one that is strong enough to prevent Véronique from meeting the same fate. (Here, one might be tempted to suggest that the Polish Weronika is sacrificed that the French Véronique might live.)

So, the film is built on the idea of different kinds of signs and on different ways of reading signs, of interpreting and constructing reality. Alexandre (Philippe Volter), the puppeteer, and Véronique are drawn together because they find significance in many of the same things. Alexandre tests Véronique by sending her a cassette tape: she will find him only if she can decode it. But while Alexandre views the whole episode as a psychological experiment, part of the research for a novel he intends to write, Véronique views it as a sign of his love and a test of hers. "I wanted to be sure," Alexandre says. "Sure of what?" Véronique asks, and her question echoes throughout the remainder of the film. All of what Alexandre learns of Véronique and her Polish counterpart, Weronika, becomes material for his stories and his puppet show. When Véronique asks him why he has made two puppets of her, he replies: "Because during performances I handle them a lot."[13] This purely pragmatic sense, this reduction which ignores the mysterious and the ineffable, drives Véronique away, and the last image of the film (in its American version) is of her embracing not Alexandre, but her father, a man who concocts fragrances and builds fine furniture, and who possesses a stethoscope (for listening to the heart/her heart).

I do not mean to suggest that the kind of intuition that Weronika and Véronique display precludes a visual involvement with the world. After all, the film opens with scenes of them as small girls being directed by their mothers: Weronika looks up at the night sky while her mother tells her that they are looking for the star that will start Christmas Eve; and Véronique examines the first leaf of spring with a magnifying glass while her mother points out its hairs and veins. The universe, macrocosm and microcosm, is examined for signs of a human significance. Later, we see that both girls possess small glass spheres through which they view the world (as Tomek does in *Decalogue Six*). In fact, the distortion of vision, which these spheres produce, is an essential part of the visual style of the film. Scenes frequently start with a shot through a refracting or reflecting surface. And a large part of the film was shot through a gold filter. Of course, the film is shot from the girls' perspective, a perspective which mingles dream visions and waking visions. But the filmmaker himself now seems allied to the idea that distortion, rather than the accurate observation which had obsessed him in his documentaries, brings us closer to the truth.

Essentially, Kieslowski was after something more ineffable than either sociological diagnosis or mythic archetype. He complained of the profane nature of film: "When you light a cigarette lighter in a film it means the cigarette lighter's lit, and if it isn't lit, it means the lighter doesn't work . . . If I have a goal, then it is to escape from this literalism."[14] *The Double Life of Véronique* shows us a character coming to the same realization, to an epiphany, to an escape from the literalism that threatens to control our lives and which renders our world mundane. But the trilogy that follows *The Double Life* demonstrates that we are faced with other threats, threats that lie in the very substance of our democratic ideals. In the *Three Colors* trilogy, liberty, equality, and fraternity appear in negative formulations: freedom to do nothing; equality in vindictiveness; a fraternity of cynicism.

In the first shot of the first film of the *Three Colors* trilogy, *Blue* (1993), we see a close-up of a car wheel speeding along the road surface; a small hand holds a candy wrapper out of the car window; the car speeds through the night; a girl sees the cars behind as menacing and meandering shapes; the girl runs to urinate behind some bushes at the side of the road; brake fluid drips from the brake line underneath the car; a boy with a skateboard stands in the fog beside a road, playing with a ball and stick; a car speeds by; the boy succeeds in catching the ball on the end of the stick; there is the sound of skidding and of crunching metal. Thus, the film begins. Two apparently irreconcilable visions are placed alongside each other; an objective view of the mechanical reality competes with a subjective view of the human reality. This same contrast of visions is repeated in the opening sequences of *White* and *Red*.

Because we associate the subjective view with the girl, Anna, we are surprised when we discover that it is not Anna who lies in a hospital bed, her breath moving a feather; it is Julie (Juliette Binoche), her mother, who is the sole survivor of the car crash. As Julie watches the funeral of her husband and daughter on a pocket TV, she caresses the image of her daughter's coffin. Like the ineffable link that makes Weronika and Véronique aware of each other's existence, this bond between mother and daughter becomes an identification. Julie pursues a childlike liberty, divorced from memories of the past and from responsibilities and expectations for the future, choosing as the only emblem of her existence a blue crystal lamp. In her childless, husbandless state, she reverts to her maiden name.

The confusion that results from Julie's attempt to maintain this absolute liberty is epitomized in the visit she pays to her mother (Emmanuelle Riva) at a nursing home. The mother's suspension in time and space reflects on Julie's detachment, so inappropriate to her age. In this no-place beyond life, this limbo, Julie is mistaken for her dead sister, Marie-France. Peculiar images arrive through the agency of the TV: an old man shuffles off a bungee-jumping platform; another dives from a helicopter. But the meaning of these images (and of the tight-rope walker in a later scene) is equivocal. Are they metaphors for life as most would wish to live it, going to great lengths to feel something, anything, even if only a momentary terror? Or are they images of Julie's liberty, a freedom which seems to mock the forces of Nature? We are left in no doubt that Julie wants to escape all connections, as she tells her mother, "Now I have only one thing left to do: nothing. I don't want any belongings, any memories. No friends, no love. Those are all traps." Yet Julie's free fall is unexpectedly arrested when she asks her mother, "Was I scared of mice as a kid?" The mother responds, "You weren't scared. It was Julie who was scared." "Now I'm scared," Julie says to herself.

Although Julie repeatedly purges herself of both memory and desire in the blue, baptismal waters of a swimming pool, the suspended state she tries to exist in is inevitably disrupted by people, by memories, and by the urgent strains of a music which represents a will greater than her individual will, music her husband was composing before his death: a Concert for the Unification of Europe. She tries not to act, but her grief and her "guilt"—here, not a moral voice but a latent response— eventually catches up with her. For instance, she ignores a man who is being beaten on the street at night and who runs into her building, knocking frantically on her

Krzysztof Kieslowski Looking at Youth

door in an attempt to escape. Later, she asks the flute player, recumbent on the sidewalk like the beaten man, if he is okay. Julie represses herself, resists the music until, close to the film's ending, she identifies to Olivier (Benoit Regent) the text that was intended to accompany it: "Tongues shall cease, knowledge shall wither away . . . And now shall abide only faith, hope, and love . . . but the greatest of these three is love."

In *Blue*, Julie chooses to become a no one, losing herself in some nameless corner of Paris. In *White* (1994), the next film in the *Three Colors* trilogy, Karol Karol (Zbigniew Zamachowski) is made a no one by the callous treatment of his wife, Dominique (Julie Delpy), and by the French divorce court which, he says, refuses to give him an equal hearing. Guilty only of a temporary impotence and an incomplete command of the French language, Karol is viewed by his wife and by the French justice system as *persona non grata*. Without money, without a passport, with only a large suitcase containing his hairdressing diplomas, Karol plays tragic Polish folk songs on his comb in the Paris *Métro*.

As with *Blue*, the opening sequence of this film also intercuts the mechanical with the human: Karol's suitcase travels along a conveyor belt, paralleling Karol's faltering journey to the Paris courtroom where his wife will declare his impotence. Karol is explicitly identified with his suitcase when he climbs into it to be smuggled back to Poland by Mikolaj (Janusz Gajos), a fellow Pole who offers to help him. Tipped out of the case by baggage thieves and beaten, Karol surveys the frozen Polish fields from the height of a garbage dump and muses: "Home at last." Home may be a dump, but at least here he can go about the process of rebuilding himself. Carrying the empty suitcase, he limps to the muddy lane where his older brother (Jerzy Stuhr) runs their hair salon. From a no one, someone without passport or bank card, Karol is able to fall back on his old identity as Polish hairdresser; then he becomes a guard at a money exchange, and eventually a successful entrepreneur.

His success paradoxically depends upon his impotence. As guard at the money exchange bureau, his job is simply to "walk around." He may possess a "gun" but the response of the loiterers to his unthreatening presence is comically overdone. His boss calls him a "clod" and, indeed, his passivity is what allows him to overhear information about a lucrative development, the building of warehouses on practically worthless farmland. And his impotence also has one other positive effect. When Mikolaj asks Karol to kill him, Karol's gun shoots only a sterile blank, and Mikolaj is forced to reconsider his desire to die. But Karol switches from passivity to activity instantaneously. Immediately after overhearing his boss's plans, he moves into action. He exchanges all his unspent reserves of Polish cash for American dollars, talks business with incredulous farmers, and concentrates on bettering his French.

By the time he engineers the plan for his fake death, Karol has complete control over his identity, has regained his sexual potency, and has mastered the vagaries of the French language. He willfully exchanges his passport for a death certificate, then takes on a new identity. In the hotel room where Dominique finds him after his fake funeral, he speaks unfaltering French to her, then proves his sexual potency. Dominique wakes alone the next morning and the police arrive to charge her with murdering Karol. But this degree of control, of mastery and self-possession is finally too much for Karol who, after all, may not be happy with his revenge on Dominique. While he was figuratively imprisoned in Paris, Dominique is quite literally imprisoned in Poland.

Dominique and Karol manipulate the justice system. How appropriate, then, that the final film of the *Three Colors* trilogy, Kieslowski's very last film, *Red* (1994), should deal with a retired judge. Judge Joseph Kern (Jean-Louis Trintignant), like Julie in *Blue*, attempts to live in a suspended, emotionless state: he speaks of having been immodest before, of having been vain in imposing judgment on those who came before him in the courtroom. So we apprehend that vanity has to do with too easy an understanding. And in this, the judge resembles Kieslowski himself who warns, "I'm frightened of all those people who show you the way, who know. Because really—and I'm deeply convinced of this, I firmly believe it—nobody really knows . . ."[15] The judge, like an omniscient but indifferent god, uses short-wave equipment to listen in on the phone conversations of his neighbors but has no interest in using his knowledge to help or harm them. He differentiates between his former life of judgment and his current one of contemplation: "I don't know whether I was on the good or bad side. Here, at least, I know where the truth is." After a life of judging on the basis of what could be revealed within the courts, a kind of moral exhaustion has set in.

But Kern's exhaustion is contrasted with the moral fervor of youth. Valentine (Irène Jacob), a young model who meets the judge after she has run over his dog, detests his voyeuristic practices, but is far quicker to judge. One of Kern's neighbors (Jean Schlegel) is a suspected heroin dealer, but the judge can't pick up the frequency of his telephone. Nevertheless, how quickly Valentine condemns the man on the basis of suspicion! Prompted by the judge to telephone the man, she uses the phone line to pronounce a sentence: "You deserve to die." The man's response—glancing anxiously around him before he runs for cover into his house—is surely a mark of guilt, *but guilt of what?* Valentine's long-distance boyfriend, Michel (voice of Marc Autheman), also accuses and judges through telecommunication; and just as quickly as Valentine herself. He phones her from various locations—Poland, England, Hungary—each time suspecting her of infidelity. So the judgment of the young is driven by love—Valentine's fierce love for her heroin-addicted brother,

Michel's jealous love for Valentine—but the judgment comes too quickly, before one really knows the truth. By contrast, Kern knows the truth about most of his neighbors, but his judgment, like his love, is suspended indefinitely.

Judge Kern's indifference is a result of the fact that his life has been sabotaged, that his love has been betrayed. In his youth, his lover was unfaithful to him and Kern has never been able to conceive the reason. The obscurity of this one woman's motives clouded the judge's life, inducing in him a suspicion of all humanity. Valentine revives his spirit: the moment of his restoration comes, quite literally, as illumination, a shaft of sunlight falling on Valentine. "Don't move! . . . The light is beautiful," says Kern to Valentine as he insists, in the sea of his indifference, that she stay with him a little longer. Through the medium of light, this seduction by beauty, Valentine's belief that humanity is not essentially bad, only weak, finally infects the judge. Valentine, as model not just of clothes, of products, but of a way of being, provides Kern with new hope.[16] And the opportunity for the judge to relive his life, at least vicariously, on the basis of this hope comes through the young law student, Auguste (Jean-Pierre Lorit), whose life mirrors the judge's own.

The protagonists of *Blue, White, and Red* do not comprise a closed community like that of the apartment complex of *Decalogue*. Kieslowski said that he believes individuals in the West are more lonely, and so these films focus on the possibility of isolated individuals making contact with one another, of a communion across the divisions of gender and age. But out of the principles of liberty, equality, and fraternity, only the fraternity that Valentine shares with Kern, that Kern shares with Auguste, is redeeming. The absolute liberty that Julie practices in *Blue* can only be maintained at the expense of both memory and desire: her evasion of all connections is essentially imprisoning. And the equality that Karol achieves in *White* allows him to be as vindictive as his wife, Dominique, has been. But Valentine is an evangel of charity and fraternity. In all of Kieslowski's films of the 1990s, the protagonists have watched as an old person struggles at some physical task: carrying heavy shopping bags home; or pushing an empty bottle into a tall recycling bin. Of all the protagonists, only Valentine helps.

While *White* has an ebullient narrative movement, the other films are quiet, brooding meditations, and all are charged with symbols. Of course, films purportedly about liberty, equality, and fraternity invite us to look for a symbolic import in the narratives, a significance, for example, in the emblematic colors of *Blue, White*, and *Red* or their corresponding emblematic animals: mice, pigeons, a dog. To Kieslowski, the symbol is important because it invites us to make connections, to see more than is readily apparent, to intuit something other than the obvious. Symbolism is an agency through which we perceive the fraternity of apparently disparate things.

But the strain of the process of converting the literal into the symbolic was evident when Kieslowski announced, after the completion of *Trois couleurs*, that he was retiring from filmmaking. He explained that "rather than subject himself to the strain and bother of making films, he would prefer to sit quietly in a room by himself and smoke. Perhaps he would watch a little television, but never, never would he go to the movies."[17] Kieslowski had stopped making documentaries because he was afraid of becoming a collaborator with the authorities, of his films being used as authoritarian surveillance. The sound rolls for *Workers '71* (1972) were examined by the police, as was the footage of *Station* (1980). But the switch to feature films did not finally excuse Kieslowski from an even greater responsibility. Like Judge Kern, the filmmaker judges which way his characters will go, imposes a sentence on them, and implies a moral. The only way the filmmaker can avoid a narrative and moral imposition is to make choice itself the subject of his film. The values that Kieslowski's characters finally subscribe to by the nature of their choices are the humanist ones of "love and life and laughter," but they must also accept the corresponding debilitations: emptiness, decay, and tears. In *White*, Mikolaj and Karol discuss Mikolaj's desire to die. "Everyone has pain," says Karol. Mikolaj replies: "Yes, but I wanted less of it."

Notes

[1] Milan Kundera, *The Art of the Novel*, trans. Linda Asher (New York: Harper & Row, 1988), 36.

[2] Krzysztof Kieslowski, *Kieslowski on Kieslowski*, ed. Danusia Stok (London: Faber and Faber, 1993), xiii.

[3] Kundera, *Art*, 7.

[4] Kieslowski, *Kieslowski*, 196.

[5] Jon Savage, "Now: Larry Clark's *Kids*," *Sight and Sound* ns 6.5 (May 1996), 7.

[6] Paul Coates, "Anatomy of a Murder: *A Short Film about Killing*," *Sight and Sound* 58:1 (Winter '88-'89), 63.

[7] Likewise, two of Kieslowski's documentaries, *Seven Women of Different Ages* (1978) and *Talking Heads* (1980) are structured as panoramas over the different stages of life, offering us a complex sense of enduring human concerns. In *Talking Heads*, 79 Poles, aged 7 to 100, respond to three questions: When were you born? What are you? What would you like most?

[8] But in defiance of either revolutionary or reactionary political stances, Kieslowski's *Blind Chance* (1981) considers how seemingly petty events (in this film, missing or not missing a train), not our seemingly momentous political commitments, have more to do with our fate.

[9] Kieslowski, *Kieslowski*, 174.

[10] Kieslowski, *Kieslowski*, 79.

[11] Geoffrey Macnab and Chris Darke, "Working with Kieslowski," *Sight and Sound* ns 6. 5 (May '96), 16.

[12] Kieslowski, *Kieslowski*, 173.

[13] The association of the human world with a puppet version of itself may be an homage to Charles Walters' *Lili* (1953).

[14] Kieslowski, *Kieslowski*, 195.

[15] Kieslowski, *Kieslowski*, 36.

[16] Think, too, of the massive poster of Valentine which is erected in a Geneva intersection that shows her looking apprehensively across the plane of the picture against a red background. The image arrests Auguste. An almost identical image of Valentine appears as the closing shot of the film: Valentine is shown on TV news as one of the survivors of a ferry disaster, along with the other protagonists of the *Three Colors* trilogy. The poster, we notice as the judge drives by it, advertises chewing gum with a small caption: *En toute circonstance. Fraicheur de vivre.*

[17] Dave Kehr, "To Save the World: Kieslowski's *Three Colors* Trilogy," *Film Comment* 30:6 (Nov./Dec. '94), 10.

Contributors

MICHAEL DeANGELIS is a doctoral candidate in Critical and Cultural Studies in the Department of Radio-Television-Film at the University of Texas at Austin. He has published in *Language and Style* and in *Spectator*. His dissertation is on gay and straight spectatorial positions of identification and desire in relation to several male Hollywood stars, including Keanu Reeves.

DAVID DESSER is Professor of Cinema Studies and Speech Communication at the University of Illinois at Urbana-Champaign, and the editor of *Cinema Journal*. He is the author of *The Samurai Films of Akira Kurosawa* (1983) and *Eros Plus Massacre: An Introduction to the Japanese New Wave Cinema* (1988); as well as co-author of *American-Jewish Filmmakers* (with Lester Friedman, 1993), *Reflections in a Male Eye* (with Gaylyn Studlar, 1993), *Reframing Japanese Cinema* (with Arthur Nolletti, Jr., 1992), and *Cinematic Landscapes: Observations on the Visual Arts and Cinema of China and Japan* (with Linda Ehrlich, 1994).

KIRBY FARRELL is Professor of English at the University of Massachusetts, Amherst. His books include *Shakespeare's Creation* (1975), *Women in the Renaissance* (1990), *Play, Death, and Heroism in Shakespeare* (1989) and the novel *Snuff* (1991). He is at work on *Post-Traumatic Culture*, exploring conceptions of trauma in narratives of the 1890s and 1990s, and his "The Economies of *Schindler's List*" appeared in the Spring 1996 *Arizona Quarterly*.

MURRAY FORMAN has taught courses in communications, cultural studies, and popular music at Concordia University, McGill University, Boston University, Northeastern University, and University of Massachusetts. He has published articles on hip hop music and culture in *Women's Studies* and *The Journal of Popular Culture*, and is currently writing about space and place in hip hop culture.

EDWARD A. GAMARRA, JR. has studied at Vassar College and New York University's Tisch School of the Arts. He is a Ph.D. candidate at Emory University's Graduate Institute of the Liberal Arts.

BARRY KEITH GRANT is Director of the Film Studies Program at Brock University in St. Catharines, Ontario. He has published widely in film and cultural studies, and has edited, among other volumes, *Film Genre Reader* (1986), *Film Genre Reader II* (1995), *Planks of Reason* (1984) and, most recently, *The Dread of Difference: Gender and the Horror Film*, forthcoming from University of Texas Press.

KEITH C. HAMPSON is a doctoral student in the Department of English at the University of Queensland, Brisbane, Australia. His current research interests include authenticity in popular culture and its relationship to Canadian middle-class audiences; and the role of the media text in consumer practice. Most of his time and effort, however, are spent trying to catch up with his baby daughter.

MICHAEL HOECHSMANN is a doctoral student at the Ontario Institute for Studies in Education in Toronto and an editorial collective member of *Border/Lines* magazine.

MARY CELESTE KEARNEY is a Ph.D. candidate in the Division of Critical Studies, School of Cinema-TV at the University of Southern California. She is writing her dissertation on the relationship of contemporary female youth cultures, feminist politics, and the popular media.

JAMES C. McKELLY is an Assistant Professor of English at Auburn University, working in 20th-century cultural studies. His scholarship has appeared in *American Literature, Arizona Quarterly, The Midwest Quarterly, Western American Literature, CEA Critic, Text and Presentation, The Eugene O'Neill Review,* and *Heritage of the Great Plains*. He is currently working on a book-length project entitled *African-American Cinema and the Culture of Ambiguity*.

E. GRAHAM McKINLEY teaches journalism, graphic design and multi-media in the Communications Department at Rider University in Lawrenceville NJ. She also works part-time as a journalist and church musician. Her book, *Beverly Hills, 90210: Television, Gender, and Construction of Identity* is forthcoming from University of Pennsylvania Press.

MARK CRISPIN MILLER is Chairman of the Writing Seminars at The Johns Hopkins University, Baltimore. He is the author of *Boxed In: The Culture of TV* (1988); *Seeing Through Movies* (1990); and the forthcoming *Mad Scientists: The Paranoid Bias in Modern Propaganda*.

ANVER SALOOJEE is professor in the Department of Politics and School of Public Administration at Ryerson Polytechnic University. He has lectured, researched and written widely on South Africa, anti-racism, human rights policy and organizational change. Currently he is co-editing a book entitled *Creating Inclusive Post-Secondary Learning Environments*.

TIMOTHY SHARY is a Ph.D. candidate in the Department of Communication at the University of Massachusetts. His dissertation is on the image of youth in contemporary American cinema. His articles and reviews have been published in *Wide Angle*, *Point of View*, *Film Criticism*, *Post Script*, and *Film Quarterly*.

SUSAN SHERR is studying at the Annenberg School for Communication at the University of Pennsylvania. She has just finished an internship in the Media Division of the Children's Defense Fund, and is writing about the symbolic resonances of children in political discourse.

SARAH E. TERES graduated from the State University of New York at Geneseo, where she is currently doing graduate work in Psychology. She has worked for *Entertainment Weekly* and has written on film and gender. She is researching female roles in science fiction films.

RAÚL TOVARES received his Ph.D. from the Department of Radio–Television–Film, University of Texas at Austin. Currently he is with the Department of Communication at the University of North Dakota, Grand Forks. He is interested in mass communications theory, television news production, ethnic minorities and mass communication, cross-cultural communication and film theory.

LAUREN R. TUCKER teaches in the College of Journalism and Mass Communications at the University of South Carolina. She has published articles in *Journalism Quarterly*, *Critical Studies in Mass Communication*, and the *Journal of Broadcasting and Electronic Media*. Her current research examines the relationship between entertainment media and the democratic process.

ELIZABETH D. WAITERS is a doctoral candidate in the Radio-Television-Film Department at the University of Texas at Austin. She is completing her dissertation on inter-ethnic interaction on *Beverly Hills, 90210*.

RINALDO WALCOTT is an Assistant Professor in the Division of Humanities at York University, Toronto. He is researching the writing of history and memory in black fiction.

STEVEN WOODWARD is engaged in writing a Ph.D. thesis on the British poet, Walter de la Mare, at the University of Toronto; while living and teaching in the Czech Republic. He was formerly a student of media production and criticism.

MURRAY POMERANCE and JOHN SAKERIS teach in the Department of Sociology at Ryerson Polytechnic University and were co-chairs of the conference, *Pictures of a Generation on Hold: Youth in Film and Television in the 1990s*. They share teaching and research interests in film, popular culture, and mass media practices.

Index of Films and Television Programs Cited